ercol
Furniture in the Making

Lesley Jackson

RICHARD DENNIS
PUBLICATIONS

For Ian and my parents,
Lorna and Derek Jackson

Photography by Magnus Dennis

Design & Typography by Tim Moore

Typeset in Sabon & Frutiger

Printed by Flaydemouse, Yeovil, Somerset

Published by Richard Dennis Publications,
The New Chapel, Shepton Beauchamp,
Somerset, TA19 0JT, England

ISBN: 978 0 9553741 9 7

Cover image
450 Love Seat, 1960

Front flap image
401 Preformed Chair,
1958

Back flap image
376 Windsor Dining
Chair, 1957

Contents

Foreword

Margaret Howell, 2012

The other day I saw a block of wood floating in the sea – with some effort
I got it home. I didn't know what to do with it – but I knew I had to rescue it
and give it a new kind of life.

We take wood for granted, though it's one of our most precious materials.
But you have to know its strengths and weaknesses to use it well. Lucian Ercolani did.

I've been living with Ercol furniture all my life. It was there in my parents' home.
The 'Modern Chair': warm, generous and secure; upholstered in red; strong,
but somehow not heavy. I didn't know the name then – perhaps I even took it for
granted, like so many things about one's parents. Then there was the kitchen
chair my mother gave me when I left to set up on my own in London. Perhaps that
too was taken for granted, but it never left me and it still sits in my kitchen today.

But the name never meant much to me until some twenty years ago, when I went into
Undercurrents, a shop selling Scandinavian design where there were two things I knew
right away I wanted to live with: a round coffee table and what I now refer to as the
Stacking Chair. Except they weren't Scandinavian: they were Ercol. A great new discovery.
Except that it wasn't.

I was recognising something special that had been there a long time. Not just for
the comfort of nostalgia, but the beauty of style. A style that joined material,
process and aesthetic vision to make something enduring and elegant. Ercol.

I can relate to Lucian Ercolani – not just for the aesthetic of those pieces and many
others, but also for his ability to innovate and sustain a business. To build a company
that depends upon satisfying public taste is a daunting task. To change that taste is heroic.
But that is exactly what Ercolani did, as Lesley Jackson's book shows *in detail*.

Inspired, driven, resourceful and inventive, Ercolani deserves to be remembered for many
things. As a designer he seized on the opportunity of a post-war commission to re-invent
the Windsor chair, working single-handedly it appears. When that succeeded he created
a range of furniture with the same family features - Shaker-simple, graceful and light,
strong and reliable – all competitively priced since technical innovation drove down
production costs. But there were also the pioneering strategies in marketing, brand,
and retail management that are now commonplace. He could spot talent in others too
– offering a job to a teen-aged Robin Day, who turned it down.

Lucian Ercolani had passion, energy, commitment and vision. I envy those generations
to come who will rediscover his best work with that same mixture of admiration and
the thrill of rightness.

Margaret Howell
August 2013

Left
392 Stacking Chair,
designed by Lucian
R. Ercolani, 1957,
customised version
with black legs
produced by Ercol
for Margaret Howell,
2012

Introduction

Edward Tadros,
Chairman ercol

When my grandfather, Lucian Randolph Ercolani, created our company in 1920, he was intent on creating an enterprise to last for many years. Lucian was evangelical in his desire to provide satisfying and long lasting employment, and to design and create beautiful and honest furniture. Furniture fit for purpose and made with integrity.

Between 1920 and 1939, he built the basis and strength of our company, skilfully navigating the economic and political turbulence of those years. The rebuilding of the country and the release of spirit and energy in the post-1945 period was Lucian's opportunity to begin to realise his ambitions for his furniture and for his people. The devotion and dedication of his two sons, Lucian and Barry, continued this progress through the later part of the 20th century.

Now, 93 years on from the start of the Old Man's enterprise, the company is flourishing and looking forward to the future. Privately owned by the same family and professionally managed, we still have a wonderful and talented workforce and a fine furniture collection.

In the intervening years we have produced vast quantities of furniture in many different styles. This book is about the story of this furniture and how it evolved. The company has always adapted and reacted to the world around it. This flexibility has enabled us to continue the Old Man's vision of offering employment and creating good furniture.

Today, like many other businesses, we are a global entity. Our factory is located in a beautiful area of rural England, but we live in a globalised economy. Many of our raw materials come from overseas, and we now collaborate with selected manufacturers in Europe and the Far East.

The success of the company would never have been possible without the combined efforts of all those who have worked at Ercol since 1920.

The Old Man had a saying:
'without loyalty, no enterprise can succeed.'

How right he was, and how much our success has benefited from this loyalty. I am indebted to Richard Dennis for having the idea and the commitment to publish this book, and to Lesley Jackson for her enormously careful research and for her empathy with our company.

Edward Tadros
Chairman ercol
July 2013

Left
909A Latimer
Armchair, 1988

Chapter 1:
Ercolani before Ercol

Opposite
Portrait of Lucian R.
Ercolani by Ruskin Spear,
1965

Bottom right
Ercolani family, c.1924.
Back row (left to right)
Mary, Fiorenzo, Eva
(née Brett, Lucian's wife),
Lucian R. Ercolani, Victor
and William. Front row
(left to right): Abdon
(father), Barry, Roma,
Benedetta (mother)
and Lucian Brett Ercolani.

Early Years in Italy and London

Luciano Randolfo Ercolani was born on 8 May 1888 in Sant' Angelo in Vado in the province of Marche near Urbino, close to the Tuscan border. The eldest child of Abdon Ercolani (1864-1957) and Benedetta Ercolani (née Gentili), he was brought up by his paternal grandmother until the age of seven when he joined his parents in Florence. Abdon, a picture framemaker who had originally trained as a cabinetmaker, was evidently highly skilled as his clients included leading museums such as the Uffizi Gallery. He was also technically ingenious and distinguished himself by inventing a machine that could carve the mouldings on oval picture frames. Abdon's profession clearly had a significant influence on his son's future choice of career. The young Luciano not only inherited his father's practical woodworking prowess but also his insistence on high standards of craftsmanship. [1]

Although Luciano was originally raised as a Catholic, the family converted to Protestantism in the mid 1890s after his father joined the Salvation Army following a spur of the moment conversion. Abdon became an avid lay preacher and would cycle around the district seeking to persuade others to embrace the Protestant faith. On a practical level this had disastrous consequences, as it not only distracted him from his work but alienated him from the community. In fact, his proselytising caused such ill-feeling that on one occasion his workshop was broken into and his frame-making equipment was thrown into the River Arno. It was as a direct result of this animosity that the Ercolani family decided to move to London in 1898, encouraged and supported by the Salvation Army.

Initially the family rented lodgings in Islington, before settling in a small house in Walthamstow. This was the first time the whole family had been reunited as Lucian's two younger brothers, William and Fiorenzo, had also previously lived with relatives. A third brother, Victor, was born a year after the Ercolanis arrived in England. [2] Adapting to life in a new country proved difficult for Abdon and Benedetta, who struggled to learn

the language. Abdon worked as a carpenter for the Salvation Army, while Benedetta supplemented the family's income through dressmaking. Money was a constant source of worry, however, and although Benedetta tried to maintain an air of gentility, the family lived in straitened circumstances. It was not until after the First World War that Abdon resumed his original profession as a picture frame-maker. Following his retirement in 1932 and the death of Benedetta, he eventually returned to Italy where he remarried.

In spite of the family's poverty, all four sons did well for themselves. The enterprising Lucian, as he became known in England, established Furniture Industries Limited (later renamed Ercol) in 1920, while Victor

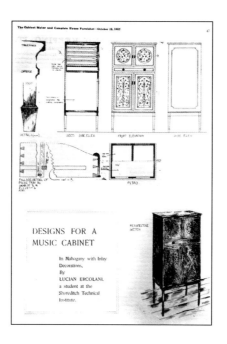

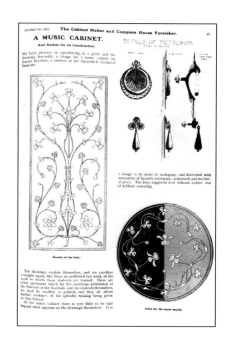

set up a highly successful wireless cabinet making business called Cabinet Industries Limited during the 1920s. William and Fiorenzo were both managing directors of this company at various times. Fiorenzo became an engineer and emigrated to Australia, but returned to Britain to take William's place following the latter's death from typhoid in 1939. Victor later became a director of Furniture Industries Limited after selling his own firm following the Second World War, so there were close professional ties between the brothers.

When Lucian arrived in London at the age of 10, he could not understand a word of English, so his education was seriously hampered. At school he was bullied for being a foreigner, so it is no surprise that he did not thrive. Although he displayed some talent for drawing, he was discouraged from going to art school by the ridicule of an unsympathetic art master. 'My whole object, to my shame, was to get away from school,' he later confessed.[3] Having left school at the age of 14, Ercolani took a job as a messenger boy at the Trade Headquarters of the Salvation Army in Kentish Town. After 12 months he transferred to the organisation's joinery department in Stepney, where he was employed for the next six years. Although the work was fairly routine, such as making doors and staircases, this practical hands-on experience would later stand Ercolani in good stead when running his own factory. He also enjoyed the comradeship of his fellow workers, many of whom were skilled craftsmen who had fallen on hard times. A keen trombonist, Ercolani became an active member of the Salvation Army band. His lifelong love of brass music stemmed from his teenage years.

Hankering for something more creatively challenging than basic joinery work, Ercolani began to attend evening classes in drawing and design at Shoreditch Technical Institute, a trade school in the East End of London providing training for craftsmen and designers in the local furniture trade. At the end of his first year Ercolani obtained a City and Guilds certificate in the theory and construction of furniture. Determined to improve himself further, he spent long hours in Shoreditch Library immersing himself in the writings of John Ruskin and Walter Crane and poring over books about Chippendale, Hepplewhite, Sheraton and Adam. His growing interest in the history of furniture was also fuelled by visits to the Victoria and Albert Museum. This intense programme of study continued for five years. 'Belatedly I realised that, while architecture was the master of all crafts, furniture was for me a good second,' he concluded.[4]

Above Left
Lucian R. Ercolani at the age of about 36

Above centre and above right
Designs for a music cabinet by Lucian R. Ercolani, *The Cabinet Maker*, 1907

Right
Music cabinet designed and made by Lucian Ercolani, 1907

Ercolani's early promise as a furniture designer was recognised while he was still at Shoreditch when, in 1907, his drawings for a music cabinet were published in *The Cabinet Maker*, cited as 'excellent examples... of the work to which these students are trained.'[5] Ercolani subsequently constructed this piece in the Salvation Army workshop.[6] Made of mahogany, with satinwood veneer and mother of pearl inlay, the cabinet combined Georgian grace with Arts and Crafts decorative detailing. The twining stems of the inlaid floral motifs evoked Art Nouveau, the prevailing fashionable style.

The insights he gained at Shoreditch had a lasting influence on Ercolani's approach to design. His favourite tutor, Mr Flashman, taught him to value the principles of simplicity and authenticity. 'Be simple in what you are designing, but however simple your design, your own personality should appear in it, blooming larger than life,' he was told.[7] Ercolani instinctively empathised with plainer idioms. He particularly admired the robustness of 17th century English oak furniture and the unaffected elegance of 18th century Georgian designs: 'This high point was reached because the furniture was designed to be fit for the purpose, to be fit for the materials with which it was made and, thirdly, to have good proportions and to be aesthetic. Furniture, so designed, takes its place as one of the fine arts,' Ercolani wrote in his memoirs.[8] His use of the phrase 'fit for the purpose' is particularly telling as it recalls the clarion cry of the Design and Industries Association, which proclaimed the virtues of the Modernist credo of 'fitness for purpose'. Although Ercolani was no Modernist, he embraced these ideals and embedded them at the core of his design philosophy. The Windsor Range - his defining creation 50 years later - enabled him to put these long-held theories into practice.

Early Career in High Wycombe

In 1909, at the age of 21, Ercolani decided to leave the Salvation Army's joinery department in order to work as a freelance draughtsman and designer. The following year he was offered the post of furniture designer by the firm of Frederick Parker & Sons. Although the company had a showroom in London, its factory was 30 miles away at High Wycombe in Buckinghamshire, the centre of the chair-making industry. Like many Wycombe manufacturers, Parker's had originally produced low-cost utilitarian chairs when it was first established in 1870, although the firm later moved upmarket, specialising in high-quality reproduction furniture in ornate period styles for wealthy aristocratic clients. The company had an extensive library of books on interior decoration, as well as a collection of antique furniture acquired by Frederick Parker, which were used as the basis for its designs.

Working under the direction of Harry Parker (1876–1962), one of Frederick Parker's sons, Ercolani's first assignment was to produce a drawing of a four-poster bed decorated in black and gold lacquer in the Chinese Chippendale style. This set the pattern for the type of designs he would undertake over the next few years. In many ways, therefore, his first job was a continuation of his design education at Shoreditch. Hard work was second nature to Ercolani, so when he was invited to give evening classes in advanced furniture design at High Wycombe Technical Institute in 1912, he jumped at the chance. Although initially somewhat diffident, he developed into an inspiring teacher, relishing the opportunity to express his ideas. Having reached the conclusion that it was impossible to teach people to design, he concentrated on trying to improve their drawing skills. He was renowned for being a hard taskmaster: if a pupil made too many mistakes, he would strike a line through their work.

Among Ercolani's students was a young man called Edward Gomme (known as Ted) from another leading High Wycombe firm, E. Gomme, later famous after the Second World War for its G-Plan furniture. The company was named after Ebenezer Gomme (1858-1931), who had founded the firm

'*No need to blow my own trumpet these days!*' says the ERCOLion.

Top
Ercol's post-war mascot, the Ercolion, playing the trombone, c.1965

Above
Frederick Parker & Sons catalogue, 1913

in 1898. Having agreed to give private design lessons to Ted, Ercolani was adopted by the Gomme family, who invited him to lodge with them. Up to this point he had been commuting from his parents' home in Walthamstow, so it was a relief to be able live on the spot.

Ted and his brother Frank Gomme were so impressed by Ercolani's knowledge of furniture that they invited him to become the company's designer in 1913. Although happy at Parker's, he was keen to progress and believed he would have better career prospects at Gomme's. The idea of designing simpler, more affordable furniture was also an attraction. Initially Gomme's had specialised in chairmaking but in 1909 a large modern factory had been built and the firm was planning to expand into new areas. The plainness of its designs and the orderliness of the new factory greatly appealed to Ercolani. 'At Gomme's they were making only a simple chair and yet everything was tidy and in order,' he noted. 'It seemed to me also that the simple chair was the outcome of very good and precise workmanship.'[9] His decision to join Gomme's was an important step, not only as a designer, but in paving the way for his future career as a factory manager.

Ercolani's prospects looked promising at this point, so in 1914 he decided it was the right time to get married. His fiancée, Eva Mary Brett (1886-1971), was a member of the Baptist Church in Walthamstow that he had been attending since leaving the Salvation Army. Eva Ercolani would prove to be a loyal and supportive wife. Although she took no direct part in her

Above
Woodcarving workshop at High Wycombe Technical Institute, c.1922-4

Left
Chairs produced by E. Gomme, c.1910

Opposite
Aerial view of Ercol factory on far side of railway line at High Wycombe, with E. Gomme's G-Plan works in the foreground, c.1965-7

husband's career, she provided vital stability. 'She accepted from the start that his life would be polarised between a family (to which he was always devoted) and a factory (with which he was always obsessed),' observed Paul Ferris in 1968. [10] Following their marriage in 1915, the couple set up home in a small flat in High Wycombe. After the birth of their first son, Lucian Brett Ercolani (1917-2010), they moved to a larger house. Two more children were to follow: Roma Kathleen Ercolani (1919-2004) and David Barry Ercolani (1921-1992). Being frugal by nature, Ercolani continued to live in modest circumstances despite his later wealth

His task at Gomme's was to oversee the setting up of a new cabinet making department and to develop a range of dining room and bedroom furniture. Although originally recruited as a designer, once in post he was encouraged to take on the role of works manager. 'Design was first and foremost in my mind, but Gomme wanted to call me a manager,' he later recalled. [11] The First World War disrupted these plans: 'It shattered the work which had begun with such great enthusiasm, but it also shattered the world's hopes,' he reflected in his memoirs. [12] Although Ercolani had lived in Britain for 16 years by this date, he was not naturalised until 1923. When war broke out he tried to enlist but, because of his specialist expertise, he was put on the reserve list and recalled to Gomme's.

His first assignment was to oversee the production of wooden bomb slings. Realising that the technical specification was flawed, Ercolani set about improving the device. He also speeded up and improved the efficiency of the manufacturing process by modifying the existing machines. Thus, as well as doing a better job for the Ministry of Munitions, he gained valuable technical experience that could later be applied to furniture making. Gomme's was subsequently commissioned by the Air Department to produce components for the De Haviland DH9 aircraft, including ribs, spars and wings. Ercolani's success in handling this contract prompted an order for wooden propellers, leading to further expansion.

Having proved himself to be extremely hard-working and efficient, Ercolani expected his achievements to be recognised by the Gomme family. After the war, the company engaged Price Waterhouse to advise on its financial affairs. Prior to this the business had been a partnership, but it now became a limited company. Ercolani had been led to believe that he would be made a director at this point, but in the end the family closed ranks and excluded him from the board, hence his decision to leave. Nevertheless, it was largely as a result of the responsibilities he took on during the war that he gained the confidence to set up his own factory.

His departure opened up a temporary rift with the Gomme family that lasted several years. 'I left Gomme's so bitterly that, going to work, I couldn't look at their factory chimneys. I had a feeling almost that I had been robbed,' he later confessed. [13] In due course, their actions proved to be a blessing in disguise. Without this impetus, Ercolani's own company, Furniture Industries Limited, might never have come into being. Over time the scars healed and friendly relations were restored.

Chapter 2:
Furniture Industries Limited

Opposite
Assembling shop at
Furniture Industries
Limited, c.1925

Below
Furniture Industries
Limited, c.1925

A Great Adventure

In his memoirs Lucian Ercolani described the setting up of Furniture Industries Limited as his 'Great Adventure'. Established in 1920, it was an ambitious enterprise for a young furniture designer, but a challenge that he was keen and ready to tackle at the age of 32. It was partly his determination to overcome apparently insurmountable odds that unlocked his creative potential and commercial drive, but also an intense feeling of relief after a prolonged period of national anxiety. Now the nightmare of the First World War was over, Ercolani was ready for a fresh start: 'Even in a small town such as High Wycombe there had been tremendous dislocation. Nevertheless, there was an aura, a magic sense of movement towards change, a feeling of wanting to take from the world no more than a normal share, and to give to it in great abundance.'[1]

The moral imperative behind Ercolani's mission comes through very forcibly in this statement. Personal gain was never a motivating factor in establishing his own company, nor was he hungry for power, except in so far as it enabled him to control his own affairs. Even after his phenomenal success during the 1950s and 60s, Ercolani disapproved of excessive remuneration and lavish expenditure. Throughout his life he remained committed to the belief that a company's profits should be reinvested in the business and the workforce.

After leaving Gomme's, Ercolani worked briefly for the firm of Edgerley's. During this period he got to know a local entrepreneur called Pa Payne who had run an aircraft factory in High Wycombe during the war. It was Payne who urged Ercolani to strike out on his own. The opportunity arose in 1919 when he was approached by a twinemaker called Frederick T. Rich, who was well-known as a supplier to the local upholstery trade and was interested in setting up in a furniture company. Rich enlisted the support of three other investors: a jute importer and sackmaker called Alex B. Peters, and two city businessmen, B. Douglas Harding and J.H. Ironmonger, the latter a director of British Merchants Incorporated.

Furniture Industries Limited was officially registered as a limited company on 16 January 1920 and its first Board Meeting was held on 3 March 1920. Alex Peters was appointed chairman, with Rich, Harding and Ironmonger as co-directors, and Ercolani as managing director. The four external investors pledged a total of £10,000. Although Ercolani wished to be a shareholder too, his personal assets amounted to a mere £300 at this date (two-thirds of which was a gift from Pa Payne), and he also had a young family to support. Rather than risking his capital, therefore, it was suggested that he should be given an upfront payment of £1000 in shares. In the future he would be allowed to increase his share holding to 52 per cent, but initially it was agreed that no single investor should have a controlling interest.

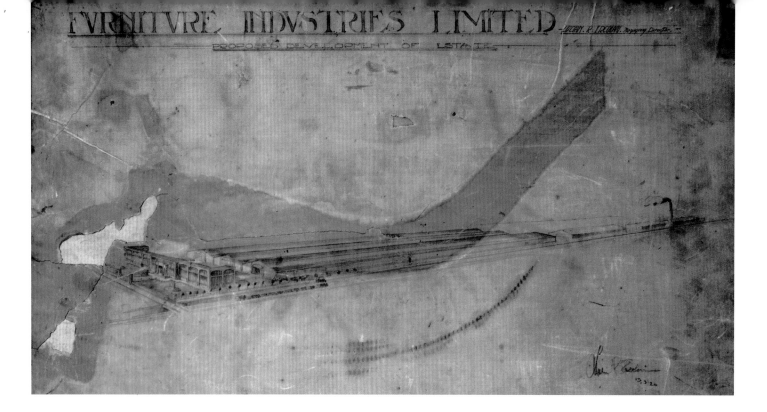

FVRNITVRE INDVSTRIES LIMITED — LUCIAN R. ERCOLANI, Managing Director.

PROPOSED DEVELOPMENT OF ESTATE

ERCOL
The RELIABILITY Mark

Above
Drawing by Lucian
R. Ercolani, 13 March
1920, showing his vision
for Furniture Industries
Limited

Far left
Lucian R. Ercolani in the
guise of the Ercolion,
juggling many different
roles, c.1965

Near left
Ercol trademark featuring
a recumbent lion, 1928

Opposite
Cutting logs into planks
at Ercol, c.1955-62

Ercolani was a man of incredible energy by all accounts. 'Recollections of Ercolani at any point in his life contain violent action,' wrote Paul Ferris. 'He is always seen running, jumping, gesturing, banging his hat on the table, talking non-stop, throwing things, exploding with wrath one minute and apologising the next.'[2] The Parkers and the Gommes had both admired his dynamism, which was why they had been so keen to enlist his services. It was his enthusiasm and vigour that convinced Harding, Ironmonger, Peters and Rich to invest in Furniture Industries Limited. They were convinced he would make it a success. 'I have never met a person with such vitality,' Peters told Ercolani, claiming that when he touched his shoulder he felt an electric shock.[3]

It was Rich who alerted Ercolani to a tract of meadow known as the Conegra Fields running alongside the railway line in High Wycombe, which eventually became the site for the new factory. As soon as he visited the plot, Ercolani could see its potential and began planning the new works, which he envisaged as a long single-storey building, housing a continuous production line, 'where a plank of wood could start at one end and finish up at the other as a piece of furniture.'[4] A perspective drawing dated 13 March 1920, sketched by Ercolani that evening, captured his heroic vision of a modern factory stretching far into the distance. Realising that such a large enterprise could not be created overnight, his idea was to develop the factory incrementally over the coming years. Resources were limited initially, so only five acres of land were acquired in 1920. It was not until 1960 that the final portion of the site was purchased. Ercolani's remarkable prescience

is indicated by the fact that, over a 50-year period between 1920 and 1970, the factory grew from 'a pimple in the desert' to occupy virtually the entire 12-acre site, eventually extending to around a third of a mile in length.

Ercolani does not explain why the name Furniture Industries Limited was chosen, but it appears on his initial drawing. Most companies were named after their founder, but because this enterprise was backed by a consortium, a more anonymous title was adopted. Although Ercolani was the prime mover, it was not until 1928 that the tradename 'Ercol' was adopted.[5] The recumbent Ercol lion logo also made its first appearance that year. Its silhouette was derived from the famous lion statues by Sir Edwin Landseer at the base of Nelson's Column in Trafalgar Square, although the angle of the lion's head was adjusted. The keystone border framing the capitalised 'ERCOL' reinforced the image of strength.

Laying the Foundations

Once Ercolani was in charge of his own company, there was no stopping him. He worked ferociously hard to make it a success and was often at the factory seven days a week. Construction work began within a matter of months - the company's first employees included a bricklayer, a carpenter and two labourers – and the building was up and running by the following winter. In the meantime, premises were rented in High Wycombe so that production could get started, the company's first order being a commission for theatre seating. Two machinists, two cabinetmakers and a polisher were recruited initially, along with an assistant to Ercolani, who later became

works manager. Sceptical locals mocked the factory as 'Erkie's Folly' during its early days, but right from the start he could see the bigger picture. Although the building and the business started on a modest scale, by the late 1920s Furniture Industries Limited had grown substantially and employed several hundred people.

Self sufficiency was one of Ercolani's primary objectives in order to keep running costs down. Water was drawn from a 200ft bore hole on the site. The machine shop was initially powered by a steam engine co-opted from an old threshing machine. This drove two shafts, one at ceiling level, the other counter-sunk in a trench, connected to individual machines by 'a forest of belts.'[6] Later the steam engine was replaced by a power plant. Ercolani was closely involved in planning the works, exploiting up-to-date woodworking machinery in order to achieve maximum efficiency, although for reasons of economy most of the original equipment was second-hand. The first pieces of plant included a band saw, two circular saws, a spindle and turning lathe, a horizontal slot-boring machine, an overhand planing machine and a thicknessing machine (used to make flat boards). Another important early acquisition was a drying stove - vital for ensuring that the timber was the correct humidity - which was fuelled by a wood-burning furnace. Other modern innovations, such as a network of internal telephones, were installed by 1928.

Ercolani's pride in the new works is indicated by the fact that in the mid 1920s he commissioned a series of documentary photographs. These images provide the earliest record of the company's operations, including its timber

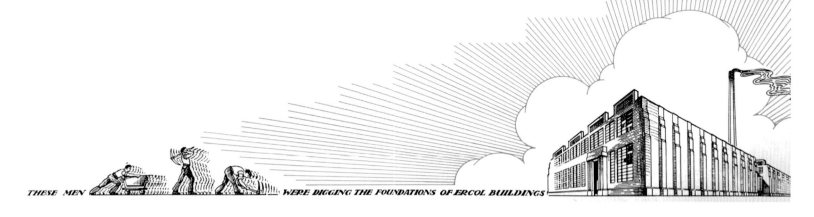
THESE MEN WERE DIGGING THE FOUNDATIONS OF ERCOL BUILDINGS

VIEWS OF FACTORY

We should like to convey some impression of the facilities our plant affords for the production of high-class furniture economically. It stands on five acres of ground situated alongside the railway lines from London, on an ideal spot surrounded by the Chiltern Hills and overlooking the town of High Wycombe. It comprises a series of one-floor shops with lofty roofs to minimise the effect of dust, beautifully lighted and kept at an evenly heated temperature, as they should be for the manufacture of furniture, day and night. The machinery is of the latest make, and laid out as on a keyboard for rapid production.

Our organisation consists of an enthusiastic staff who realise that with each transaction we have our customers' reputation at stake.

The Directors extend a cordial invitation to all our customers and their clients to visit the works at any time and see our furniture in course of manufacture.

ERCOL
The RELIABILITY Mark

FURNITURE INDUSTRIES LTD.

A CORNER OF THE MAIN BUILDING · ENGINE ROOM · MACHINE SHOP · CABINET ASSEMBLING SHOP · UPHOLSTERING SHOP · POLISHING DEPARTMENT · CORNER OF DESPATCH

A SECTION OF THE TIMBER YARD · BOILER HOUSE · MACHINED PARTS STORES · CHAIRMAKING ASSEMBLING SHOP · UPHOLSTERING SHOP · CUSHION MAKING SHOP · INSPECTION DEPARTMENT

Top
'Digging the foundations
of Ercol buildings',
Exclusiveness in Design
leaflet, 1935

Above left
'Views of Factory',
Furniture of Today
catalogue, c.1928

Above right
Furniture Industries
Limited's workforce in
front of the factory, c.1925

Opposite top
Drawing office, c.1925

Opposite bottom
Engine room, c.1925

yard, engine house and drawing office, as well as the machine shop, chair-making and cabinet-making workshops, and the finishing and upholstery departments. Even at this early date Ercolani's priorities as an industrialist were readily apparent, his aim being to produce well-made furniture in a civilised and humane way. 'We should like to convey some impression of the facilities our plant affords for the production of high-class furniture economically,' states an early catalogue. 'It comprises a series of one-floor shops with lofty roofs to minimise the effect of dust, beautifully lighted and kept at an evenly heated temperature, as they should be for the manufacture of furniture, day and night. The machinery is of the latest make, and laid out as on a keyboard for rapid production.'[7]

Ercolani hated waste and inefficiency and sought to eliminate it wherever possible, not because he was mean-spirited (quite the opposite, philanthropy was second nature), but because he believed that everyone in the organisation benefited from the collective gains of being economical. His concern for the welfare of his workforce was entirely genuine, his aim being to provide steady, well-paid employment in a safe and benign environment. Ercolani did not regard himself as intrinsically superior to his employees. Having risen from a humble background himself, he understood the importance of treating his staff with respect, providing good working conditions and fair rates of pay so that they could live decently, both during their working lives and in retirement.

Setting up a manufacturing enterprise literally from scratch, however, is fraught with problems. As managing director, Ercolani was personally accountable to the board for the firm's commercial success. 'I should warn anyone starting a business that there can be periods, inevitably, when a person suffers from loneliness beyond understanding, because only he is responsible,' he later confessed.[8]

American Interlude

In 1923 Ercolani was sent on an expenses-paid holiday to the US at the instigation of his fellow directors, partly to reward him for his strenuous endeavours in establishing the company, but also because they were worried that he was in danger of burning himself out. On the eve of his departure from New York, Ercolani chanced upon a room in the Metropolitan Museum of Art featuring a display of Shaker furniture. With its focus on utility rather than decoration, Shaker furniture looked completely different to other historical artefacts and bore no resemblance to contemporary commercial furniture. It made an indelible impression on Ercolani, who remarked: 'I was struck by how beautiful and satisfying a thing can be without adornment of any kind.' [9]

The Shakers were a religious group headed by Ann Lee who had settled in North America in 1774. Originally known as the United Society of Believers in Christ's Second Appearing, they established close-knit, insular communities with strict rules and a rigorous moral code. Furniture-making was just one aspect of the Shakers' self-sufficiency and a practical demonstration of their faith. Radically pure and simple in design and construction, its pared down forms and sound craftsmanship embodied the strict puritan ideology of its makers. It was the integrity of Shaker furniture that particularly appealed to Ercolani: 'their essential quality; not just because of their simple fitness for purpose, in the sense of being useful for what is required, but also for that added elegance which is in the realm of aesthetics.' [10]

Although 20 years would pass before Ercolani achieved a similar simplicity in his own designs, it was this early encounter with Shaker furniture that planted the seed for the later Windsor Range. Even at the time, he recognised this experience as a life-changing moment: 'Would it were possible to convince people that if they work honestly and follow the purest ideas, they are themselves on the threshold of creating work that will live for all time. This is the thought that came to me on that last day. It has remained in my mind ever since.' [11]

Above
Cabinet shop, c.1925

Opposite top
Upholstering shop, c.1925

Opposite bottom left
Finishing department,
c.1925

Opposite bottom right
Machined parts store,
c.1925

Left and below
Living room and dining
room furniture, *Furniture
of Today* catalogue, c.1928

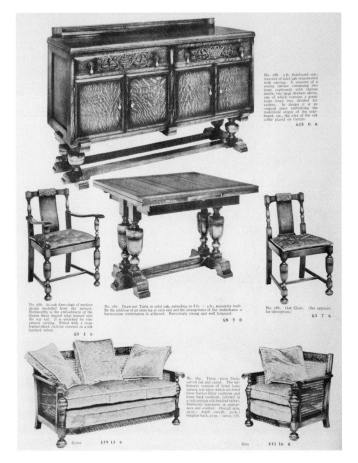

Decent Furniture for the Masses

Ercolani's aim at Furniture Industries Limited was to produce good quality, practical, affordable designs. 'My idea was to make decent furniture for the masses such as they had never had,' he declared. [12] Whilst catering to the prevailing fashion for period styles, Ercolani was instinctively drawn to simpler idioms, placing great store on functionalism and value for money: 'I had it in mind to bring to the ordinary man and woman the comfort and the taste which had been the privilege of the well-to-do,' he told *Furnishing Trades Organiser* in 1936. [13] Retailers exerted considerable influence over the market at this date, so their views could not be ignored. Their buyers were notoriously conservative, so Ercolani had to take care not to be too original in his designs.

Initially Furniture Industries Limited was represented by two agents connected with the large Tottenham-based furniture manufacturer Harris Lebus. Later, from around 1925, the company employed its own sales representatives, the first of whom, John Wright, had trained as an interior decorator and previously worked for Waring and Gillow. [14] During the early days, sales staff were issued with large photographs of the latest furniture models to take round to the stores. By 1928, the company had begun producing illustrated catalogues, often in ring binder form so they could be easily updated. All the early catalogues up to 1939 were entitled *Furniture of Today*. The Ercol logo – promoted as 'The Reliability Mark' - was emblazoned on the cover, reinforcing Ercolani's commitment to 'a high standard of taste and workmanship hitherto not associated with such low priced productions'.

Ercolani himself also played a key role in selling. His talent for this (largely due to his persuasiveness) is indicated by the fact that, in a good year, he brought in up to 25 per cent of the company's trade. He would regularly spend a day visiting buyers in furnishing stores in Knightsbridge and the West End. Efficient as ever, he would arrange for a car and a driver to meet him at Marylebone Station so that he could travel speedily from one shop to the next. The fact that he made the effort to call in person seems to have made all the difference, although he was uncompromising on price and operated by a strict moral code: 'A buyer always thinks, if he's dealing with the boss, that he'll get the best possible price. But I taught him that, with Ercolani, there was only one price. I think we were giving good value for money.' [15]

The company's early collections consisted of two main areas: dining room suites and upholstered easy chairs and settees. Solid, well proportioned and not overly ornate, the restrained character of these designs and the preponderance of dark oak proclaimed the virtues of sobriety. Period designs predominated, variously described as 'Jacobean', 'William and Mary', or 'Queen Anne', although these terms were somewhat loosely applied. The 626 Sideboard, one of the most popular models of the late 1920s, combined 'all the charm of the Jacobean style with a modern rendering, enriched with dog-tooth carvings and strapwork from authentic examples', according to the catalogue. Cane-sided Bergere armchairs and settees also featured prominently in the company's inter-war collections. The French term 'Bergère' originally referred to a partially upholstered armchair with a high back. Ercolani's 506 Bergere Chair was less formal, with a carved walnut frame, a deep seat and comfortable down-filled cushions.

One of the most successful designs during the interwar period was the 472 Adjustable Armchair (1930), marketed as 'the famous chair with the big soft downy cushions'. Made of solid oak, it had wide flat armrests and a patented adjustable seatback, which allowed the sitter to recline safely without toppling backwards. [16] Targeted specifically at men, the merits of this design were outlined in a series of explanatory photographs and diagrams in fold-out pages of the catalogue. Apart from its reclining mechanism, its

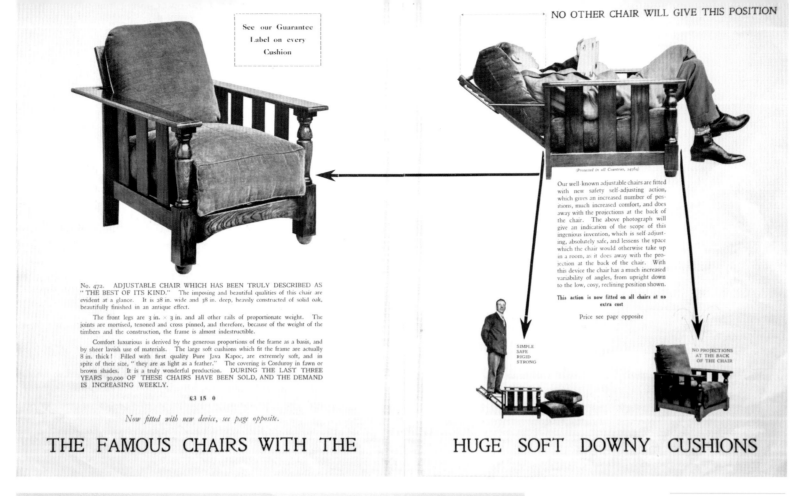

See our Guarantee
Label on every
Cushion

No. 472. ADJUSTABLE CHAIR WHICH HAS BEEN TRULY DESCRIBED AS "THE BEST OF ITS KIND." The imposing and beautiful qualities of this chair are evident at a glance. It is 28 in. wide and 38 in. deep, heavily constructed of solid oak, beautifully finished in an antique effect.

The front legs are 3 in. × 3 in. and all other rails of proportionate weight. The joints are mortised, tenoned and cross pinned, and therefore, because of the weight of the timbers and the construction, the frame is almost indestructible.

Comfort luxurious is derived by the generous proportions of the frame as a basis, and by sheer lavish use of materials. The large soft cushions which fit the frame are actually 8 in. thick! Filled with first quality Pure Java Kapoc, are extremely soft, and in spite of their size, "they are as light as a feather." The covering is Corduroy in fawn or brown shades. It is a truly wonderful production. DURING THE LAST THREE YEARS 30,000 OF THESE CHAIRS HAVE BEEN SOLD, AND THE DEMAND IS INCREASING WEEKLY.

£3 15 0

Now fitted with new device, see page opposite.

Our well-known adjustable chairs are fitted with new safety self-adjusting action, which gives an increased number of positions, much increased comfort, and does away with the projections at the back of the chair. The above photograph will give an indication of the scope of this ingenious invention, which is self-adjusting, absolutely safe, and lessens the space which the chair would otherwise take up in a room, as it does away with the projection at the back of the chair. With this device the chair has a much increased variability of angles, from upright down to the low, cosy, reclining position shown.

This action is now fitted on all chairs at no extra cost

Price see page opposite

SIMPLE
SAFE
RIGID
STRONG

NO PROJECTIONS
AT THE BACK
OF THE CHAIR

THE FAMOUS CHAIRS WITH THE HUGE SOFT DOWNY CUSHIONS

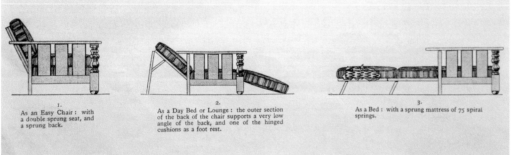

1. As an Easy Chair : with a double sprung seat, and a sprung back.

2. As a Day Bed or Lounge : the outer section of the back of the chair supports a very low angle of the back, and one of the hinged cushions as a foot rest.

3. As a Bed : with a sprung mattress of 75 spiral springs.

Above and left
472 Adjustable
Armchair, 1930

Overleaf
Exclusiveness in Design
leaflet, 1935, showing
furniture produced since
1920

primary appeal was its strength: 'The joints are mortised, tenoned and cross pinned, and therefore, because of the weight of the timbers and construction, the frame is almost indestructible.' Initially launched in 1930, the 472 Armchair proved astonishingly popular: 30,000 were sold in the first three years, and more than 100,000 by 1937.

Economic Vicissitudes

Although Furniture Industries Limited made a loss during its first two years because of the initial setting up costs, by 1923 it was in profit and was producing around £1,000 worth of furniture a week. Ercolani was naturally cautious, but even he admitted to 'a sense of buoyancy' at this point. [17] His success in establishing the company's reputation is indicated by the fact that, only two years after it began operating, one of its dining sets was selected as an example of good workmanship at an industrial art exhibition in London. Growth continued steadily for the rest of the decade. By 1926 turnover was £55,000, and by 1930 it had risen to £101,878. In February 1930 Ercolani reported that the company had 'made greater progress than in any other year in establishing good will for high-class furniture at prices within the reach of the great buying public.' [18]

The Cabinet Maker also applauded Ercolani on his achievements as 'head of one of the most progressive furniture manufacturing concerns in the country, the rise of which has been one of the romances of the Wycombe industry since the war.' [19]

Following the stock market crash of 1929, however, there was a dramatic downturn in the British economy. Furniture Industries Limited was not immune from these financial vicissitudes. After making a net profit of £5,637 in 1930, its sales declined by more than 20 per cent over the next two years and, by 1932, the firm was making a loss. Ercolani's top priority for the rest of the decade was simply to make the company profitable again. In order to increase sales, his strategy was to produce lower cost ranges and to be more responsive to changing fashions. If this meant compromising on originality in favour of saleability, temporarily at least, then so be it, he accepted. By August 1932 he was able to reassure the board of directors that, although 'trade in general was very bad in the town, the amount of orders received showed that the company was receiving more business than most of the other firms in the furniture trade, due to the policy which had been pursued of adapting the factory to the manufacture of cheaper furniture to meet present-day demands.' [20]

EXCLUSIVENES

The business of furnishing is not merely sellin
customers now no longer come to you for just "a
Neither do they come to you for good taste and go
are attracted to your shop if PLUS good taste and
EXCLUSIVENESS IN DESIGN.

Year after year Furniture Industries Ltd. has shown leadership in desig
are offering furniture which excels in saleability because in addition t
EXCLUSIVENESS IN DESIGN our furniture also appears worth much
We cordially invite you to visit our Showrooms now displaying
our new mid-year range of furniture of ABSOLUTELY
OUTSTANDING INTEREST.

S in DESIGN

rchandise.   Your
ing room suite.''
alue alone.   They
d value you show

ay, more than ever, we
taste, good value and
han its price.

1931

1932

1933

1934

1935

ATIONS OF ERCOL BUILDINGS

Increased competition between furniture manufacturers during the 1930s prompted widespread copying of designs, a direct knock-on effect of the Depression. Because retailers demanded cheaper prices and constant novelty in order to stimulate trade, plagiarism was rife in the industry, something that Ercolani abhorred, but over which he had no control. Most designs were incredibly short-lived; some only lasted a month before being copied by another firm, often in a cut-price variant. Although Furniture Industries Limited still managed to produce 'some good clean stuff' during the 1930s, the company consciously embraced popular styles that it knew the public would readily accept. [21] Streamlined armchairs with jazzy abstract upholstery patterns reflected the vogue for *Moderne* styling, but Ercolani was never entirely comfortable with purely modish design.

His higher aspirations were encapsulated in a publicity leaflet produced in 1935 urging retailers to promote originality: 'Your customers now no longer come to you for just "a dining room suite." Neither do they come to you for good taste and good value alone. They are attracted to your shop if PLUS good taste and good value you show EXCLUSIVENESS IN DESIGN.' The typography and graphics adopted in this leaflet were strikingly modern. At the bottom of the page was a perspective drawing of the factory showing three labourers hard at work, 'digging the foundations of Ercol buildings.' Running diagonally across the page was a staircase with 16 steps dated from 1920 to 1935 recording the progress of the firm.

The furniture perched on each step provided a potted history of the company's designs. Early pieces reflected the more ornate tastes and grander aspirations of the 1920s: a throne-like chair in 1922; an imposing Jacobean-style sideboard in 1926; and a sumptuous sofa with an elaborate carved scrolling back in 1929. In 1930 there was a distinct change, indicated by the solid, practical 472 Adjustable Armchair. From this point onwards, designs became plainer, squarer and bulkier. Sideboards remained 'statement' pieces, but dining tables and chairs were increasingly utilitarian and armchairs became much heavier and more rectilinear.

Humanising the Machine

In 1936 Furniture Industries Limited announced in its catalogue: 'Herein we present a selection of designs of beautiful furniture built to an ideal to "humanise the machine" and bring to the public at moderate prices a high standard of design and manufacture.' This statement highlights the dilemma faced by the company: how to reconcile the conflicting demands of mechanisation and craftsmanship, tradition and modernity, continuity and novelty, quality and price. In an article in the *Furnishing Trades Organiser* published later that year, the factory was presented as a model of efficiency, 'mechanised to the limit' in order to reduce costs. At the same time, Ercolani took pains to emphasise that there was still a role for craftsmanship, particularly hand carving, recognising that this was vital in order to inject 'soul' into precision-made products. This is what he meant by 'humanising the machine'. The description of the factory at this date is very evocative:

> Thousands of pounds worth of machinery rips and planes and turns and bores to the thousandth part of an inch. By going back to first principles, by releasing his men from the drudgery of handcraft; by planning functionally first and later working out the cost; by using every latest invention and scrapping ruthlessly everything that did not serve his purpose and its own, it has been possible to produce machine-made goods that in every detail are products of the twentieth century. This is the measure of Ercolani's success. He has used the machine to its uttermost limits – and no further. He has reduced costs by its means to the lowest level. Each piece of furniture is as perfect as the machine can make it. What is further needed is provided by the craftsman's hand. [22]

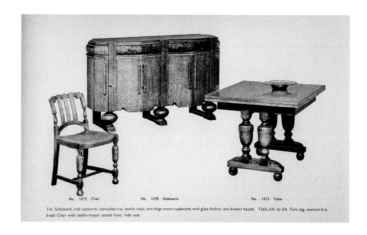

No. 1272 Chair   No. 1239 Sideboard   No. 1273 Table
5 ft. Sideboard, end cupboards, concealed tray, bottle racks, two large centre cupboards with glass shelves, one drawer baized. Table, 6 ft. by 3 ft. Twin leg, nominal 6 in. Small Chair with saddle-shaped canted front, hide seat.

No. 1767 Three Piece Suite
Covered in silk tapestry No. 439 Range 6a. Soft pocketted sprung arms, spring back and extra deep double sprung platform. Carved oak wood plinth.
Sizes: Width over arms   36 ins.
        Height of Back   33 ins.
        Depth overall   39 ins.
        Settee   4 ft. 9 ins.
No. 1767 Easy

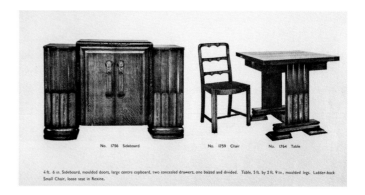

No. 1756 Sideboard   No. 1759 Chair   No. 1764 Table
4 ft. 6 in. Sideboard, moulded doors, large centre cupboard, two concealed drawers, one baized and divided. Table, 5 ft. by 2 ft. 9 in., moulded legs. Ladder-back Small Chair, loose seat in Rexine.

Above
Living room and dining room furniture, *Furniture of Today* catalogue, c.1936-7

Right
Easy Chair in the style of Charles II, made for Torre Abbey, Torquay, 1934

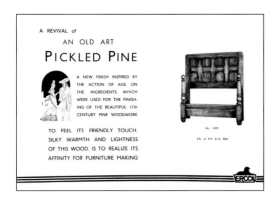

A REVIVAL of
AN OLD ART
PICKLED PINE

A NEW FINISH INSPIRED BY THE ACTION OF AGE ON THE INGREDIENTS WHICH WERE USED FOR THE FINISHING OF THE BEAUTIFUL 17th CENTURY PINE WOODWORK

TO FEEL ITS FRIENDLY TOUCH, SILKY WARMTH AND LIGHTNESS OF THIS WOOD, IS TO REALIZE ITS AFFINITY FOR FURNITURE MAKING

Top left
1823 Pickled Pine
Bed, 1936

Bottom left
1831 Anglo-Spanish
Sideboard, 1936

Right
Chairmaking workshop
at Walter Skull & Sons,
c.1920s

An Anglo-Spanish Suite (1936) exemplified the type of high-calibre craftsmanship that Furniture Industries Limited could offer. Made in oak, finished in off-white gesso with traces of gilt, it was inspired by 'Spanish designs made in this country at the time of the English Court's connection with the Spanish Court'. A Bedroom Suite decorated in relief with sprays of flowering plants in 'real antique silver' provided another illustration of the company's repertoire of special effects. More in keeping with Ercolani's personal design ethos was the 'dignified simplicity and fitness for purpose' of the Pickled Pine Range (1936). Described as 'a new finish inspired by the action of age on the ingredients used for the finishing of the beautiful 17th century pine woodwork', this collection of bedroom and dining furniture, with its 'friendly touch, silky warmth and lightness', was a precursor of the Old Colonial Range (1937) launched the following year.[23]

Securing Commissions

Although the bulk of Furniture Industries' business came through the retail trade, Ercolani was always on the lookout for commissions to supplement the firm's income and enhance its prestige. This became particularly pressing during the 1930s when the domestic market was slack. Ercolani could be quite a showman when making a pitch to potential clients, dazzling his audience with his historical and technical expertise. His flair for public speaking and colourful turn of phrase served him well on these occasions. He was adept at persuading cost-conscious clients that his company offered good value for money and was the best firm for the job.

In 1933, for example, Ercolani secured a commission to furnish the Council Chamber of Morecambe Town Hall, a neo-Georgian building completed in 1932, designed by the Borough Engineer, P.W. Ladmore, and funded through the Unemployment Grants Committee. When a group of town councillors visited High Wycombe in the hope of purchasing furniture at wholesale prices, Ercolani hijacked their mission, convincing them that it would be better if the furniture was custom-designed. Having insisted on viewing the building in person, he drew a plan of the proposed desks and

seating on the bare walls of the room. The councillors were so stunned by Ercolani's theatrical performance that they gave him carte blanche.

Another commission that Ercolani went to great lengths to secure was for a new Agricultural College in Durham. Having familiarised himself with the building in advance, Ercolani so impressed the committee with his detailed drawings that he not only secured the job, but even managed to persuade them to increase the budget: 'I expounded on the fact that they were putting up a lovely building and that I was anxious to match its quality with furniture which I had designed personally – furniture fit for the purpose and suited to the excellence of the building.'[24] Once again his adroit preparations and persuasiveness won the day.

In Torquay, Ercolani's strategy proved less successful. Here, the project was to supply period furnishings for a house in the grounds of Torre Abbey, which was being restored by the local council for use as function rooms. Again, Ercolani did his homework, preparing a series of colour-wash drawings of furniture in the style of Charles II, but on this occasion his zeal backfired. The councillors were so enthused by his argument for respecting the historical character of the Abbey that they decided to furnish the building with genuine antique furniture. As a result, Ercolani only secured a modest order for four easy chairs and two settees.

Walter Skull & Sons

The furniture manufacturers worst affected by the Depression were those operating at the top end of the market, such as the High Wycombe firm of Walter Skull & Sons. Founded in 1872 by two brothers, Walter and Edwin Skull, the company had originally produced Windsor chairs and rush-seated chairs. Its reputation for good workmanship was such that, in 1874, it supplied 4000 chairs to St Paul's Cathedral. Walter's son, Charles Edwin Skull, later repositioned the company as a manufacturer of period furniture. Like Frederick Parker & Sons, the company became renowned for making accurate reproductions of historic pieces: seeking 'inspiration from authentic antiques, it soon established a market for reproductions

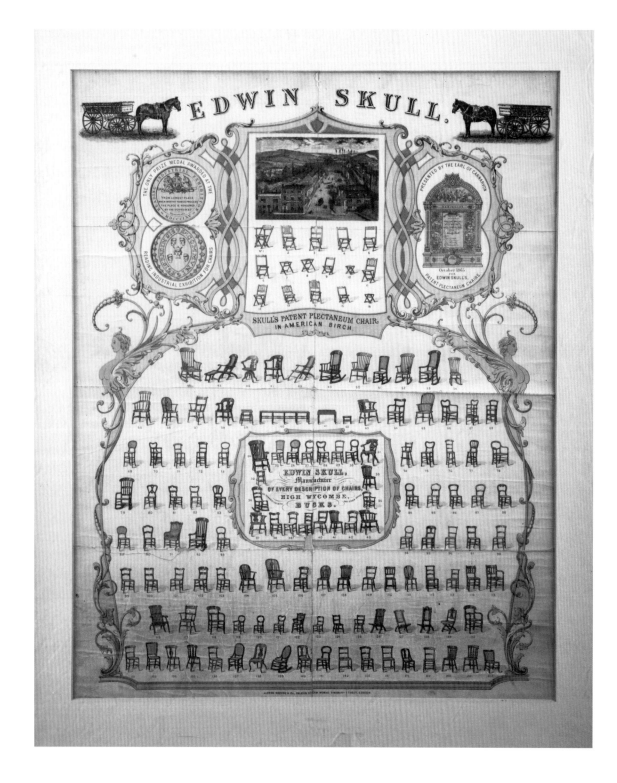

of design and workmanship not inferior to the originals.'[25] Examples of Skull's furniture were presented to the Prince of Wales (later Edward VII) and the Duke of York (later George V).

During the 1920s a significant part of Skull's business derived from large furnishing contracts for ships. This hitherto lucrative trade was badly affected by the financial crash and, by 1930, the company was losing money and on the verge of collapse. Recognising the seriousness of the situation, Charles Edwin Skull invited Ercolani to become joint managing director in the hope that he could save the company. Although Ercolani had problems of his own at this date, he agreed, on the understanding that 20 per cent of any profits would go to Furniture Industries Limited. His initial alliance proved short-lived, however, as Skull's other directors were not prepared to

implement the rescue package he proposed. Frustrated that his advice was not being heeded, Ercolani resigned, but following C.E. Skull's death, his son, Fred Skull, offered to sell him the company as neither he nor his two younger brothers, Percy and Charles, wished to remain involved.

Although Ercolani had grave reservations about taking over a failing firm, he realised that Skull's was a valuable asset and that the skills of its employees could enhance the reputation and extend the range of his own company. In April 1932, therefore, he struck a deal whereby he arranged to purchase the Skull family's shares for £11,000, payable over the next ten years. A new company called Walter Skull & Son (1932) Ltd. was subsequently absorbed into Furniture Industries Limited after Ercolani sold 40 per cent of his shares in Skull's to his fellow directors, Harding and Rich, while retaining a controlling interest himself. From this date onwards, the two firms operated side by side.

In order to reverse the decline at Skull's, Ercolani introduced drastic economies, rationalising production methods, improving efficiency and simplifying designs. The new range, which was 30 per cent cheaper, was marketed through a catalogue called *Oak down the Ages*, which stressed the 'sincerity' of these plainer designs, sincere in the sense of being 'free from pretence or deceit: not assumed or put on: genuine, honest and frank.'[26] The starting point for the designs was 17th century English oak furniture, a period to which Ercolani was instinctively drawn, when: 'luxurious effects gave way to plainer frames and simple loose cushions: decorative needlework to plain leather: ornamental braids and heavy fringes to leather banding and simple studs.' In his introduction to the catalogue, the historian W.A. Gibson Martin drew a direct link between these historical precedents and Skull's new collection: 'Tudor... Stuart...Cromwell... Charles... the halcyon days of oak, now brought to life again in a range of superbly designed furniture, retaining all the quaint charm which has immortalized these periods, yet adapted to the needs of to-day.'[27]

Retrospectively, what Ercolani was most proud of at Skull's was not so much the furniture, but the fact that, against the odds, he had managed to turn the factory around. By cutting waste and slashing prices, he stimulated new orders and succeeded in returning the firm to profit. After the Second World War, there was no longer sufficient demand for this more decorative style of furniture to warrant resurrecting Skull's as a brand in its own right. By the 1950s it had been absorbed into Furniture Industries Limited and the Skull tradename disappeared.[28]

Dutch Debacle

Two years after the takeover of Skull's, Furniture Industries Limited faced an unexpected crisis. Latterly, as a result of a successful agency agreement with a Dutch merchant, the company had been exporting around 20 per cent of its output to Holland. In 1934, however, the Dutch government introduced a trade embargo out of the blue. This hit Ercolani's firm hard and its revenue suddenly plummeted. Finding itself in debt to the tune of £30,000, Furniture Industries Limited applied for an overdraft but was turned down by the bank. Faced with the prospect of bankruptcy, Ercolani was forced to take urgent action. In order to reduce the firm's outgoings, he managed to persuade some of its creditors to be paid in shares rather than cash. The company also took up the offer of a private loan of £10,000 from Frank Gomme by mortgaging some of its machinery. Although Ercolani felt humiliated by having to take such drastic measures, had he not acted so decisively, the company would have gone under. It was not until 1947 that he finally managed to pay off this loan. Eventually, with the help of his brother Victor, he bought back the shares that he had been forced to sell. Victor became a director of Furniture Industries Limited at this point.

Despite these trials and tribulations, by 1938 Ercolani had managed to restore Furniture Industries Limited's turnover to £122,481. Although the company only made a small profit of £1,024 and no shareholder dividends were issued because of debt repayments, this recovery was miraculous under the circumstances. The relentless pressure to generate sales by bringing out increasing numbers of new models inevitably took its toll creatively. By the late 1930s the company's products had become much more formulaic, with only slight variations between designs. Ercolani later dismissed the 1930s as a 'dreadful period' in the company's history. 'That wasn't design; that was trade,' he declared.[29] Whilst proud of keeping the firm afloat, he felt he had betrayed his design principles. The Second World War, although disruptive, at least brought some respite from these anxieties. 'The rat race was over for the moment, and Ercolani vowed never to go back to it,' concluded Paul Ferris.[30]

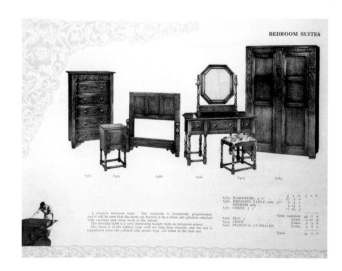

Above

Oak down the Ages catalogue, Walter Skull & Sons (1932) Ltd, 1939

Left

Toby Chair, *Furniture of Today* catalogue, c.1936-7

Chapter 3:
Windsor Utility

'It's a family affair,'
pants the ERCOLion.

Wartime Heroics

The Second World War had a huge impact on the operations of Furniture Industries Limited and on Ercolani personally, as both his sons, Lucian and Barry, were away on active service in the RAF. As children, the boys had spent a lot of time at the factory. They would walk down to meet their father after school and play tennis on the courts next to the works. 'They were always interested,' recalled Ercolani. 'Lucian used to stand on large lumps of coal in the boiler house to make him tall enough to start the machines running.' [1]

Lucian Jnr felt so at home at the factory that he was keen to get involved immediately after leaving school. He began working alongside his father in 1934, having joined the firm at the age of 16. Ercolani was a hard taskmaster, though, as he did not wish to be seen to be giving his son any favours: 'I was very strict with him when he came to work for me,' he later admitted. [2] Lucian's first three years were spent in the drawing office, which gave him a thorough grounding in how the furniture was designed and made. Being technically minded, with a natural flair for engineering, he quickly developed a good understanding of woodworking machinery and learnt how to operate every machine in the factory. By 1937 he was fully trained and by the end of the decade he had effectively taken on the job of works manager. Lucian would later play a key role in designing new machines, patenting his first machine design at the age of 22. Although he was away for most of the war, he kept in close contact with his father, discussing technical matters and helping out whenever he was on leave.

As a pilot, Lucian was in constant danger during the war, so this was an extremely worrying time for the Ercolani family. After completing his training in Canada, he embarked on active service in May 1941, carrying out regular bombing raids over Germany. In November of that year he gave his family a real scare after he was reported missing following a mission to Berlin. His plane was set alight by anti-aircraft fire and came down in the Channel, but miraculously he and his crew were washed ashore in their dinghy on the Isle of Wight three days later, a huge relief for his parents and siblings. Lucian was subsequently posted to India, where he continued to make many daring long-distance bombing raids in Burma, Malaya and the South China Seas over the next few years. He rose to the rank of Wing Commander and was awarded two Distinguished Service Orders and a Distinguished Flying Cross for his bravery. His brother, Flight Lieutenant Barry Ercolani, also had an illustrious war record, being posted to India and Burma where he served as an Air Force Gunner.

Wartime Efficiency

Although Furniture Industries Limited remained in operation throughout World War II, normal manufacturing quickly ground to a halt. For the next six years the factory was mainly engaged on government contracts of one sort or another, mostly military-related. During this period the company applied its woodworking expertise to a diverse array of products, from snow shoes, munitions boxes and picketing posts to wooden pulley blocks for hoisting tents. Although domestic furniture production was severely restricted, the company was commissioned to make chairs and beds for air-raid shelters, kitchen units for prefabs and several thousand Suffolk chairs.

Ercolani's factory was already a model of efficiency during the 1930s, but the war made it even more imperative to increase productivity and eliminate wastefulness. Twelve indoor kilns were built to speed up the drying of timber, for example. Because of the shortage of wood, Ercolani developed ways of utilising substandard timber from trees that were too thin, crooked or stunted for other applications. One of the firm's largest wartime commissions was for wooden tent-pegs made from tree tops. Ercolani devised a way of maximising these offcuts using poor quality beech trees from Bloom Wood near High Wycombe, which he bought specifically in order to guarantee supplies. Special jigs were developed to hold the small pieces of timber while they were shaped by the cutters. This greatly speeded up production, enabling the factory to manufacture 25,000 tent-pegs per day. This number later doubled and eventually the company would produce over 36 million tent-pegs.

It was the wartime drive for increased productivity that prompted Ercolani's interest in work studies - the science of workplace efficiency. The principle behind work studies was that, by analysing the manufacturing process and breaking it down into a logical sequence of coordinated operations, productivity could be increased and cost-savings achieved by identifying where time and effort was being wasted. Although some of the new working practices adopted as a consequence were simply common sense - such as ensuring that machinists were supplied with timber, rather than having to fetch it themselves – without the impetus of the war, these improvements might not have been implemented. Yet, while keen to reap the benefits of mechanisation, Ercolani did not pursue this blindly at any cost. After the war, for instance, some processes were deliberately not automated because it would have had such a negative impact on morale.

'Work study is a scientific thing and a moral thing,' Ercolani asserted.[3] He was deeply offended when an official from the Ministry of Supply referred to his men as 'robots', simply because they were so much better organised and more efficient than workers elsewhere. As well as benefiting the company, increased productivity had significant advantages for its staff because it meant that the firm could afford to pay them more. Workers at Furniture Industries Limited earned around a third more than the standard union rate. This caused ructions among other local manufacturers, who accused Ercolani of being a communist, but as he pointed out, the reason he was able to pay higher wages was because he ran such a tight ship.

Opposite left
Illustration showing Lucian
Brett Ercolani and his crew
climbing into a dinghy
after their plane came
down in the Channel in
November 1941

Opposite right
Stacks of machined parts
at Ercol, c.1955-62

Above
Ray Brown holding the
clamps of a jig to shape a
component on a spindle
moulder, c.1962

Right
Utility Furniture catalogue,
Board of Trade, 1948

Although Ercolani was a staunch supporter of trade unions, he characterised himself as a humanist rather than a socialist. A caring employer, albeit strict, with a keen social conscience, he valued his workers and treated them with consideration. As well as setting up a generous company pension scheme, he took his staff on summer outings to the seaside and gave each individual a Christmas present, such as a chicken or a joint of pork. In later life Ercolani was particularly proud of the fact that there had never been a strike at the factory. 'To have a dispute would be a terrible thing. I'd never get over it,' he confessed.[4] His views reflect a curious mix of hard-nosed pragmatism, paternalism and sensitivity. It was all about striking the right balance.

Utility Regulations

During the war furniture-grade timber was strictly rationed and many skilled labourers were conscripted. The destruction of so many houses in the Blitz, however, meant that some replacement furniture was needed for 'bombees'. In 1942, therefore, the Board of Trade established the Utility Furniture Advisory Committee, succeeded the following year by the Utility Furniture Panel, chaired by Gordon Russell. The purpose of the Utility scheme was to regulate supply by licensing production of a basic range of standard furniture designs that were simply constructed and economical in their use of materials. Utility restrictions remained in operation until the end of the 1952, although from 1948 onwards manufacturers were permitted to develop their own designs, as long as they complied with Utility specifications.

The furniture industry resented these strictures, but adherents of the Modern Movement welcomed the Utility scheme as an opportunity to instigate design reform. Ercolani, although hardly a Modernist, was one of those who viewed Utility in a positive light, because it established minimum standards and fostered plainer styles. As there was a guaranteed market, manufacturers no longer had to compete with each other or pander to popular taste, another advantage from Ercolani's point of view. The Utility scheme prompted him to go back to basics and develop a much simpler approach to furniture design. This was why he was so enthusiastic about Utility, describing it as 'the greatest movement which has ever taken place in any country in trade.'[5]

His direct involvement with the Utility scheme began in 1944 after he was commissioned by the Board of Trade to produce 100,000 basic Windsor chairs, mainly for use in canteens, with the prospect of further large orders if the initial contract was fulfilled. The design, known as the 4A Chair, had first appeared in a Utility catalogue in 1943, so it was not Ercolani's invention, although by working out how to manufacture it efficiently in bulk, he effectively made the design his own. Although Ercolani was keen to take on the contract, the job was problematic because the Board of Trade stipulated that the chairs should be produced at a very low unit cost – only 10s 6d per chair. This appeared to be uneconomic, but Ercolani was prepared to consider it because of the large quantities involved. He realised from the outset that the only prospect of making the chair cheaply was by industrialising the manufacturing process and greatly speeding up production. This would involve designing new machinery and setting up a new assembly line, which might take up to a year, he informed the Board of Trade, but the long-term benefits were considerable, both for the client and the company. On a personal level, Ercolani relished the technical challenge so, despite all the risks, he agreed to take the project on.

Embracing the Windsor Chair Tradition

Ercolani had been interested in the history of English furniture since his student days. His admiration for 17th century oak furniture had already influenced his Pickled Pine and Old Colonial Ranges. He also appreciated the elegance of English 18th century furniture, particularly Chippendale, because it was furniture that people could actually use. 'We are great simplifiers in this country,' he believed. [6] The Windsor chair had also flowered during this period, evolving organically, largely immune from metropolitan fashions. Growing spontaneously out of vernacular traditions, its origins lay in the humble three-legged stool. Essentially this was practical everyday seating made by, and for, country people, but also co-opted as 'below stairs' furniture and garden seating on country house estates.

The 'Cinderella' of English furniture, the Windsor chair was so familiar and ubiquitous that its merits were often overlooked. In spite of its enduring popularity, it had largely been omitted from official histories of furniture as it was considered too commonplace and unremarkable to warrant being recorded. Embodying centuries of tradition, it had a timeless quality that transcended a particular period and was equally well-suited to historic and contemporary interiors. Like Shaker furniture, its materials, proportions and construction were all intrinsically satisfying. Plain, functional and unpretentious, it appealed to the hand, heart and eye.

As a designer, Ercolani felt a strong personal affinity with the Windsor chair and had long been fascinated by the technical processes involved in its manufacture. There was something about the design that captured his imagination. An archetype created by the common man, it was a marvel

Left
Traditional Windsor chair owned by Lucian R. Ercolani

Top right
Chiltern bodger rough-hewing billets before turning them on a pole lathe

Right
472 Chairmaker's Chair, produced by Ercol, 1962, a double bow fireside chair inspired by Ercolani's Windsor chair (left)

of simplicity, constructed from as few as 14 pieces of wood. For him, it epitomised all that was best about English furniture: 'a very simple article born out of jolly good native methods.'[7] The Windsor chair also carried a special local resonance, being so closely associated with the Chilterns, where it had been made for centuries, due to the abundant beech woods in this area. Although production had greatly declined during the early 20th century, Windsor chairs were still being made by a few local craftsmen during the 1930s.

Even in the industrial age, Windsor chair-making remained rooted in vernacular idioms and rural craftsmanship. Traditionally, the beech legs, stretchers and sticks for the seatback had been produced by 'bodgers' (itinerant turners) using a portable pole lathe erected in the woods next to where the trees were felled. Alternatively, some bodgers used a metal-framed treadle wheel lathe installed in a shed.[8] Pole lathes were activated by means of a foot-operated treadle mechanism connected by a cord to one end of a fine beech pole. A second cord tied to the other end of the pole was wrapped around a length of wood held in a spindle. As the treadle was operated, the pole moved up and down and spun the wood. By holding the blade of a chisel against the wood while it revolved, the surface could be smoothed and regular or tapered forms could be created.

The bow-shaped seat backs were bent while the timber was still 'green' (in other words, unseasoned) using a simple jig with pegs to hold the stave in place. The chairs were assembled either by the bodgers or by specialist craftsmen known as framers, based in the surrounding towns and villages. While the frames were made from beech, the seats were traditionally carved from elm, with saddle-like depressions in the seat created by scooping out the wood with an adze, a process known as 'bottoming'. Holes were bored in the seat and bow to accommodate the sticks for the seatback (also known as lists or spindles) and the legs of the undcrframe. As the timber dried out, all the various elements became fixed together.

The bodgers also supplied components to the large chair-making workshops established in High Wycombe during the 19th century. By 1874 the industry was considerable, with an annual output of around 1,250,000 chairs. Yet, although furniture making became increasingly industrialised from this date onwards, Windsor chair making remained essentially a manual process. Boring the holes in the bow and the seat was done by eye, and unless they were exactly the right diameter and set at the correct angle, the chair would fall to bits. All the components had to be carefully adjusted, otherwise the timber would crack. Windsor chairs could only be assembled by a skilled craftsman, therefore, even though they were produced in bulk.

During the 1930s Ercolani had felt increasingly frustrated at being obliged to produce commercial furniture designs that he did not particularly like. Although keen to make a fresh start after the war, until the Board of Trade approached him with the Windsor chair commission, it was unclear which direction he should pursue in the future. 'During the war I made up my mind to develop the simplest thing there was. It took me all my lifetime to see that,' he later reflected.[9] By putting the humble Windsor chair into production, Ercolani felt as though he was compensating for the aesthetic deficiencies of his earlier work. Speaking in overtly moral and quasi-religious terms, he declared: 'We were learning to shun fancifulness and holding factually to the principle of making our work a living spirituality of goodness.'[10] For him, the Windsor chair offered 'salvation'.

Although Ercolani had always instinctively favoured plain furniture, he never claimed to be progressive and would later characterise himself as 'a retrograde, a regressionist.'[11] Rather than creating something self-consciously novel or modern, he preferred to explore tried and tested solutions from the past as a starting point for new improved designs. In taking up the challenge of modernising the Windsor chair, he planted a seed that would grow into a mighty tree over the next 25 years through the Windsor Range.

Industrialising the Vernacular

Most furniture is made from seasoned timber, in other words, wood that has been left to dry in the open air for several years after being cut into planks so that the moisture content is reduced. This is a pre-requisite in order to ensure the wood does not move after a piece of furniture has been made, otherwise it may crack or fall apart. Because wood is an organic material, it is acutely sensitive to atmospheric conditions: 'On a dry July day, the outside of that board might contain only 14 per cent of moisture but the inside will contain 20 per cent,' explained Ercolani. 'Now if you make that wood into a chair and put it in a room where the air is dry, the wood will shed its surplus moisture, bend and possibly crack. That's why seasoning wood is such a slow process.'[12]

The crucial point about the Windsor chair was that, although it had been produced in large quantities for over two centuries, in manufacturing terms it was still basically hand-crafted and each chair was essentially a one-off. One of the reasons why it was so difficult to make was because elm is a notoriously 'twisty' wood, prone to warping, so it is not easy to handle. It also tends to be knotty so there is often a lot of wastage. Although elm trees were commonplace in the British countryside at this date, elm had not previously been widely used in furniture making. In spite of its rich colour and beautiful grain, it was generally avoided by cabinetmakers because it was considered too 'wild', its main application hitherto being for utilitarian items such as gates, wheelbarrows, coffins and clapboards on building sites.

Beech, by contrast, being fine-grained, is a much more workable and stable timber, hence its widespread adoption as the standard material for chair frames. 'It can be sawn, turned on a lathe, shaped and even bent in a bow, far more easily than most other timbers, as well as taking stain and colour very well,' the company pointed out.[13] Yet, even the bow frames of Windsor chairs were difficult to bend in a standardised way and required careful adjustments by hand. The reason for combining beech and elm in the Windsor chair is that they complement each other perfectly, not only in colour and texture, but in their structural properties. Although beech is strong and pliable, it lacks the visual and tactile richness of elm. As Ercolani summed up succinctly: 'Elm has got the surface but it hasn't got the strength.'[14] The traditional juxtaposition of beech and elm was not only logical in terms of construction, it was vital aesthetically in order to capture the essence of the traditional Windsor chair. In spite of the problem of 'taming' the elm, therefore, Ercolani wanted to stick to these materials for reasons of authenticity.

Having acquired a classic Windsor chair from Fred Skull, who ran an antiques business, Ercolani analysed its construction. In order to produce Windsor chairs speedily and in bulk, the key problem, he realised, was how to control the movement of the wood. Unless the wood was stable, it would 'dance', necessitating time-consuming and fiddly adjustments while the chair was being assembled: 'How could it be prevented from warping or "moving" with changes in the weather or environment?' he asked himself.

Far left
Sawn planks being air-dried in Ercol's timber yard, c.1955-62

Top left
Detail of elm seat on Ercol Draughtsman's Stool, c.1959

Bottom left
Detail of beech frame and elm seat on 391 All Purpose Windsor Chair, 1957

Right
Shaping the steam-bent bow of a 365 Quaker Chair, c.1957-62

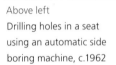

Above left
Drilling holes in a seat
using an automatic side
boring machine, c.1962

Above right
Logs being delivered
to Ercol's timber yard,
c.1965-7

Bottom right
Automatic steam kiln at
Ercol, c.1955-62

Opposite top
Loading timber into a
steam kiln, c.1955-62

'And supposing these problems could be solved, how could the bend of the bow be made precise or machines take over where the "Bodgers" left off?'[15]

The two central aspects of Windsor chair-making are bending the beech bow to exactly the right curvature so that it slots into the seat and holds the sticks in place; and stabilising the elm seat so that it does not warp or crack. In industrial production, both these processes need to be controlled. Furthermore, in order to be cost-effective, the cutting of the wood must be standardised and the machining, bending and assembly operations need to be carried out in multiples, rather than one by one. These were the challenges faced by Ercolani in industrialising the manufacture of the Windsor chair:

> It was necessary, of course, to be certain of having a fixed seat and to be certain of a bend retaining its shape, because I had in mind the possibility of pre-forming all the sticks ready to insert into the back of the seat, without fitting. This would avoid the time-consuming operation of placing each stick into that particular shape and making it take the shape of the bend.[16]

The difficulties of overcoming the technical problems of mass-producing the Windsor chair should not be underestimated. Everyone in High Wycombe was highly sceptical of Ercolani's aspirations, not least the bodgers from the nearby villages of Stokenchurch and Penn, whose secrets had been passed down from generation to generation. They, of all people, knew how tricky it was to control the movement of the wood. When they got wind of Ercolani's experiments, they sent him messages saying, 'Tell Erkie he'll never make a Windsor chair.'[17] Nevertheless, Ercolani was confident that he would eventually solve the problem, and eventually he triumphed: 'I found out their secret – timber only half baked, so they could bang the sticks in as they liked – so, as the timber shrank, it held the wood in all the better.'[18]

Taming Timber

Timber was still extremely hard to come by during 1944-5, so when Ercolani was alerted to the existence of 20,000 cubic feet of elm boards in East Anglia, he quickly snapped them up. Traditionally, the elm used for the seats of Windsor chairs had been seasoned in the open air, yet although this timber had been standing for five years and should, in theory, have been fully seasoned, Ercolani later discovered that only the top planks had actually dried out properly. Determined not to allow his precious timber to go to waste, he started thinking of ways in which the damp timber could be dried artificially in a controlled way without causing it to warp.

In order to make furniture, the moisture levels in timber have to be reduced from about 20 per cent to 10-11 per cent. Although kilning was relatively commonplace in the furniture industry by this date as a means of speeding up the drying process, elm was too unstable to be dried in a conventional kiln. The solution arrived at by Ercolani, therefore, was to use steam kilns. With steam kilns, the timber was first saturated and then dried out slowly in a more gradual and controlled way, so that the moisture content was reduced evenly throughout the wood, which was stabilised in the process. As some new steam kilns were available locally at the Forest Products Research Laboratory in Princes Risborough, not far from High Wycombe, Ercolani was able to pursue his experiments there. Having ascertained that his theory worked, as long as the temperature and humidity were carefully regulated, he adapted one of the existing kilns at the factory and then set about building a series of others. The first automatic steam kilns were installed at the works during the early years after the war.

The adoption of steam kilns was central to the firm's post-war expansion. Eventually, as the scale of production grew during the 1950s and 60s, the number of steam kilns at the factory rose to 32, each holding 1,000 cubic

Engineering Wood

Another significant breakthrough in 'taming' elm was to glue lengths of timber together to make composite boards. Joining several pieces of wood not only overcame the problem of warping by making the timber more stable, it also meant that knots could be avoided. This process also resolved another dilemma faced by Ercolani with the elm planks he had acquired which, being only one inch thick, were not strong enough to be used for seats in their existing form. Although still solid, the composite boards were considerably stronger than timber in plank form, so they could support more weight.

The lengths of timber combined to create a board were carefully selected by a matcher so that the grains were complementary in colour and texture. Adjacent blocks were jointed with dowels and glued with synthetic resin adhesives, then clamped in a press to ensure the joints were secure. Radio-frequency heating jigs were used to accelerate the setting of the adhesives. Rather than pressing each block individually, a mechanised multi-press was developed so that several blocks could be formed at the same time under controlled pressure. This technique proved so successful that it became a mainstay of production at the factory for several decades. Although initially developed for seats, the same principle was later successfully applied to elm boards for table tops and cabinets.

Standardising components in this way was a key aspect in mass-producing the Windsor chair. Precision was absolutely vital. There was no room for error in any aspect of the machining. The holes had to be bored in exactly the right place, for example, and the sticks and legs had to be exactly the right dimensions so that they fitted perfectly into the holes. 'What the old framers did was to adapt the chair to the distortion. What we did was to remove the distortion,' Ercolani explained.[23] Cutting the wood to shape with a high level of accuracy to engineering standards was central to the process.

feet of timber, making it one of the largest kilning plants of its kind in Europe. In 1967 the company reflected proudly on this transformation through the voice of the company's advertising mascot, the Ercolion: 'Today, mile-after-mile of seasoned beech and elm pass through my kilns daily and emerge accurately conditioned with an unheard of stability that prevents any possibility of movement, warping, twisting or splitting over the years. Without this complex and costly pre-manufacturing skill, Ercol Windsor furniture could never have been made.'[19]

The elm was placed in the steam kilns for up to two to three weeks. 'This process is not merely drying, it is a conditioning of the wood and it is very important that it is done slowly and very exactly,' wrote one observer.[20] 'Hygrometers report the progress of each batch of timber hourly so that central control knows exactly how each load is progressing at any time during the drying cycle,' noted the trade journal *Forestry and Home Grown Timber*. 'The even tempo of the factory's output is based on the assumption that the timber being processed is constant in its density, moisture content and lack of defects.'[21]

Steaming was also vital in bending the beech bows. The staves were placed in a special retort for 45 minutes, which raised the moisture content of the wood, making it temporarily as pliable as rope. During this brief interval, lasting only about two minutes, the softened staves were secured in metal braces and either bent individually or as a group using a hydraulic bending machine. The bows were then removed from the press, but the straps were left in place. The whole unit was then baked in a drying oven to reduce the moisture content, a process known as curing. When they emerged, the bows retained their shape and the wood was perfectly stable: 'a perfect arc of beech, with a strength, spring and resilience that will last through generations of use.'[22]

Above
Kiln office at the back of the steam kilns, 1960s

Left
Jack Holmes filling a steam oven with machined timber, 1976

'Each operation is wholly foolproof due to the perfect jig designs produced for each component,' noted *The Scotsman* in 1960. 'There is no measuring and marking of wood allowed. Mr Ercolani says that no two people with a tape measure get exactly the same measurements. Each item is therefore fitted exactly on to the jig and cannot vary by a blade of a millimetre as the cutters do their work.'[24]

Although the 4A Chair appeared quite simple as a design, working out how to manufacture it industrially was extremely complex. After analysing the production process, Ercolani concluded that as many as 80 separate operations were involved in the machining, assembly and finishing of a single chair. Each operation had to be addressed individually in order to work out the best way of tackling it, and the whole production process needed to be considered together as an assembly line. Ercolani had championed the adoption of woodworking machinery from the outset, but to manufacture the 4A Chair meant either adapting existing machines or developing new equipment to undertake specific tasks. The challenge was to develop machines that could shape large quantities of standardised components quickly and reliably to precise specifications. Spindles were turned using a Fell lathe, for example, with square blocks of wood being fed into a cutter with rotating knives, then turned to the desired profile.

As well as machining individual components, other devices were developed to facilitate and speed up the assembly process, such as a machine to push the legs firmly into the holes on the seat. Initially there were problems because the elm seat had a tendency to split when all four legs were pushed in together. The solution was to reverse the process and press the seat down onto the legs, rather than the other way round, a good example of lateral thinking. Resolving all these issues was a painstaking process. One tiny miscalculation could have disastrous consequences. Because there were no industrial precedents for what Ercolani was attempting to do, there was

no model to follow so he was breaking new ground. Although extremely time-consuming, in the longer term all this careful development work paid off because, once he had resolved all the manufacturing problems for the 4A Chair, he was able to apply the same principles to other designs. 'Automation is his achievement, the production of solid, cheap, attractive, well-constructed chairs at a low price for a mass market,' confirmed *The Observer* in 1959. [25]

Another significant factor affecting the speed and efficiency of Windsor chair production was the layout of the factory. Until the end of the 1930s, machines were arranged in rows as they were powered by a line shaft, but during the war, this system was abandoned as it was too inflexible. From this date onwards each machine was powered individually, which meant that they could be positioned in a more logical way. Another wartime innovation that proved lastingly useful was a system of fixed rollers linking different sections of the production line. Acting like a conveyor belt, this equipment proved highly effective in moving products and components around the building.

The 4A Windsor Kitchen Chair

Because of the long lead time in refining the 4A Chair and putting in place the new machines and systems to enable it to be manufactured, it was late in 1945 before the first chairs came off the production line. By this date the Board of Trade had doubled their order from 1000 chairs a week to 2000. They later agreed to raise the unit cost from 10s 6d to the more realistic figure of 13s 6d. [26] As a result of Ercolani's shrewd wartime investment in this new area of production, therefore, Furniture Industries Limited emerged from the war in a much healthier state than many other manufacturers, with a staff of 300 and a turnover of £300,000, making it well-placed to capitalise on the expected post-war surge in consumer demand. Because the Utility scheme remained in place until the end of 1952, the 4A Chair was manufactured in large quantities throughout this period. Whereas other Utility designs were dropped as soon as the scheme ended, the 4A Chair proved lastingly popular. It remained in production in its original form until 1953 and continued to be made in variant designs for several decades.

Ercolani's achievement in industrialising the Windsor chair greatly

Top left
Cabinets being moved
around the factory
on fixed roller system,
c.1955-62

Top right
121 Table and variant 4A
Chairs produced for *Britain
Can Make It*, 1946

Right
120 Sideboard produced
for *Britain Can Make It*,
1946

Above
Windsor Range furniture
in Ercol catalogue, 1951

Left
370 Windsor Dining Chair
and 370A Armchair, 1957,
descendants of 4A Chair

enhanced his reputation within the furniture trade. Fellow manufacturers were all too aware of the technical problems he had managed to overcome. In fact another High Wycombe firm made an unsuccessful attempt to produce Windsor chairs after the war, but failed and gave up. In 1945 Ercolani was chosen by the British Furniture Manufacturers (the trade organisation representing the industry) to act on its behalf in preliminary discussions with the selectors of *Britain Can Make It*, a high-profile design exhibition being organised by the Council of Industrial Design, scheduled to take place at the Victoria and Albert Museum the following year. Ercolani was very positive about this event, which he regarded as a great opportunity for manufacturers to display their wares to the British public and international buyers.

To complement the 4A Chair, he designed two other pieces of dining room furniture for *Britain Can Make It*: the 120 Sideboard and the 121 Dining Table. Because Utility restrictions were still in force, the company was given a special licence to produce these pieces, which were both made from beech (rather than beech and elm, as their successors would be). As well as being listed in the catalogue, they were also illustrated in a souvenir guide called *Design '46*. [27] The chairs were actually a variant of the 4A Chair, with four sticks in the seatback and a plain central splat. Although described as 'wheel back' in the caption, they did not actually incorporate the traditional carved wheel motif, perhaps because decoration was discouraged at this date. After the exhibition only the 4A Chair remained in production. It was not until 1951, after Utility regulations had been relaxed and timber shortages eased, that the other designs were revived, although at the time they were significant in being the first additions to the expanded Windsor Range.

Significantly, the wood used for these pieces was waxed in natural colours to allow the texture and tone of the grain to be appreciated. This in itself was an innovation as light-coloured woods were still a novelty at this date. During the inter-war years oak had been the standard timber used at Furniture Industries Limited, almost invariably stained dark brown. Walnut, too, was another inter-war staple. The shift to pale beech and warm honey-coloured elm was revolutionary, therefore, not only for the company but within the industry. The unusual combination of beech and elm and the fact that solid wood was used gave the Windsor Range a unique character. The conscious decision to retain a natural finish carried moral overtones, symbolising a new transparency and a fresh start after the war.

A Chair for Everyman

Following its debut at *Britain Can Make It*, the 4A Chair was exhibited in the Homes and Gardens Pavilion at the Festival of Britain in 1951. By that date the Council of Industrial Design was more apprehensive about endorsing a 'historical' design, but, having worked so hard to create a standardised Windsor chair, Ercolani knew how radically different his industrialised version was from its hand-crafted predecessors: 'The Festival was against my doing the Windsor chair. They said there wasn't any design in it, but there was,' he asserted. [28] The growing nervousness of the design establishment about being associated with anything that might smack of reproduction furniture escalated during the 1950s. Whereas overtly Modernist firms, such as Hille and Race, were actively championed by the COID, Furniture Industries Limited – or Ercol as it became known - did not receive the same accolades, not that this really mattered in the end as the public enthusiastically embraced the 4A Chair and the whole Windsor Range.

Having re-established his firm's reputation through this design, Ercolani realised that it made good business sense to develop the Windsor theme. As well as bringing him creative satisfaction and enabling him to fulfil his potential as a designer, the commercial success of the Windsor Range secured a healthy future for Furniture Industries Limited, helping him to re-build the business which had had to be scaled down during the war. Developing a collection that was so challenging to make from a technical point of view deterred other manufacturers from copying. Ercolani made it so difficult for potential plagiarists that very few attempted to follow his lead. It was not until the 1960s that Windsor Range look-alikes began to appear. Even then, none of these had the grace or elegance of his designs.

Ercolani's achievement was to devise a way of mass-producing the Windsor chair industrially in a factory whilst preserving the essence of the craft-based archetype. One of his great strengths as a manufacturer was his ability to treat furniture making as a form of engineering and analyse technical processes in a systematic and scientific way. 'He's very broad in his sense of design and highly practical in his approach,' remarked his son Lucian. 'He has an astonishing mechanical grasp, and he applied this to working with wood, so that we were able to work on engineering principles, as though we were dealing with steel.' [29]

Ercolani's success in manufacturing the Windsor chair in large quantities at low cost was a source of personal pride. 'I thought the Windsor chair, born out of adversity, was worth creating,' he reflected in later life. [30] 'I had seized the opportunity, not for the creation of the greatest thing, or a clever article which could be purchased only by the rich; instead, as a personal fulfilment, I had chosen to provide a work of simple originality for the people.' [31] As *The Scotsman* confirmed in 1960: 'Lucian Ercolani has always been obsessed by the idea that the ordinary, average person should be able to possess beautifully-proportioned and finished craftsmen-made furniture.' [32] It brought him great satisfaction to produce a well-designed, well-made chair that his own workers could afford. His 4A Windsor Chair was truly a chair for Everyman.

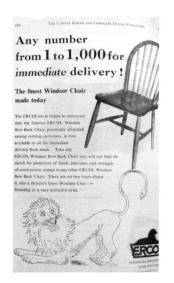

Top left
Advertisement for 4A
Chair, *The Cabinet Maker*,
April 1950

Top right
Kitchen furniture in *Utility
Furniture* catalogue, 1948,
including 4A Chairs

Above left
909A Latimer Armchair,
1988, later variant of 514
Armchair

Right
514 Windsor Bow
Armchair, 1967

Chapter 4:
Windsor Contemporary

Opposite
'Comfortable and
so ERCOLourful'
advertisement in
House & Garden, 1956

Below
4A Chair, Ercol
catalogue, 1951

Ercolani in Charge

The 4A Windsor Kitchen Chair marked a turning point for Furniture Industries Limited. Produced in large quantities from 1945 onwards, it sustained the company until 1950 when the Windsor Contemporary collection was launched. Modest though it might seem compared with the fully developed Windsor Range, the 4A Chair contained the seed of everything that followed. This explains why it retained such an enduring mystique for Lucian Ercolani. It took pride of place in the company's 1951 catalogue, where its story was presented as a fairytale told by the company's 'mascot', the Ercolion (Ercolani in disguise):

> "Once upon a time... there was a lovely thing condemned to the kitchen. No! it was not Cinderella – it was the Windsor Chair – and nobody realised how beautiful it was till I rescued it and put it in its proper place... First I had to smarten it up – even Cinderella didn't go to the ball in her working rags. Then I invented machines to turn out the Ercol Windsor Bow Back Chair, and wax polish it, as well as any craftsman would... Having put all this mechanical efficiency to work I found myself able to sell these beautiful chairs for a very low price... So if anyone wants to lend distinction to their dining room, there is no more economical way." [1]

The success of the 4A Chair gave Ercolani a new lease of life as a designer and as an industrialist. Although he had turned 60 in 1948, he felt completely reinvigorated. 'My energy was that of a person of thirty years.

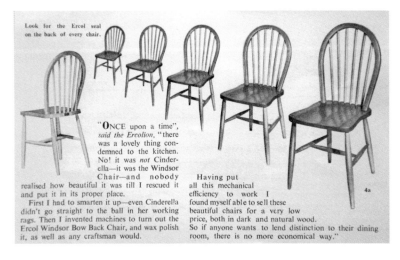

Look for the Ercol seal on the back of every chair.

"ONCE upon a time", *said the Ercolion*, "there was a lovely thing condemned to the kitchen. No! it was *not* Cinderella—it was the Windsor Chair—and nobody realised how beautiful it was till I rescued it and put it in its proper place.
First I had to smarten it up—even Cinderella didn't go to the ball in her working rags. Then I invented machines to turn out the Ercol Windsor Bow Back Chair, and wax polish it, as well as any craftsman would. Having put all this mechanical efficiency to work I found myself able to sell these beautiful chairs for a very low price, both in dark and natural wood. So if anyone wants to lend distinction to their dining room, there is no more economical way."

I was full of optimism and I felt that with my two sons we could recapture the world.' [2] He approached the task of rebuilding the company with a moral fervour, almost like a crusade: 'I had learnt that there is something religious about a craft, a craft which has a bearing on people's happiness,' he averred. 'I am sure that when a new piece of furniture enters a house – if it is a well made piece of furniture, as it should be – it is greeted by all with happiness.' [3] Ercolani's missionary zeal was infectious. Although he made heavy demands on his sons and on the company's workforce, he inspired great loyalty and commitment because his motivations were so obviously genuine and altruistic.

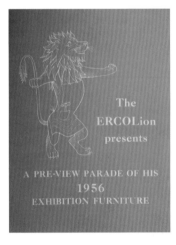

The
ERCOLion
presents

A PRE-VIEW PARADE OF HIS
1956
EXHIBITION FURNITURE

When *New Homes* ran a feature on the company in 1955, the article opened with a paeon to the 'Old Man' (as he was affectionately known at the factory): 'Lucian Ercolani – philosopher, raconteur, enthusiast, host, and Furniture Designer par excellence! One might also add Philanthropist since his aim is to turn out high-quality furniture at a price within the reach of all.'[4] Ercolani remained perennially popular with the media, who admired his tireless energy and drive. 'Now 76, bald and squarish, his eyes still sparkle behind black-rimmed spectacles and he brims with confidence and fervour,' wrote *House Beautiful* in 1965. 'He has watched his early dream turn into reality but in the process has lost none of his ardent youthful belief in the value of a craftsman's skill.'[5]

Another reason for Ercolani to feel positive about the future was that, by April 1947, he was both chairman and managing director of Furniture Industries Limited. The company's shares were now almost entirely family-owned as the original investors had gradually been bought out. Furthermore, the shares he had been obliged to issue to the firm's creditors as an emergency measure in 1934 when the company faced bankruptcy had also been bought back with the help of his brother Victor. By this date Ercolani was also the outright owner of Walter Skull & Son (1932) Ltd., as he had completed his purchase of the Skull family's shares in 1942. Another milestone for the firm in 1947 was paying off its mortgage to the Gomme family, so the business was untrammelled by debt. Although the name Furniture Industries Limited was retained until 1958, when a trading company called Ercol Furniture Ltd was established to sell all furniture manufactured by Furniture Industries Limited and Walter Skull & Son (1932) Ltd., the firm was widely known as Ercol throughout the preceding decade.[6] Ercolani now had complete control over the entire enterprise for the first time in his career. It is no wonder he saw this as a new beginning. In spite of his age, the last thing on his mind was to retire.

With his eldest son, Lucian, back at his side helping to develop and expand the factory, and with his younger son, Barry, now in harness on the sales side, restoring and nurturing vital links with retailers, the company had a strong management team. Lucian's input was particularly crucial as he played a key role in developing the machines to produce his father's designs, as well as the day-to-day running of the works. 'Most of the plant has been specially designed by Lucian Ercolani junior, whose delicate task it is, among others, to work out the machinery for the particular design, and to ensure that large-scale production is practical and economical,' noted *The Scotsman*.[7] A trade journal called *Industrial Safety* pointed out that Lucian 'designed most of the special jigs and machine attachments… designed to ensure a high degree of accuracy, with great speed – and in a way that keeps the operator's fingers well away from the workface.'[8]

Lucian's aptitude for engineering was matched by his organisational skills and diplomacy. He was appointed as a director in 1946 and later became joint managing director with Barry, who joined the board in 1950. 'Everyone in this works is free to come direct to me with any problems,' confirmed Lucian. 'Apart from the fact that I'm available around the works a great deal of the time, my office door is open to anyone who wants to get something off his chest.'[9] Barry was equally well-suited to his role in sales and marketing, being highly articulate and a natural showman like his father. Despite his initial reservations about joining the family firm, having originally contemplated a career as a writer, he made a very positive contribution. His flair for publicity proved vital in imprinting the Ercol brand in the minds of consumers during the 1950s and 60s.

Working in a family company has its pros and cons, however, and making the transition from one generation to the next can be problematic. Having ruled the roost single-handedly since 1920, Ercolani Snr was used to getting his own way. A passionate individual who cared deeply about the enterprise that he had created from scratch, he was prone to lose his temper and had

an extremely short fuse. At heart, though, he was essentially considerate. 'The Old Man can get mad about some things, to the point where you feel he's going off his head,' admitted Lucian Jnr. 'But when there's a real problem, he's as cool as a cucumber.'[10] Barry neatly summed up the two contrasting sides of his father's character, describing him as 'possibly the kindest and most tolerant man I know if someone is in trouble, but when it comes to the vocation, to the work itself, I suppose he's the most intolerant man I know.'[11]

As these comments indicate, Ercolani was a complex character. A man of principle, he was an unconventional businessman and took a highly personal approach to running his company. Although financially astute, he refused to see business in purely economic terms. For Ercolani, running a furniture company was about long-term investment in human beings and humane design. What mattered most was the sincerity of his furniture and the welfare of his workforce. When his sons joined the company, Ercolani infused them with the same ideals: 'I aimed to impress upon them that we were not in business to make money. We were in business to make furniture,

to make it well and to make money with which to make more furniture.'[12] The fact that Ercol is still a family company and has never passed into public ownership underlines how effectively Ercolani's founding principles were communicated to his heirs. 'It's not easy for the boys working with me,' he admitted. 'I'm much harder on them than I would be on anyone else. But for me it is wonderful. I have planted two acorns, and watched the growth of two fine sturdy oaks.'[13]

Ercolani Finds his Voice

One of the advantages of bringing his sons on board was that Ercolani had more time to devote to designing. Although he had originally trained and practised as a designer, over the years he had been diverted from his original calling because of the day-to-day demands of running the business. As managing director he retained overall creative control, but some of the furniture produced during the 1930s is likely to have been designed by other in-house staff, generally recruited from the somewhat narrow confines of the High Wycombe industry.

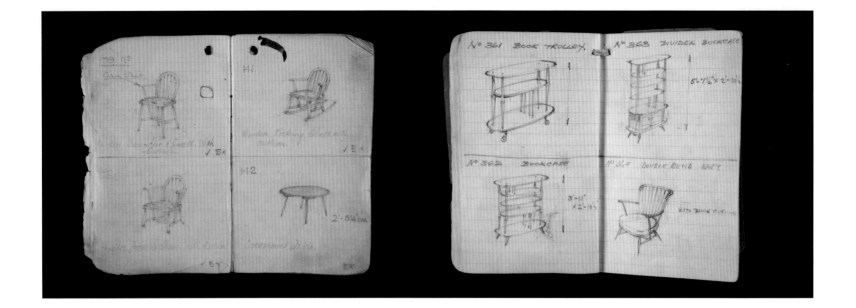

Interestingly, one of the locally trained designers who Ercolani had attempted to enlist in 1934 was Robin Day (1915-2010), later renowned as the consultant designer at Hille after the war. Day had been working as a draughtsman for a local firm, having recently finished his studies at High Wycombe School of Art. Recognising his potential, Ercolani approached the young designer and offered him a job. By this date, however, Day had already been awarded a scholarship to the Royal College of Art so he turned the job down in order to continue his education. It is intriguing to speculate what might have happened had he accepted the post.[14]

What this anecdote reveals is that, even before the war, Ercolani was already on the lookout for new blood. 'It is most necessary that you employ inventive men or have an inventive brain yourself with which to create articles which are not only pleasing to your own eye but also to the other person's eye,' he confirmed.[15] In the end, the fresh ideas that he was seeking emerged from within Ercolani himself in his newly re-energised state. Determined to avoid the vicious circle of copying that had bedevilled the furniture trade during the 1930s, Ercolani re-oriented the company in a positive new direction through the Windsor Range. By effectively re-learning how to make furniture through the 4A Chair, he reinvigorated the whole enterprise, bringing its products 'more into harmony with an emerging world without disowning all that was best in the world.'[16]

During the 1920s and 30s, no designers were identified in the firm's catalogues, even Ercolani himself. This is hardly surprising as anonymity was the norm in the furniture industry at this date. Manufacturers themselves were also largely unknown to the public as retailers took the credit for the products they sold. After the war, however, Ercol pioneered the concept of branded furniture and Ercolani himself became personally associated with Ercol's designs and its public image. From the late 1940s onwards, he was openly credited as the designer of the Windsor Range. His memoirs also confirm that Ercolani himself was personally responsible for designing this collection.

An early post-war photograph entitled 'Modern Furniture Design' shows Ercolani, pen in hand, with a group of furniture models on the desk in front of him. Generally, the starting point for a new design would be a sketch by Ercolani, which a draughtsman would work up into a scale drawing. Ercolani would spend hours refining a particular detail such as the arm of a chair. 'He used to draw with a 4B pencil or with felt tip pens when they first came on the market,' recalls his grandson, Edward Tadros.[17] A small model would then be produced, followed by a full-scale prototype. Following adjustments, detailed technical drawings would be prepared.

Another key part of the design process was photography, as outlined by a journalist who visited the factory in 1959: 'A model of a chair, two inches high, will be photographed from all angles, thirty or forty times, the prints of details blown up to life-size, cut out of cardboard, and pinned up on the wall so that "space shapes" can be studied.'[18] The 'space shapes' were the spaces between the arms and legs. 'Mr Ercolani is intense about space shapes,' noted the journalist. Another press visitor recorded a similar incident:

"Have you ever noticed the fascinating angles a chair makes from this position?" asked Ercolani. Soon we – and he – were grovelling about on the floor getting an entirely new aspect of a chair, marvelling at all the rectangles, triangles and many other shapes made by the supports, the verticals and the back... Mr Ercolani sounded as if he could write a thesis on the importance of all these shapes being a delight to the eye.[19]

Designing furniture for mass production is a collaborative process. Although the creative ideas for the Windsor Range originated from Ercolani, he was supported by an able team of draughtsmen, craftsmen and engineers who helped to fine tune the designs as they were being developed. Ercolani regarded his furniture as a collective endeavour by everyone in the company, even those not directly involved in the design process. 'Ercolani modestly

accepts some responsibility for the design of his furniture, but emphasises that the result is due to the co-ordinated work of his team, which includes his sons, Lucian (an expert machinery designer) and Barry (Sales Manager),' reported *New Homes* in 1955.[20]

Two key members of staff who assisted Ercolani in developing the Windsor Range were the production engineers, Ted Summers and Tom Redrup (1912-1999). Ercolani also relied heavily on two skilled craftsmen: jig-maker Ted Cann and carver Arthur Gray. The production engineers were the designers of the manufacturing process. They ensured that a design was practical to produce and that it was manufactured as efficiently and cost effectively as possible, providing a vital link between the drawing office (later known as the design studio) and the factory. [21] Redrup, who had joined the company in 1928, worked very closely with Ercolani and was adept at turning his ideas into reality. 'They were like brothers,' recalls Mike Pengelly, who joined the

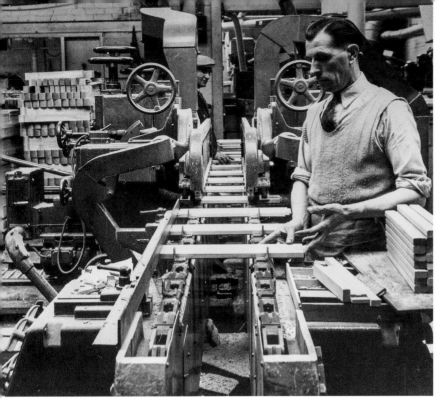

design team in 1966 when Redrup was still in charge of the drawing office:

> The Old Man had the vision – there was no doubt about that – but it was
> Redrup who was responsible for the detailed design development. Redrup was
> highly skilled technically. He designed the jigs that enabled very difficult machine
> operations to be undertaken. The Old Man's motto was, if there was no
> machine for the task, they would invent one. [22]

In an interview in 1955, Ercolani outlined his definition of the essential characteristics of good design:

> Clearly the foremost is efficiency, the ability to fulfil the required function. After
> that, design must be pleasing to the eye without being ostentatious. Something
> which catches the eye at first glance can become very tiring to live with and a
> design which is deliberately exaggerated for the sake of being obvious or ornate
> has no place in the home. [23]

Over and over again in his memoirs he repeated the words 'simple' and 'simplicity' and reiterated the phrase 'fitness for purpose' to signify his approval: 'Fitness for purpose is the basis of all design, coupled with the fitness of the materials which you are going to use in making your article,' he wrote. [24]

Ercolani alluded to his 'catechism' - the declaration of core design principles that he set down for his sons - in quasi-religious terms. Top of the list, as ever, was fitness for purpose, closely followed by proportion, materials and form. Proportion he defined as 'that which fulfils the practical requirements when the dimensions are suitable and aesthetically pleasing.' With form, he urged designers to introduce 'some movement of the object into the design, some aesthetic touch tending to make the article as happy as your vision and as elegant as possible.' Sculptural awareness was another valuable asset: 'It might be necessary to add some element to produce light and shade, or apply some idea which has suggested itself for sculpting part of your work.' But ornament was much less significant, he reiterated: 'Pure decoration, by itself, could be useless to your design.' [25]

With its subtle details and satisfying proportions, the Windsor Range, provided an eloquent demonstration of these principles. As Ercolani recognised, however, good design cannot be taught; it is largely dependent on personal instinct about balance and scale. 'There is right and wrong in everything,' he acknowledged; 'there are good aesthetics and bad aesthetics, but no encyclopaedia will tell you what it is.' [26]

Ercolani knew he had hit a rich seam when he came up with the idea of the Windsor Range but he was not prepared to release any further designs until they had been refined to his satisfaction and the production

infrastructure was in place. Good design was not something to be hurried, he believed. Having come up with such an inspired concept so late in life, he was determined to ensure that the designs were as good as they could possibly be. 'I was very slow over the planning and the developing,' he acknowledged. 'I felt that the future was so precious and when a design comes to life through skill and sheer vocation the complete article lives a long time.'[27]

Tapping Traditions

Although the Windsor Range was at the forefront of post-war British 'Contemporary' design, Ercolani made no attempt to ally himself with Modernism, a concept that was completely alien to him. Even Scandinavian design, closer though it was to the aesthetics and values espoused by Ercolani, had no direct bearing on the Windsor Range. Although there were certain parallels, they sprang from the fact that the Danes and the Swedes were drawing on the same source of inspiration as Ercolani: the English Windsor chair. There is no evidence to suggest that there was any direct cross-fertilisation, although consumers with a taste for Ercol were likely to appreciate Scandinavian furniture and vice versa.

Ercolani may have been Italian by birth but he was English by adoption. It was on native English traditions that he drew and to the English temperament that his work was designed to appeal. 'It has always been my opinion that one of the traits of the Englishman is that pleasantness should come through simplicity,' he observed. 'And I found eventually that furniture could, in fact, develop in a very lively manner with simplicity, being original and friendly rather than strange.'[28] The phrase 'friendly rather than strange' is very revealing. What Ercolani was suggesting was that familiar home-grown ideas expressive of the English character were more in tune with his designs than imported foreign concepts. 'This contemporary interpretation of the original Windsor theme provides furniture fit to grace a palace yet priced to suit the popular purse,' affirmed the Ercolion. 'It is English furniture – English furniture at its very best for English homes.'[29]

One of the quintessentially English features of the Windsor Range, apart from the bow and stick seatbacks, was the use of beech and elm, timber that looked 'good enough to eat', in Ercolani's words.[30] Until their decimation through Dutch elm disease in the 1970s, elm trees, like beech, were ubiquitous in the English countryside. Yet, although commonplace, they took hundreds of years to reach maturity, hence the significance of using solid wood as a mark of respect to the trees themselves. Through the Windsor Range these precious resources were preserved in furniture of lasting value, which became a symbol of regeneration: 'When timber such as elm or beech is handled with the skill of a craftsman it assumes a new life,' declared Ercolani.[31]

The idea of solid wood being precious, something to be prized and cherished, was enshrined in the ethos of the Windsor Range from the outset and still underlies Ercol's philosophy today. 'There's nothing like the feel of solid wood,' enthused the Ercolion. 'You know instinctively as you touch and handle it, that here is something that will grow in beauty as it mellows and matures through the years.'[32] The fact that Ercolani nurtured these values at the dawn of the space age, when other manufacturers were starting to experiment with plastics and promoting the merits of knock-down furniture, is highly significant. He was literally going against the grain in championing the virtues of natural materials and longevity. In the light of present-day concerns about sustainability, his prescience seems all the more remarkable now.

The impulse to produce furniture that was 'Contemporary' and reflected the spirit of the age was balanced by Ercolani's desire to create designs that transcended their own time. Although the Windsor Range drew on historical idioms, however, it was not actually retrogressive. The Windsor theme was simply the starting point for a series of forward-looking creative experiments harnessing a combination of advanced technology and traditional craft processes. 'Each chair has a sculptural feel deriving from a true appreciation of form,' noted *Art and Industry*. 'Effective sanding of curved members is accomplished by air-filled rotary balloon type abrasive drums which yield to the contours, and hand-waxing completes the job.'[33]

Although inspired by vernacular furniture, the Windsor Range was far from anonymous or derivative. A highly original concept, it embodied the unique personality of its creator. 'It seemed simple but it had a recognisable individuality,' Ercolani acknowledged.[34] In reality, he had departed from the Windsor chair 'proper' virtually from the start. Structurally, functionally and stylistically, there were significant differences between traditional Windsor chairs and Ercolani's Windsor Contemporary Furniture, although the two were clearly linked conceptually. 'Our furniture came to my mind from proportions entirely different from the Windsor chair,' stressed Ercolani. 'Nevertheless, within the simple design of the Windsor chair there are many possibilities.'[35]

Another important source of inspiration for the Windsor Range was the Shaker furniture that Ercolani had first encountered in the Metropolitan Museum of Art in New York back in 1923. Shaker furniture impressed him in two respects, partly for the purity and unaffected simplicity of its design and craftsmanship, but also for the idealism and values of the people who made it:

> I asked myself why that person two or three hundred years ago was so careful to clean the underneath of a table top or inside the mortise – the unseen parts as well as the visible parts. It dawned on me forcibly that it was because those early settlers had in mind that He, God, was also there watching to see that the unseen part was as cleanly finished as the rest.[36]

Although Ercolani was no longer a churchgoer, he was still a puritan at heart. Spiritual aspirations and moral principles continued to guide and motivate him throughout his life. 'If I put into a chair something which is vainglorious, something which is there to catch the eye, then I'm cheating,' he confessed.[37] In developing the Windsor Range he was able to implement his aesthetic and ethical ideals: 'Above all, truthfulness and pride in one's work usually bring their own reward. I think that is why my original simple designs did set a pattern which I hope will be good enough to meet the changes in times to come.'[38]

Having overcome the technical hurdles associated with Windsor chair production, Ercolani had much greater confidence when he began exploring and extending the Windsor theme. Because his designs were so difficult for other manufacturers to replicate, this reduced the risk of plagiarism.

Opposite
Assembling the seatback of a 472 Chairmaker's Chair, c.1962

Top
428 Quaker Rocking Chair, 470 Tub Rocking Chair and 435 Goldsmith's Rocking Chair, 1959-66

Centre left
Elm veneer on moulded plywood seat of 401 Preformed Chair, 1958

Bottom
Inspecting a 455 Sideboard, c.1961-62

However, the main hurdle for Ercol's competitors was the high standards and meticulous attention to detail that characterised the company's work. 'People say that our furniture is uncopyable, but it's not,' admitted Barry Ercolani. 'They could make it exactly as we make it, but they would have to do everything we do, from the buying of the tree, through the seasoning procedures to the machining of the wood. What my father has done is to make it unattractive for other manufacturers to copy him.'[39]

The Ercolion Finds his Feet

The development of the Windsor Range began in earnest in 1947, although it would be another three years before the collection could be launched. Realising that, once the economy recovered and Utility restrictions were lifted, there would be a surge in demand, Ercolani's plan was to ensure that the company was geared up to capitalise on this as soon as normal trading conditions were resumed. His prediction proved correct. Demand for furniture was so great during the early 1950s that it was a sellers' market. Ercolani took advantage of this unusual situation to influence public taste for positive ends.

In the meantime, Furniture Industries Limited (as it was still known at the time) was partly sustained by contract work for the firm of Harris Lebus, which commissioned large quantities of Utility chairs. Lebus was the largest furniture manufacturer in the country at this date and the order was substantial: around £250,000 worth of furniture per annum. Along with Board of Trade's orders for the 4A Chair, Lebus provided steady work for Ercolani's company during the late 1940s, enabling him to focus on developing the Windsor Range. The Lebus chairs were recorded in the firm's design notebooks from 1946 onwards, alongside Ercolani's new Windsor Range designs.

This arrangement lasted until 1956 when the two companies fell out. Ercolani had become increasingly incensed by the penny-pinching attitudes of Herman Lebus, the firm's chairman. Losing the Lebus contract so suddenly had serious implications, as it accounted for 25 per cent of Ercol's turnover. Although the Windsor Range was thriving by this date, Ercolani was still obliged to lay off 70 men as a consequence. Thankfully, over half were speedily re-engaged before they had time to spend their six weeks' redundancy money.

Opposite
Waxing a cabinet by
hand, c.1961-2

Above
Fixing the underframe
to the seat of a 376
Chair, c.1957-62

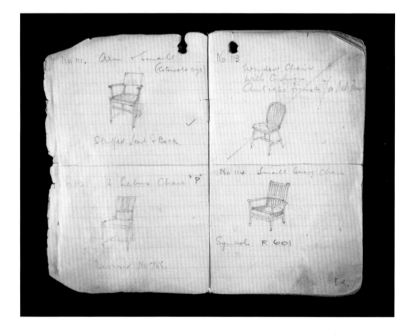

Although Utility restrictions were eased from 1948 onwards (the so-called 'freedom of design' period when manufacturers could develop their own Utility designs), the Utility scheme remained in operation until December 1952. As well as manufacturing large quantities of 4A Chairs, Ercol produced other Utility furniture during this period, such as a mahogany dining set in 1948.[40] Because Utility furniture was tax free, it had a decided advantage in terms of price. All the early designs in the expanded Windsor Range were also designed to meet Utility criteria, partly for this reason. Normal free market conditions did not, in fact, return until the end of 1955, when the government's D scheme (which replaced the Utility scheme) was finally abolished. Until then, higher-priced furniture was subject to additional purchase tax. This explains why only a limited range of Windsor Range furniture was issued during the early 1950s. From 1954 onwards the collection was steadily expanded, with a big push in 1957 when the first full printed catalogue was produced.

It was at the Furniture Exhibition at Earl's Court in February 1950 that the Windsor Range was officially launched, heralded as 'a new range of contemporary furniture.' The accompanying advertisement marked the debut of the Ercolion, the jovial cartoon character who became the public face of Ercol for the next 20 years.[41] Enthusiastically championing the Windsor Range, the Ercolion played a vital role in the rebranding of Furniture Industries Limited as Ercol, supplementing (and eventually supplanting) his stately recumbent lion predecessor. The reinvigorated Ercolion was the invention of the advertising agency, Pemberton's, which handled Ercol's publicity from 1947 until 1970. Initially, the Ercolion's front legs were still firmly planted on the ground and he clasped the old pre-war lion logo in his paw, but from 1950 he was depicted standing on his hind legs, symbolising the new-found confidence and dynamism of the company he represented.

Top left
Dining room alcove with Windsor Range furniture, *House & Garden*, 1954

Top right
Dining room featuring 306 Chairs, *House & Garden*, 1955

Bottom left
Utility furniture in Ercol Design Notebook, c.1949: 112 Chair was manufactured for Harris Lebus

Top left
Utility dining set in sapele
mahogany, produced
by Furniture Industries
Limited, 1948

Near left
The post-war Ercolion
holding Ercol's inter-war
logo, 1951

Below
139 Small Chair and 139A
Armchair, 1949, in Ercol
catalogue, 1951

ERCOL WINDSOR
CONTEMPORARY STYLE FURNITURE
finished natural colour waxed.

No. 139 Windsor chair.
and No. 139a Windsor armchair,
both with pallet cushions.

Reverse shows the above
together with
No. 177 Side table and
No. 176 Windsor Tub chair.

139   139a

The 4A Chair was still the mainstay of production at this date, promoted as 'the famous Ercol Windsor Bow Back Chair... The finest Windsor Chair made today.' By 1950 the company was keen to flag up that, whereas hitherto these chairs had been reserved for existing contract customers, they were now generally available from stock: 'Any number from 1 to 1,000 for immediate delivery!' proclaimed an advertisement.[42] Robin Day was one of the first to applaud Ercolani's initiative. Writing in the *Journal of the Royal Society of Arts*, he observed that, in recent years, it had been the Scandinavians who had shown the most appreciation of 'our fine invention, the Windsor chair,' so it was gratifying to see 'a new and highly successful version' by a British company. 'This has an elm seat, with legs, spindles and bows of beech, and is remarkably well-finished for a very inexpensive chair,' he remarked.[43]

Although Ercolani was keen to extend the Windsor concept to other forms of seating, Utility regulations constrained his early designs. For example, the 114 Small Easy Chair (1950) had a rectilinear stick-back frame rather than a bow.[44] The first fully upholstered chair associated with the Windsor Range, the 169 Easy Chair (1950), was also designed to comply with Utility requirements. Advertised in July 1950 as 'An Ercol Production made by Walter Skull & Son (1932) Ltd', it had an upholstered sprung seat and a square seatback with beech legs and arms. By this date the Ercolion was standing upright and addressing his audience more directly. Not only had the Ercolion found his feet but he was also finding his voice:

The ERCOLION has departed newly in all directions with his latest chair. The chief deviations from the path of the usual (not that he ever uses a path – he is too busy breaking trails) are in price (very low); standard of comfort (very high); feeling (highly contemporary); and beauty (extreme). He has, as usual, stayed close to his habit of craftsmanship, classic design and impeccable taste.[45]

Above
139A Armchair, 177 Side
Table, 169 Easy Chair and
176 Tub Easy Chair in Ercol
catalogue, 1951

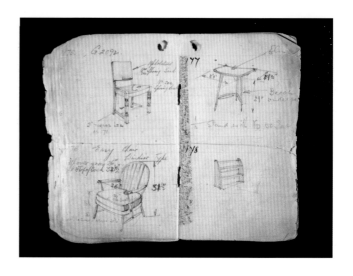

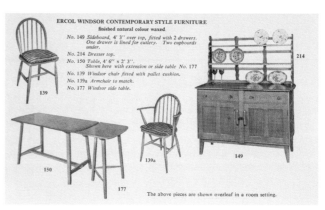

Windsor 'Contemporary'

It was not until the following year, with the launch of the 176 Tub Easy Chair (1951), that the term 'Windsor Furniture' was adopted.[46] Described as 'a contemporary development from the traditional style', this semi-upholstered chair marked a significant breakthrough as it successfully extended the Windsor theme into the field of upholstered seating. A curious hybrid, it combined a spring-filled cushion supported by tension cables with a Windsor bow seatback. Ercolani had been unsure whether to put this chair into production initially as there had been teething troubles with the spring mechanism, but following its debut at the Furniture Exhibition in February 1951, it proved an immediate hit. Its success was clinched when it was shown at the Festival of Britain three months later. 'The Ercolion makes his Festival Offering' announced an advertisement in April 1951: 'He designed it himself and there was nothing ambiguous about his intention, it being to combine the sturdy grace of the traditional Windsor with extreme comfort.'[47] To emphasise its technical merits and aesthetic appeal, the chair was illustrated from both the front and back, and with and without its cushion. Promoted for its flexibility, it was described as: 'A chair to delight in by the winter fireside or in the summer garden, a chair in which to work or idle – completely at ease.'

As well as providing a showcase for the 176 Tub Easy Chair and the 139 Chair (by this date produced in an armchair version as well), the Festival enabled Ercol to display the new versions of the sideboard and dining table created for *Britain Can Make It* in 1946. These designs, modified to fit Utility criteria, were renumbered as the 149 Sideboard (1951) and the 150 Trestle Table (1951). The sideboard was complemented by the 151 Plate Rack (1951) and the table was supplemented by the three-legged 177 Side Table (1951), which could either be used as an extension or as a standalone piece.[48] Whereas the earlier pieces had been produced in beech, the new variants were made from a combination of beech and elm. Although the large stock of elm planks purchased by Ercolani had ultimately proved too thin for the seats of Windsor chairs, he was able to use this timber for cabinets instead so that these precious materials did not go to waste. Practical considerations of this kind were typical of the external factors affecting the development of the Windsor Range. The company also exhibited these pieces at an exhibition organised by the High Wycombe Furniture Manufacturers Society in the summer of 1951 to tie in with the Festival.[49]

From this date onwards the range was marketed as Windsor Contemporary Furniture, the term 'Contemporary' having been widely adopted in the furniture trade and in the media to denote the self-consciously modern style of design popularised by the Festival. Significantly, when explaining the concept behind the Windsor Range, Ercolani dwelt little on its historical

Top left
176 Tub Easy Chair in Ercol catalogue, 1951

Top right
176 Tub Easy Chair and 177 Side Table with two non-Windsor Range designs, Ercol Design Notebook, 1951

Above centre
149 sideboard and other Windsor dining furniture in Ercol catalogue, 1951

Bottom
Ercol stand at Furniture Exhibition, Earl's Court, 1953

The Windsor Furniture Family

The idea of developing the Windsor Range as a coherent furniture family evolved during the Festival of Britain. A small portfolio-style catalogue entitled *The Ercolion Presents his Furniture Family*, issued in November 1951, presented the Windsor Range as a coordinated collection, illustrated through photographs of room settings showing how pieces could be combined.[53] While projecting an image of modernity, the collection was presented in such a way as not to alienate consumers unfamiliar with Contemporary design.

New additions in the 1951 catalogue included the circular 142 Coffee Table, the 140 Fireside Chair and the 141 Rocking Chair. Both chairs had bow seatbacks, outward projecting armrests and wooden seats with pallet cushions. The catalogue also featured two fully upholstered easy chairs categorised as 'Ercol Windsor Contemporary Style Furniture'- the 192 Easy Chair and the 191 Wing Easy Chair - both with turned legs. Right from the start, therefore, the 'Windsor' tag was applied to a wider range of furniture than just bow-framed Windsor chairs.

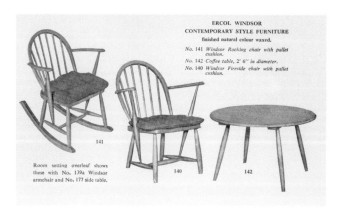

origins, emphasising instead its functionalism and suitability for modern open-plan interiors: 'I had in mind, then, a group of furniture to complete the house, with particular reference to a dining room-cum-living room or a lounge-cum-living room.'[50] Although Ercolani pursued his own agenda with the Windsor Range, which always stood somewhat apart from prevailing trends, the collection harmonised with the vogue for 'Contemporary' design, especially the preference for lighter, airier furniture that floated above the ground. The clean lines, organic forms and tapered splayed legs of the Windsor range were all classic 'Contemporary' features.

Ercol was at the vanguard of British furniture at this date, leading consumers in new directions and influencing trends industry-wide. Capitalising on the upbeat mood of the early post-war era, the Windsor Range chimed with the Zeitgeist. 'I had a feeling that – immediately after the war, and relieved of the constant dread and restraint brought about by it – the consumer would want to redecorate the house with vivacious colours and would be glad of an opportunity to buy joyous furniture,' observed Ercolani astutely.[51] The phrase 'joyous furniture' is telling, suggesting that the Windsor Range embodied the hopes and aspirations, not just of its creator, but of the nation as a whole. The chirpy Ercolion captured this mood and the rejuvenated personality of Ercolani himself. This interpretation is confirmed by contemporary media coverage. 'The fiery but friendly little lion which is Ercol's well-known trade mark is affectionately thought, in High Wycombe, to resemble the Old Man,' commented the *Daily Herald*.[52]

Top left
The Ercolion introducing a booklet called *What the Press Says About Ercol*, c.1965

Top right
140 Fireside Chair, 141 Rocking Chair and 142 Occasional Table in Ercol catalogue, 1951

Bottom left
Cover of Ercol catalogue, November 1951

Bottom right
191 Wing Easy Chair and 213 Small Coffee Table in Ercol catalogue, 1952

The 1951 catalogue, which remained current throughout the following year, was noteworthy in its own right. Described in *The Cabinet Maker* as a 'tastefully designed brochure', it received special notice for its 'postcard illustrations with descriptions, inserted neatly in a pocket on the inside of a handy size blue cover.' This catalogue consolidated the role of the Ercolion, who was depicted as a craftsman wearing an apron with a hammer in his pocket. An amiable ambassador, dignified but down-to-earth, the Ercolion served as a spokesman for the company, conveying useful information in a witty and humorous way. At this date his message was to reassure customers that Ercol was keen to expand production as soon as possible. Standing at a drawing board holding up a crystal ball, he was described as a 'famous fidget, seldom without a pencil in hand... unless it is to doodle furniture in ink on the glass top of his desk,' recalling Ercolani himself. Apologising for the company's difficulties in meeting demand due to external factors, he confidently announced that: 'Whatever the future holds in store, stores will certainly hold further ERCOL designs.'

As with subsequent catalogues, 'dark finished Old Colonial furniture' was presented in tandem with 'the lighter type of contemporary Windsor.' Although, retrospectively, these two ranges seem incongruous, this juxtaposition of the traditional and the modern was not unusual in the furniture industry during the transitional years after the war. *The Cabinet Maker* drew attention to the advantages of the 'happy combination of the old and the new in Mr Ercolani's designs that makes it possible for his furniture to harmonise with almost any good furniture one already possesses.'[54]

To explain the concept of the two parallel Ercol furniture families, the Ercolion was shown watering a 'family tree' with a forked trunk, one branch labelled Windsor Contemporary, the other, Old Colonial. Enthusing about the adaptability of the Windsor Range, he urged consumers to:

> Take, or rather buy, my Windsor Chair, or its sprung and cushioned cousin, the Windsor Tub. In its blonde, natural wood complexion it takes its place gracefully in any setting of contemporary mood. Put it in the lounge or the dining room, the bedroom or the nursery – it is handsomely at home. Sit in it, knit in it, rest, read or write in it, it will give you comfort in repose and support in employment.

The bubbly prose style, full of puns and alliteration, encapsulated Ercol's confidence, poised on the brink of success.

Improving on the Improved

When tracing the evolution of the Windsor Range, one of the recurrent features is the constant tweaking of designs. Ercolani was a perfectionist. If he thought a design could be improved, a new or modified version would be introduced. This relentless drive for perfection had been evident from the moment he accepted the Board of Trade's invitation to manufacture the 4A Chair. He refused to be rushed, insisting that he needed time to address all the underlying technical issues before putting the design into production, arguing that this would save time in the long run because he would be able to manufacture the chair in larger quantities at a faster rate. Similarly, after conceiving the idea of creating a fully-fledged Windsor collection, Ercolani

Far left
877 Windsor Chair, 1987, later variant of 370 Windsor Dining Chair, 1957

Top near left
400 Chair and 391 All Purpose Windsor Chair in Ercol catalogue, 1969

Bottom near left
393 All Purpose Table, 1957, and 400 Chairs, 1958

took his time before releasing these new designs to the public, partly because of early post-war manufacturing constraints, but also because it gave him a longer gestation time. He wanted to savour the moment and ensure that the collection satisfied him before sending it forth into the wider world.

The 4A Chair remained in production in its original form until 1953. A slightly modified version with five spindles instead of six was issued the following year as the 100 Windsor Chair (1954). By 1949 the 4A Chair had been supplemented by the 139 Small Chair, a more clean-lined compact variant, smart enough for dining room as well as kitchen use.[55] Like the 4A Chair, the seatback of the 139 Chair had six sticks, but the seat was D-shaped rather than fiddle-shaped, with a thin pallet cushion. 'The fifteen component items of the chair, the bow, seat, sticks, legs and struts, are all turned out by specialist machines, and when they are brought together for assembly they fit like eye-balls into sockets,' noted *Punch* admiringly in 1950.[56] In the 139A Small Armchair (1949), the diagonal supports for the armrests rose from the stretcher rather than the seat, marking the first appearance of a memorable Ercol feature, a staple of future designs.

In 1957 the 139 Chair was subtly modified to create the 370 Dining Chair, a more sophisticated and elegant version with slender splayed legs, which made its straight-legged predecessor look rather clumsy by comparison. 'The legs are beautifully shaped and more widely spread, and the underframe is closer to the oyster-shaped seat,' explained a publicity leaflet.[57] Another improvement was that the detachable latex foam cushion was now secured to the underside of the seat by means of straps and press studs, rather than being tied to the spindles. The 400 Chair (1958) marked a further

development of the original Utility chair. Initially identified as 4A/400, this was a simpler variant of the 4A Chair, with a rounded oyster-shaped seat, rather than a fiddle-shaped seat, and four sticks in the back instead of six. As with the 370 Dining Chair, the underframe was positioned closer to the seat and the finely-contoured legs were set at an angle. 'Never were two chairs of such high quality produced at such low prices,' bragged the Ercolion. 'Everyone loves them. They are a real joy to handle, or to sit upon…Solidly built in solid wood, they are as sturdy as they are good looking. There's nothing *cheap* about these chairs except the price!'[58]

Apart from their bow and stick backs, the common thread linking all these models from 1953 onwards (and all the subsequent chairs in the Windsor Range) was the wedged joint, a distinctive Ercol device still in use at the factory today. Hitherto wedged joints had been used for fixing the staves of the bow to the seat, but the legs were attached to the underside of the seat so the joint was not visible from above. In 1953 the company adopted the wedged joint technique for attaching the legs to the seat as well. Because the legs come right through the seat, this makes them much more secure. No screws are used in these joints, which are held simply by means of pressure and glue. A small wooden wedge is tapped into a notch at the top of the leg, pushing the wood outwards so that it fills the hole, thereby holding the leg securely. After the glue has dried, the projecting sections of the leg and wedge are sanded down so that they are flush with the seat, although they remain clearly visible as a circular motif with a line through the centre. As the company proudly proclaimed, this 'cunning construction enables it to withstand the roughest treatment and come up smiling.'[59]

Top far left
Detail of 'wedged-through-seat-legs' on Draughtsman's Stool, c.1959

Bottom far left
Knocking a wedge into a chair leg protruding through seat

Top near left
338 Fireside Chair, 1956

Bottom near left
Windsor Range furniture in Ercol catalogue, 1951

Opposite
Windsor Contemporary Furniture Family Reference Sheet, 1956

An advertisement in July 1953, which included a diagram of these 'wedged-through-seat legs', confirmed that the device had only recently been adopted: 'The Ercolion has arranged a marriage of strength and beauty. The legs of his Windsor chairs are from henceforward to be wedded to their rounded edge D-shape seat in a manner that no man may put asunder.'[60] A 1954 leaflet referred to the: 'The new Blue Seal Ercol Windsor 4A/100 Chairs with wedged-through seat legs and chamfered seat' as 'a perfect example of the Ercolion's skill in improving on the improved!'[61] The same distinctive 'wedged-through' joints were used to connect armrests to their supports and coffee table legs to their tops.

Compatibility and Flexibility

One of the appealing characteristics of the Windsor Range was its informality, a natural expression of its democratic roots. Whereas period furniture was essentially aspirational (lower cost furniture in the guise of expensive upper class designs), the Windsor Range was more honest, elevating decent below-stairs or cottage furniture to the living rooms and dining rooms of many different types of homes. When the collection was shown at the Furniture Exhibition at Earl's Court in February 1952, Ercol announced that it was aiming for 'a higher note than has previously been struck in high-class furniture within reach of the lower income groups, which should also prove attractive to the higher income groups for taste.'[62] Yet there was nothing snobby or condescending about the Windsor Range: it appealed to a wide audience, irrespective of wealth and class, not just an educated elite.

Apart from the aesthetic and practical appeal of individual items, compatibility and flexibility were two key factors in the success of the Windsor Range. As well as blending with other furniture, it harmonised with a remarkably wide spectrum of interiors, so it was both coherent and cohesive, hence its popularity with consumers. Ercol produced a series of reference sheets promoting the concept of the Ercol Furniture Family, illustrating how different pieces could be combined, a concept known as 'grouping'. The first leaflet, distributed to retailers in June 1953, outlined the rationale behind 'grouping', emphasising that this was 'an entirely new idea in furniture buying':

> This method of choosing the component pieces in any furnishing scheme supersedes the "suite" and improves on the "unit" method of design. It not only allows the greatest latitude of choice, but gives the utmost scope for individual taste whilst still ensuring a harmonious effect within any rooms. The principle of grouping has been made possible by the Ercol method of design. Every individual piece in the range is part of a family – a family which has been built up slowly and is still growing… Within each of these groups any piece will group successfully with any other piece and an almost endless variety of room settings can be built up entirely to your choice. Moreover, any additional Ercol design that you may decide to add in the future will marry in perfectly.[63]

In this respect there were similarities to G-Plan, the coordinated furniture introduced by E. Gomme in November 1952 and marketed from 1953. The fact that the Ercol Furniture Family had been promoted in this way

Top left
438 Circular Mirror on 437
Dressing Table, 1959

Top right
439 Drawer Fitment, 1959,
on 479 Writing Table, 1962

from 1951, however, suggests that the Windsor Range may have influenced G-Plan, rather than vice versa. At the very least, the two manufacturers deserve to be jointly credited for pioneering the concept of coordinated furniture. The idea promoted by both was that customers could furnish their homes incrementally over time, as their means permitted, confident in the knowledge that each item would synchronise with others within the range. This notion of buying furniture more casually, piece by piece, or in clusters, rather than in predetermined suites, was a revolutionary concept at the time. Ercol took the lead in educating consumers about the merits of this approach.

The growing popularity of the Windsor Range was indicated by its increasingly widespread appearance in the media from 1952 onwards. A firm favourite with stylists, it was regularly featured in interiors magazines and was frequently displayed in show houses and exhibitions. In 1952, for example, a Windsor Sideboard and Plate Rack were included in a show house in Birmingham sponsored by the *Birmingham Mail*, furnished by Joan Patrick on behalf of the Council of Industrial Design.[64] Ercol's Windsor chairs and tables were selected for two years running for the People's House at the Ideal Home Exhibition in 1952 and 1953.[65] Windsor furniture was also used extensively in a show house at Harlow New Town in 1957.[66]

When the Whitechapel Art Gallery mounted an exhibition of room settings in 1952 called *For Bill and Betty*, intended to educate people in the East End about the merits of modern furniture, the 4A Chair (a perennial favourite) was selected for a boy's bedroom. Whilst conceding that, 'This kind of educational exhibition may not have sent contemporary sales in East End shops sky-rocketing immediately,' *Furnishing* magazine believed it was a positive development: 'In the long run... it can only be beneficial to both consumer and retailer alike.'[67]

Above
203 Windsor Bergere
Easy Chair and Settee,
261 Sideboard and 266
Occasional Table in *House
& Garden*, 1953

Opposite
Windsor Range furniture,
including 349 Loveseat,
House & Garden, 1956

Retail Appeal

Following the excitement generated by the Festival of Britain, retailers began to respond to the surge of interest in 'Contemporary' design. Ercol was well-placed to capitalise on this. When Jones & Co. of Bristol mounted an exhibition of modern furniture in 1952 focusing on the needs of low-cost housing, for example, chairs and tables from the Windsor Range featured prominently in the displays.[68] Although it fell into the low to mid-range price categories, the Windsor Range was readily stocked by high-end stores and discerning independent shops, as well as more mainstream furnishing houses with a broader customer base. When Harrods remodelled its Modern Furniture Section in 1952, a dining table and chairs from the Windsor Range were featured in a model kitchen-breakfast room.[69] Initiatives of this kind gathered steam as the decade progressed. Significantly, at the Midlands Ideal Home Exhibition in Birmingham in 1953, the hitherto conservative Times Furnishing Company signalled its conversion to 'Contemporary' design by showcasing the Windsor Range.[70] Likewise, when Jones Brothers of Holloway created a new circular showroom for 'Contemporary' furniture in 1954, a whole section was devoted to the Windsor Range.[71]

Ercol's Windsor chairs were also regularly included in Heal's furniture catalogues during the 1950s. The 176 Tub Easy Chair first appeared in Heal's *Living Room Furniture* brochure in 1952, and the 139A Armchair made annual appearances in Heal's *Dining Room Furniture* brochures from 1954-6.[72] This in turn influenced the furniture produced by Heal's themselves. A stick-back tub dining chair in beech and sycamore designed by Ronald Ingles for Heal's Furniture in 1954 was clearly indebted to the Windsor Range. Ercol also proved a popular choice for more cautious retailers because its two parallel furniture families, Windsor Contemporary and Old Colonial, catered to the tastes of different consumers. Harrison Gibson, which had stores in Ilford, Bromley, Ipswich, Bedford and Doncaster, made a point of highlighting that it stocked both ranges. 'Whether your choice be Traditional – or the Modern Trend' was the heading of its advertisement in *House & Garden* in October 1954. Significantly, though, it was the Windsor Range that was illustrated in this advertisement, suggesting that the pendulum had swung in favour of 'Contemporary' by this date.

Keen to promote its brand through as many retailers as possible, Ercol took the unusual step of supplying its stockists with a special display model of the Ercolion in July 1952. Made of reinforced 'stonecast' with a silver metallic finish, the lion held a circular frame in which a showcard could be inserted, labelled either 'Windsor Furniture' or 'Old Colonial', depending on which range was being displayed. Ercolani told *The Cabinet Maker* that 'the Ercolion standing in the window will tell the public where they can buy Ercol furniture and will link up with the national press advertising, giving an extra sales boost.'[73] Strategies such as this established a direct personal link between the company and the consumer, an initiative that retailers had hitherto resisted but which they now actively embraced. Although other companies would soon follow suit – namely E. Gomme with its G-Plan range - Ercol was one of the first manufacturers to promote the concept of branded furniture. Its pioneering initiatives revolutionised the marketing of furniture throughout the industry over the next 20 years.

Top left
Ercolion promotional display model supplied to retailers, 1952

Centre and bottom
428 Quaker Rocking Chair, 1959

Opposite
391 All Purpose Windsor Chairs stacked up in the factory, c.1957-62

Public Recognition

Because Ercol was equipped to handle large orders and was used to working with government departments, it was well-placed to operate in the contract market. When the retailer William Perring & Co. resurrected its contract department in 1953, Windsor Range chairs were amongst its staple products. Ercol's 139 and 139A Chairs were also included in a Heal's Contracts leaflet entitled Chairs for Offices in 1956.[74]

Educational institutions became major clients during the 1950s, attracted by the strength and durability of Ercol's chairs. In 1952 the company supplied furniture to Warnham Court, a 19th century country house near Horsham in Surrey which had been converted into a special school by London County Council. The LCC's architect, Robert Matthew, had recently co-designed the Royal Festival Hall, so it is significant that he chose Ercol's chairs for this scheme, rather than other modern furniture on offer at the time. According to *The Cabinet Maker*, the interiors of the building were transformed using 'well designed furniture and furnishings against a background of bold colours and bright and spacey surroundings.'[75]

Kidbrooke School at Blackheath, a new secondary school for girls built by the LCC in 1954, was an even larger contract. One of the first comprehensive schools in the country, it became a showpiece for modern design, with £55,000 of the £600,000 budget being assigned to furniture and furnishings. The 139 and 139A Chairs were used extensively in various parts of the building, including the library, staff room, medical suite and administrative offices.[76]

On 24 June 1952, the 139A Armchair appeared in a Giles cartoon in *The Daily Express*.[77] Within a year of the Festival of Britain, therefore, the Windsor range was already established as a firm favourite in the nation's homes, familiar enough to warrant being taken for granted in a joke. Another sign that the collection had struck a chord with post-war consumers was that, by 1953, sales of the Windsor Range were far outstripping Old Colonial. Barry Ercolani attributed the surge in popularity to the influence of women's magazines, which now devoted so much more space to home furnishings, ensuring that young people setting up home were better educated about design.

Yet, although publicity and marketing played a vital role in establishing the Windsor Range, ultimately it was the allure of the furniture itself that accounted for its phenomenal success. This was entirely due to the unique attributes of the designs and the outstanding quality of its manufacture. 'You must never forget the people,' Ercolani stressed.[78] It was because of his instinctive understanding of the needs of post-war consumers that the Windsor Range took off in such a big way. Nevertheless, even though the factory had geared up for expansion, demand escalated at such a rate that the company was unable to meet orders. For the next few years it would be full steam ahead for the Old Man and his sons. The pressure was on to extend the factory in order to increase production and to develop and expand the collection to its full potential.

The ERCOLion proudly presents his
ERCOL furniture family

No. 268 (top) *Plate Rack*
OVERALL WIDTH 38″ HEIGHT 19¾″
Natural Colour Waxed Finish

A hanging Plate Rack in solid elm. Can be used either together with any of the sideboards shown, or separately. Fitted with metal plates for screwing to the wall.

No. 351 *Sideboard**
LENGTH 4′ 0½″ DEPTH 1′ 6″ HEIGHT 2′ 9″
Natural Colour Waxed Finish

The top of this neat Contemporary Sideboard is of solid elm and the remainder is a light contrasting wood. Note the extra wide linen drawer; the right-hand drawer is divided for cutlery. A shelf is fitted in each cupboard.

*Please note that on this particular sideboard only, some of the unseen interior parts and the back are of plywood.

See page 18 for low price ERCOL tables and chairs that are especially suitable for use in the Kitchen or in Restaurants, Halls, etc.

No. 430 *Serving Cabinet*
HEIGHT 3′ 7″ WIDTH 2′ 8″
DEPTH OVERALL 19″
Natural Colour Waxed Finish

The latest development of the Ercol solid elm serving cabinet is even more useful. It has been enlarged and is now mounted on semi-concealed ball castors. It can be wheeled close to the dining table at meal times for handy serving, or it can act as a room divider. Notice the refinement of the sculptured wood handles.
Roomy top cupboard accommodates breakfast, dinner and tea services. When open it acts as a serving flap, strong enough for carving. The large two-door cupboard has an adjustable shelf. At the base is a long deep drawer.

No. 386 (top)
Panelled Hanging Back
OVERALL WIDTH 3′ 6″
HEIGHT 1′ 7″
Natural Colour Waxed Finish

Made entirely from solid elm. Fully polished on the outside back. The end uprights have keyhole slots for flush fitting to the wall.

No. 366 *Sideboard*
(middle and right)
LENGTH 3′ 9″
DEPTH 1′ 8″
HEIGHT 2′ 8″
Natural Colour Waxed Finish

Made entirely in solid elm with a contrasting beech underpart. Fully polished outside back and interior. Can be used as a Room Divider. Cupboards fitted with adjustable half shelves and the right-hand cupboard has a solid elm "cutlery tidy."

No. 429 *Sideboard*
HEIGHT 2′ 6″
WIDTH 4′ 3″
DEPTH OVERALL 19½″
Natural Colour Waxed Finish

Two long, deep drawers at the base. Two convenient cupboards above, one large cupboard with two doors and long, wide, adjustable shelf: smaller cupboard fitted with cutlery tray and adjustable partitions. Made entirely of solid elm, natural colour, wax polished inside, outside and at the back.
It stands just off the floor on semi-concealed ball castors and, at the touch of the hand, moves easily, silently, so convenient for easy positioning and of course cleaning. Because of its fully polished back it can be placed at right angles to the wall as a room divider.

No. 265 *End Table*
WIDTH 2′ 3″ DEPTH 1′ 6″ HEIGHT 2′ 4″
Natural Colour Waxed Finish

Designed specially to be used as an extension to No. 382 or No. 383 Dining Tables, but can also be used as a separate serving or writing table. Made in solid elm and beech.

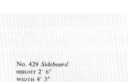

No. 384
Round Shaped Dining Table
SIZE OPEN 4′ 1″ × 3′ 8½″
SIZE CLOSED 2′ 0″ × 3′ 8½″
HEIGHT 2′ 4″
Natural Colour Waxed Finish

The top and leaves are in solid elm and the legs in a contrasting beech. The flaps are supported on metal rods of great strength. Designed when opened to seat six people.

No. 382 *Dining Table*
LENGTH 5′ 0″ WIDTH 2′ 6″ HEIGHT 2′ 4″
Natural Colour Waxed Finish

This table, though primarily designed to seat six people, can accommodate eight because of its length and width. The top is in solid elm with the legs in contrasting beech.
(*Note:* The No. 265 End Table can be used at the end of this table to provide additional seating.)

No. 383
Dropleaf Dining Table
SIZE OPEN 4′ 6″ × 2′ 5½″ SIZE CLOSED 2′ 0″ × 2′ 5½″
HEIGHT 2′ 4″ *Natural Colour Waxed Finish*

This Dropleaf Table with its most pleasantly shaped top seats six people when fully opened. Especially useful for smaller rooms, as it seats two comfortably when folded. The top and leaves are in solid elm and the legs in a contrasting beech.
(*Note:* The 265 End Table can be used at the end of this table to provide additional seating.)

No. 370 *Windsor Dining Chair*
No. 370A *Windsor Dining Armchair*
Natural Colour Waxed Finish
The most simple design of Windsor Dining Chair, but notice the widely spread, beautifully shaped legs, and the under-frame close to the oyster-shaped seat. The foam filled seat cushion is fixed by straps and press-studs, and the cushion covers are detachable for easy dry cleaning.

No. 365 *Quaker Back*
Windsor Dining Chair
No. 365A *Quaker Back*
Windsor Dining Armchair
Natural Colour Waxed Finish
An extremely comfortable high-back version of the traditional Windsor Chair. Rounded oyster-shaped seat with foam filled seat cushion, fixed to the frame with straps and press-studs. Covers are detachable for easy dry cleaning.

No. 333 *Small Chair*
No. 333A *Armchair*
Natural Colour Waxed Finish
An elegant Windsor Chair with matching Armchair. The solid elm seat is unusually thick to allow very deep shaping for comfort. The curved back and rails are in beech.
Note: Loose seat cushion is not normally supplied or recommended with this design but prices are available on request.

No. 349 *Love Seat*
LENGTH 49"
HEIGHT OVERALL 30"
Natural Colour Waxed Finish
An entirely new piece of Ercol furniture for the dining room—a Settee Love Seat. The thick solid elm seat is deeply and comfortably shaped with graceful moulded edges. Very light in weight and easily carried with one hand; this love seat can also be used as an occasional settee.
Note: A loose seat cushion is not normally supplied or recommended with this design, as it is extremely comfortable owing to its deeply shaped seat.

No. 338 *Fireside Chair*
WIDTH OVER ARMS 21½"
DEPTH 20½"
HEIGHT 26"
Natural Colour Waxed Finish
A new Chair with deep oyster-shaped seat tooled out from 2" thickness elm for comfort. It is also available with foam filled seat cushion and plastic foam filled back cushion. The cushion covers are detachable for easy dry cleaning.

No. 339 *Rocking Chair*
DEPTH *(including skids)* 30½"
WIDTH OVER ARMS 21½"
HEIGHT 28"
Natural Colour Waxed Finish
Well-balanced lightweight Rocker, with skids so shaped that it is impossible to tip over backwards. The deep oyster-shaped seat is tooled from 2" thickness solid elm. Also available with foam filled seat cushion and plastic foam back cushion, with covers that zip off for easy dry cleaning.

No. 369 *Goldsmith's Windsor Dining Chair*
No. 369A *Goldsmith's Windsor Dining Armchair*
Natural Colour Waxed Finish
A wonderfully comfortable development of the traditional Goldsmith's Chair. The seat is oyster-shaped and the foam filled seat cushion is fixed with straps and press-studs. Covers are detachable for easy dry cleaning.

No. 376 *Windsor Dining Chair*
Natural Colour Waxed Finish
This is an extremely elegant Dining Chair with widely spread legs and underframe close to the oyster-shaped seat. The foam filled seat cushion is fixed with straps and press-studs. Cushion covers are detachable for easy dry cleaning.

No. 428 *Quaker Rocking Chair*
HEIGHT 2' 8½"
OVERALL WIDTH 2' 0"
Natural Colour Waxed Finish

No. 435 *Goldsmith's Rocking Chair*
HEIGHT 2' 9½"
OVERALL WIDTH 2' 0"
Natural Colour Waxed Finish

Two interesting developments in Rocking Chairs. One is based on the well-known Ercol Quaker Chair, the other on the Ercol Goldsmith's Chair. Both have solid elm seats and solid beech frames. The long rocker skids avoid tipping over backwards. Foam filled cushions are attached to the frame by press studs and the cover is detachable for easy dry cleaning. Various qualities of covers are available.

Preformed dining chair in elm and beech

No. 401 *Windsor Dining Chair with Preformed Back. In Elm and Beech. Natural Colour Waxed Finish*
This Chair marks a milestone in the development of furniture making. It is a marriage between the traditional Windsor under-frame —as developed by Ercol over the years—and the great technical potentiality inherent in preforming laminated wood to an exact shape. Hitherto laminations for preforming have had to be extremely thin in order to achieve the desired curved shapes. Now after intensive investigation the Ercol research team have developed a technique that makes possible the use of thick laminations. Thus, one of the outstanding characteristics of all Ercol furniture— the friendly feel of solid wood—is maintained. This new Dining Chair is extremely elegant and of great comfort; its strength is immense. It is designed to be used without a seat cushion.

No. 361 *Trolley Bookcase*
WIDTH 3′ 0″ DEPTH 1′ 0½″ HEIGHT 2′ 5½″
Natural Colour Waxed Finish
This Trolley Bookcase, made entirely in solid elm and beech, is quite unique. It is easily moved about on its ball castors, even when fully loaded. Ideal for use by the fireside with Chair No. 248 and placed by Occasional Table No. 213.

Natural Colour Waxed Finish
This Room Divider is made entirely in solid elm and beech. The top shelf is fixed, the other two are adjustable. The roomy cupboard has an adjustable half shelf. Fully polished on the outside back, in the inside of the cupboard, and on the underside of the shelves.

No. 437/438
Dressing Table with mirror
HEIGHT OF MIRROR 1′ 4″
WIDTH OF MIRROR 1′ 0″

No. 437/439 *Writing Table*
HEIGHT 3′ 1″
WIDTH 2′ 3″
DEPTH 1′ 7″
Natural Colour Waxed Finish
Light, graceful, charming, this writing table has a full width drawer, and a most beautifully detailed escritoire which must be handled to be appreciated. Notice the new refinements of design—the triangular section of legs, the positioning of the underframing, sculptured table edges. It's a masterpiece in natural solid elm and beech with a craftsman-like natural colour waxed finish.
The table can be bought separately and makes a very useful occasional table. Or with the addition of the delightful circular adjustable mirror it becomes an excellent small dressing table.

No. 437
Hall or Side Table
HEIGHT 2′ 5″
WIDTH 2′ 3″
DEPTH BACK TO FRONT 1′ 7″

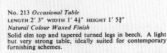

No. 213 *Occasional Table*
LENGTH 2′ 3″ WIDTH 1′ 4½″ HEIGHT 1′ 5½″
Natural Colour Waxed Finish
Solid elm top and tapered turned legs in beech. A light but very strong table, ideally suited for contemporary furnishing schemes.

No. 308 *Folding Occasional Table*
SIZE OPEN 24″ DIAMETER
SIZE CLOSED 24″ × 13½″ HEIGHT 16″
Natural Colour Waxed Finish
A new circular Coffee Table of contemporary design with a drop leaf, enabling it to be used as a side table for an easy chair. The top is solid elm with the contrasting underpart in beech.

Supper Table in Two Sizes
No. 436 *Table*
DIAMETER 2′ 10½″ HEIGHT 1′ 5½″
No. 142 *Table*
DIAMETER 2′ 5½″ HEIGHT 1′ 5½″
Natural Colour Waxed Finish
Solid elm top and tapered turned legs in beech. A graceful addition to any room. The extra large topped table is most convenient at T.V. suppers or for other occasional meals.

No. 354 *Nest of Three Tables*
SIZE OF LARGEST TABLE 25½″ × 17½″
HEIGHT 16″
Natural Colour Waxed Finish
An elegant simply designed nest of three tables made in solid elm with beech legs. Note the attractive oyster-shaped tops of the tables.

No. 425 *Saddle Shaped Fireside Stool*
HEIGHT 16″
WIDTH OF SEAT 13½″
Natural Colour Waxed Finish
A saddle shaped fireside stool with elm seat and beech wedged-through-seat legs. Until you have a stool in the house you will never realise how useful it can be.

No. 398 *Occasional Coffee Table*
LENGTH 3′ 5½″ WIDTH 1′ 3″ HEIGHT 14½″
Natural Colour Waxed Finish
A new Coffee Table with an elm top and underparts of beech. The really capacious top can cope handsomely with any group of guests—or any number of papers from a brief case! The handy rack keeps magazines out of the way but not out of reach.

The ERCOLion's entirely new comfort principle
FREE FLOATING SITTING

"A new dimension in ease and softness" says the ERCOLion. Never have you relaxed so completely as in the gentle embrace of this amazing new chair. Designed on a revolutionary new principle which allows the entire sitting area of the seat and back to be completely free of any cross rails. Thus the reinforced rubber webbing supports, and deep foam cushions comfort you every single inch of the seat and back with the same cherishingly resilient softness. This new sensation of 'free floating sitting' brings deep, deep comfort never before possible in a chair so strong, so light weight and so compact in size.

Put three or more of these easy chairs together—and make a luxuriously restful settee. You simply multiply your comfort when you take your ease with Ercol's exclusive 'free floating sitting'.

Registered Design Application
Nos. 891/888 891/887
Provisional Patent Application
No. 35840/58
Reinforced Webbing Patent
Nos. 800, 828

No. 427 *Easy Chair*
HEIGHT 31"
WIDTH 20"
DEPTH OVERALL 2' 6"
Natural Colour Waxed Finish
With its new principle, the construction of this latest Ercol chair entirely dispenses with the uncomfortable rigid cross rails essential in the construction of normal chairs. The reinforced rubber webbing, securely attached by a special patented method, ensures relaxing elasticity and also acts as a shock absorber. Covers zip off the luxurious foam cushions in a flash for easy dry cleaning.

No. 305 *Windsor Tub Chair*
WIDTH OVER ARMS 27½"
OVERALL DEPTH 26"
HEIGHT OVERALL 31½"
Natural Colour Waxed Finish
The tub-shaped back and framing are beech with contrasting solid elm seat. Foam filled seat cushion. Also available with foam filled back cushion. Zip off seat and back cushion covers for easy dry cleaning.

Left: **No. 315** *Grandfather Rocking Chair*
WIDTH OVER ARMS 29½"   OVERALL DEPTH 31"
HEIGHT OVERALL 37½"
Natural Colour Waxed Finish
Right: **No. 317** *Grandfather Easy Chair*
WIDTH OVER ARMS 29½"   OVERALL DEPTH 29"
HEIGHT OVERALL 37½"
Natural Colour Waxed Finish
Two tall-backed Grandfather Chairs of large dimensions. The framing is of beech and the seat in solid elm. Foam filled seat and back cushion. Seat and back cushion cases are zip fastened and are detachable for easy dry cleaning. The rocker skids on design No. 315 are specially shaped to prevent tipping over backwards.

No. 335 *Easy Chair*
WIDTH OVER ARMS 27½"
OVERALL DEPTH 31½"
HEIGHT OVERALL 34½"
Natural Colour Waxed Finish
A tall back Easy Chair with fabric reinforced rubber suspension to support the foam filled seat cushion. The back cushion is also foam filled. Seat and back cushion covers are reversible and zip off for easy dry cleaning.

No. 415 *Tall Back Easy Chair*
WIDTH OVER ARMS 28½"
DEPTH OVERALL 32" HEIGHT OVERALL 40½"
Natural Colour Waxed Finish
A new Windsor Easy Chair with a very tall back and most graceful curved bow. Its clean lines make it an attractive chair for any room. Seat and back cushions are foam filled and have zip covers for easy dry cleaning. The seat cushion rests on fabric reinforced rubber suspension.

No. 364
Double Bow Easy Chair
WIDTH OVER ARMS 28½"
DEPTH OVER SEAT FRAME 23½"
HEIGHT 34"
Natural Colour Waxed Finish
A most elegant Easy Chair with a widely swept bow-shaped back. Fabric reinforced rubber suspension supports a deep foam filled seat cushion. The back cushion is also of specially moulded foam. Both seat and back cushion cases zip off for easy dry cleaning. *Note: A larger rear illustration of this chair is shown in the foreground of the room-setting on page 17.*

No. 359 *Easy Chair*
WIDTH OVERALL 27½"
DEPTH OF SEAT FRAME 21½"
HEIGHT OVERALL 33½"
Natural Colour Waxed Finish
This Easy Chair is specially designed for the smaller room. Fabric reinforced rubber suspension supports a deep non-reversible foam filled seat cushion. The back cushion is also foam filled. Both seat and back cushion covers zip off for easy dry cleaning.

No. 248 *Easy Chair*
WIDTH OVER ARMS 26"
DEPTH OVERALL 26"
HEIGHT OF BACK 31½"
Natural Colour Waxed Finish
Small Easy Chair with polished seat rails and shaped arms. Fitted with the new rubber suspension and non-reversible foam filled seat cushion. The seat cushion is zipped for easy dry cleaning.

All covering materials used on ERCOL Windsor Contemporary furniture are made by manufacturers of international reputation and are tested and guaranteed to the very rigid requirements of the British Standards Institution (B.S. 1960 Pt. V), both in regard to light fastness and stress and strain. The collection consists of three separate price ranges ('Standard,' 'L' and 'XL' ranges). Samples are available from your retailer.

ERCOL floating back upholstery

Where is the rubber webbing? Anchored to each side of the chair back, it passes through the zip off cushion cover to comfort you unseen. The seat cushion also rests on fabric reinforced rubber webbing. That is why your body 'floats' on the new ERCOL upholstery.

No. 236 *Upholstered Arm Easy Chair*
WIDTH OVER ARMS 28½"
DEPTH OVERALL 29"
HEIGHT OVERALL 32"
Natural Colour Waxed Finish
Graceful upholstered Easy Chair of contemporary design with buttoned back and arms. Fitted with the new rubber suspension. The reversible foam filled cushion is zipped for easy dry cleaning.

No. 403 *Easy Chair*
WIDTH OVER ARMS 27"
DEPTH OVERALL 33½"
HEIGHT OVERALL 34"
Natural Colour Waxed Finish
An entirely new design with the 'floating back' fabric reinforced rubber webbing suspension. Foam filled seat and back cushions fitted with zip off covers for easy dry cleaning.

No. 403 *Settee*
WIDTH OVER ARMS 51"
DEPTH OVERALL 33½"
HEIGHT OVERALL 34"
Natural Colour Waxed Finish
This Settee matches No. 403 Easy Chair, and the cushion cases, as with the chairs, are of course zip fastened and detachable for easy dry cleaning.

No. 341 *Extension Stool*
LENGTH 27½" WIDTH 20"
HEIGHT (TO TOP OF CUSHION) 13½"
Natural Colour Waxed Finish
An addition that makes the 203 Easy Chair into a *chaise longue*. Fitted with foam filled cushion on fabric reinforced rubber suspension. It is a very comfortable stool in its own right. The cushion is reversible and is zipped for easy dry cleaning.

No. 203 *Easy Chair*
WIDTH OVER ARMS 27½"
DEPTH OVERALL 35"
HEIGHT OVERALL 30½"
Natural Colour Waxed Finish
Windsor Bergere style Easy Chair with deep seat and the extra comfortable, fabric reinforced rubber suspension. Foam filled reversible seat cushion and specially shaped foam filled reversible back cushion. Seat and back cushions have zip off covers for easy dry cleaning.

No. 334 *Easy Chair*
WIDTH OVER ARMS 27½"
DEPTH OVERALL 28½"
HEIGHT OVERALL 30"
Natural Colour Waxed Finish
A low-backed well-shaped Easy Chair. Fitted with fabric reinforced rubber suspension which supports a deep foam filled seat cushion. Specially shaped foam filled back cushion. Both seat and back cushions are reversible and have zip off covers—easy to detach for dry cleaning.

No. 203 *Windsor Bergere Settee*
WIDTH OVER ARMS 53½"
DEPTH OVERALL 36"
HEIGHT OVERALL 30½"
Natural Colour Waxed Finish
Windsor Bergere style Settee with deep seat and the extra comfortable, fabric reinforced rubber suspension. Foam filled reversible seat cushions and specially shaped foam reversible back cushions. Seat and back cushions have zip off covers for easy dry cleaning.

No. 334 *Settee*
WIDTH OVER ARMS 51½"
DEPTH OVERALL 28½"
HEIGHT OVERALL 30½"
Natural Colour Waxed Finish
A new low-backed Settee. Superbly designed with fabric reinforced rubber suspension supporting the deep foam filled seat cushions. Specially shaped foam filled back cushion. Both seat and back cushions are reversible and have easily detached zipped covers.
Note: See also Easy Chair No. 335 (on page 14) which can be used with this settee to form a three-piece suite.

The ERCOL Studio Couch

An entirely new piece of furniture. This Studio Couch is large enough to be used as a settee for four persons, and has the advantage that the back can be taken off completely, and the couch can then be used as a single bed. The seat cushion is supported on fabric reinforced rubber suspension. The cases of all cushions (including the seat cushion) are zip fastened and are easily detachable for dry cleaning. The backboard is of solid elm mounted on gracefully shaped beech supporting columns.

No. 355 *Studio Couch*
DEPTH OVERALL 2' 5½" WIDTH OVERALL 6' 9½"
HEIGHT OVERALL 2' 8"
Natural Colour Waxed Finish

Page 18

No. 395 *All-purpose Breakfast Room or Restaurant Table*
SIZE OF TOP 2′ 3″ × 2′ 3″
HEIGHT 2′ 4¾″
Natural Colour Waxed Finish
A simple and practical table with a solid elm top and beech underpart. Note the useful rack under the table top. Designed specially for the small kitchen/breakfast room.

No. 393 *All-purpose Breakfast Room or Restaurant Table*
SIZE OF TOP 3′ 3″ × 2′ 3″
HEIGHT 2′ 4¾″
Natural Colour Waxed Finish
A Breakfast Room Table with a solid elm top and beech underpart. Seats four people. Useful rack under table top. Although this table has been designed primarily as a breakfast room table, it can of course be put to many other uses such as writing table, T.V. stand, etc.

No. 396 *All-purpose Breakfast Room or Restaurant Table*
SIZE OF TOP 3′ 3″ × 2′ 11″ HEIGHT 2′ 4¾″
Natural Colour Waxed Finish
A nicely shaped oval table with under rack. Solid elm top and beech underpart. Designed to seat four people. Useful for breakfast rooms where neither a square nor rectangular table would be suitable.

No. 391
All-purpose Windsor Chair
(Registered design No. 884923)
Finished Natural or Medium Dark Colour
A simple well-proportioned and graceful chair for use with the breakfast room tables illustrated, or as a simple desk or bedroom chair. This chair with its seat of solid elm is very comfortable and quite inexpensive.

No. 4a/400
Finished Natural or Medium Dark Colour
The newest version of the well-known Ercol 4a Windsor Chair. Stylish enough to grace any room in the house. Look at the new elegant raised underpart — what could be smarter or more practical. For lasting sturdiness, the beech legs are wedged through the comfortably shaped elm seat.

No. 392 *Windsor Stacking Chair*
(Registered design No. 884892)
Finished Natural Colour or Medium Dark Colour
Also: No. 440
Same design but slightly smaller for use in schools
An elegant Windsor Stacking Chair of immense strength and light weight. Any number can be stacked absolutely vertically. The back uprights and the top rail are shaped to give full back support for the whole of the back. Solid elm seat, the remainder in beech. This chair has successfully completed the very rigid performance tests sponsored by the Ministry of Education in their new draft performance standards for School chairs.

No. 394 *Pair of Bogey Wheels*
Finished Natural Colour or Medium Dark Colour
Designed as a simple carrier for as many chairs as can be conveniently stacked. Ball-bearing wheels make the movement of a whole stack finger-tip light.

Page 19

No. 431 *Wardrobe*
HEIGHT 6′ 0″ WIDTH 4′ 0″
DEPTH 21¾″
Natural Colour Waxed Finish
You'll bless the many virtues of this solid elm wardrobe. It is extra roomy, and, poised on its semi-concealed castors can be moved at finger touch, even when full of clothes. It 'knocks down' into two units for easy transport. Wax polished inside and outside, back and front, which makes it perfect as a bedroom divider. Finally—peep inside and admire the optional interior drawer fitment, the shoe rail and hanging rail.

"... and now ERCOL SOLID WOOD furniture for your bedroom" *says the ERCOLion*

"Allow me to present," said the ERCOLion, "my latest and greatest adventure in solid wood. Superlative furniture for your bedroom, of solid elm and beech. Perfectly proportioned. Superbly made. Every piece a polished essay in craftsmanship. Yes, mellow wax polished inside, outside and at the back to fit it for my lady's chamber. And to appeal to her practical nature, I have concealed large ball castors under each cabinet piece. Thus, at finger-tip touch, she can glide even the big wardrobe around for dusting and cleaning more easily than a tea trolley.

"You will notice," continued the ERCOLion, "that masterly simplicity is again my keynote for design. In keeping with the best modern trends, every item is precisely fitted for its purpose. Everything is easy to keep clean, easy to move around —and wholly delightful to live with! For every piece has the warmth and friendliness, the satisfying and *enduring* quality that only solid wood can give.

"Whether you want just one or two items or a whole bedroom full of furniture, you will find the right answer here. For this is a *complete* bedroom range. There are two sizes of wardrobe, a chest of drawers, a dressing chest and a dressing table both with adjustable mirror, and triple dressing-table units fitted with cheval-type mirrors and a dressing chair. All the mirror fittings are neatly designed in wood too—nothing to rust, get shabby or look unsightly.

"ERCOL Windsor beds, of course, match this new furniture perfectly. Being also made of solid wood, they have no metal frames or springs to work loose, rattle or squeak—ever. They are heavenly to look upon and heaven to lie on.

"Half the secret of their comfort is their hygienic and permanently resilient fabric reinforced rubber webbing instead of the usual dust-harbouring, and often hard, base. The other half of the secret lies in the specially designed foam-rubber mattress, beneath the gay and debonair exteriors of which there is a technical triumph of cavity shape moulding to ensure that the initial bliss shall be permanent."

(Detachable headboards in solid elm are also available as separate pieces if you already have your own divans.)

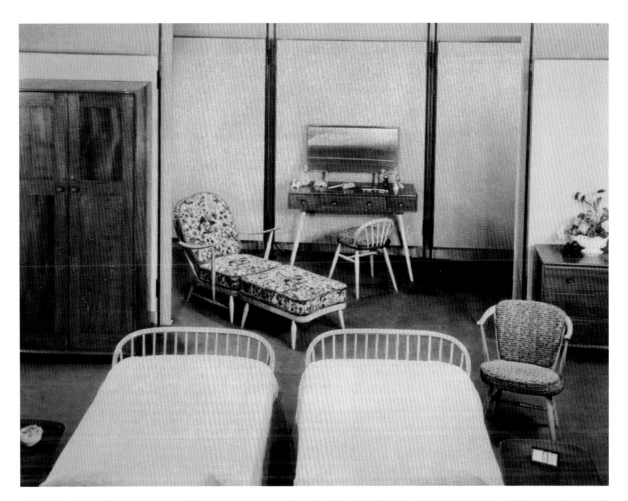

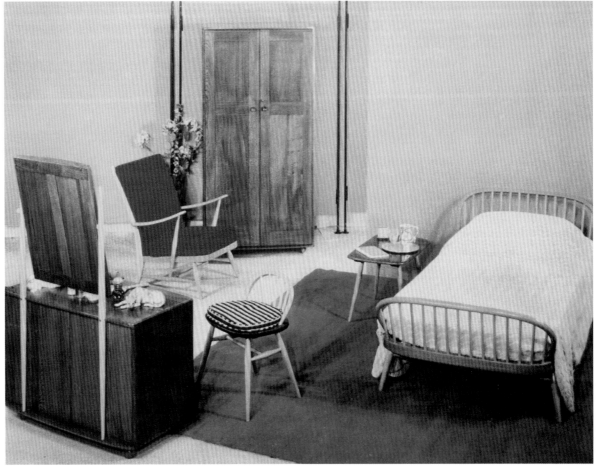

No. 408 *Dressing Chest with Mirror*
WIDTH OVERALL 3′ 0″
DEPTH OVERALL 1′ 7½″
HEIGHT 2′ 2½″
HEIGHT TO TOP OF MIRROR 4′ 6½″
SIZE OF MIRROR FRAME 25½″ × 20″
Natural Colour Waxed Finish
A three-drawer Dressing Chest of solid elm and beech. Top drawer fitted with sliding in-built plate-glass shelf. Easy-running ball castors simplify moving and cleaning. The adjustable mirror fitments are also of wood, fully polished.

No. 412 *Dressing Chest*
No. 438 *Adjustable Mirror*
WIDTH OVERALL 3′ 0″
DEPTH OVERALL 1′ 7½″ HEIGHT 2′ 2″
Natural Colour Waxed Finish
This handsome chest, in solid elm throughout, is already well known as one of the most beautifully proportioned pieces of its kind. Notice the interesting new refinement of the sculptured wood handles. Add a free standing circular adjustable mirror and you have a dressing table that is a joy to look at from every angle wherever you place it in the room. It is fully polished outside, back and interior. Mounted on semi-concealed ball castors, the chest moves easily for housework or can be brought to the bedside.

No. 407 *Hanging Wardrobe*
WIDTH OVERALL 3′ 0″
DEPTH OVERALL 1′ 10″
HEIGHT OVERALL 6′ 0″
Natural Colour Waxed Finish
A Hanging Wardrobe made entirely in solid elm and beech—including the interior hanging rail. Beautifully polished outside, inside and on the fully panelled back. Smooth-running ball castors ensure easy moving and easy cleaning. This wardrobe has been designed with really practical depth; clothes will hang perfectly straight and not askew, as they so often do.

No. 406 *Dressing Table*
WIDTH OVERALL 3′ 9″ DEPTH OVERALL 1′ 9″
HEIGHT 2′ 5″ HEIGHT TO TOP OF MIRROR 4′ 0½″
SIZE OF MIRROR FRAME 34″ × 16½″
Natural Colour Waxed Finish
A beautifully elegant dressing table with a strength that belies its slim grace. In wax polished elm and beech, with three drawers. The vanity drawer at each end is fitted with a handy in-built sliding glass shelf. Another notable point is adjustable all-wood mirror fitments.

No. 414 *Dressing Chair*
A stylish development of the Ercol Windsor Chair, designed for the bedroom. In natural, wax polished elm and beech. Handy straps hold the foam filled cushion to the seat. Detachable cushion cover.

Here is the most cunning contrivance ever—triple dressing table units! Three mirrors are mounted, each on a separate compact unit—two being drawers and one a cupboard. Each unit stands on smooth-running ball castors, so it moves at a finger-tip touch. Seated comfortably between them, you can position each piece to enjoy an all-round view of yourself. Another special feature is that even the adjustable mirror movements are of wood. No metal to rust or squeak. Finished in natural wax polished elm and beech, these units can be bought separately; but together they make a strikingly handsome and practical *ensemble*.

No. 411 *Side Cheval Unit with Cupboard*
WIDTH 1′ 7″
DEPTH 1′ 8½″ HEIGHT 1′ 9″
HEIGHT TO TOP OF MIRROR 4′ 9¾″
SIZE OF MIRROR FRAME 33¾″ × 15½″
Natural Colour Waxed Finish

No. 409 *Centre Cheval Unit with Drawer* WIDTH 2′ 2″
DEPTH 1′ 9″ HEIGHT 12½″
HEIGHT TO TOP OF MIRROR 4′ 11½″
SIZE OF MIRROR OVER FRAME
44½″ × 19¾″
Natural Colour Waxed Finish

No. 410 *Side Cheval with Drawers*
WIDTH 1′ 7″ DEPTH 1′ 8½″
HEIGHT 1′ 9″
HEIGHT TO TOP OF MIRROR 4′ 9¾″
SIZE OF MIRROR OVER FRAME
33¾″ × 15½″
Natural Colour Waxed Finish

"No-one can hold a candle to ERCOL beds" *says the ERCOLion*

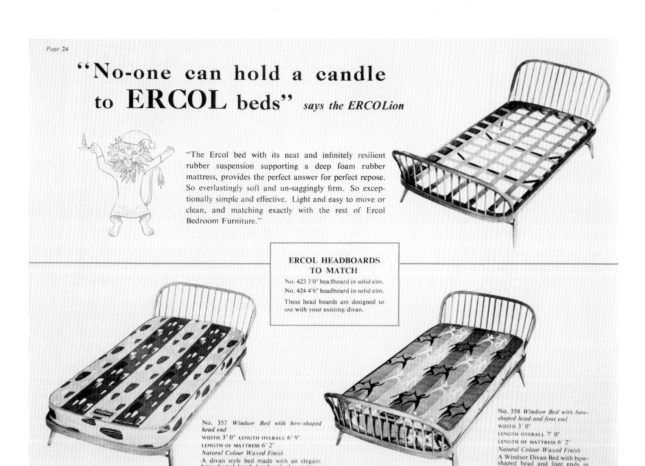

"The Ercol bed with its neat and infinitely resilient rubber suspension supporting a deep foam rubber mattress, provides the perfect answer for perfect repose. So everlastingly soft and un-saggingly firm. So exceptionally simple and effective. Light and easy to move or clean, and matching exactly with the rest of Ercol Bedroom Furniture."

ERCOL HEADBOARDS TO MATCH

No. 423 3'0" headboard in solid elm.
No. 424 4'6" headboard in solid elm.

These head boards are designed to use with your existing divan.

No. 357 *Windsor Bed with bow-shaped head end*
WIDTH 3' 0" LENGTH OVERALL 6' 9"
LENGTH OF MATTRESS 6' 2"
Natural Colour Waxed Finish
A divan style bed made with an elegant bow-shaped beech head end, the mattress is foam rubber filled and is of special design for use on fabric reinforced rubber suspension.

No. 358 *Windsor Bed with bow-shaped head and foot end*
WIDTH 3' 0"
LENGTH OVERALL 7' 0"
LENGTH OF MATTRESS 6' 2"
Natural Colour Waxed Finish
A Windsor Divan Bed with bow-shaped head and foot ends in beech. The mattress is foam rubber filled and is of special design for use on fabric reinforced rubber suspension.

The ERCOLion proudly presents his
ERCOL furniture family

Chapter 5:
The Windsor Furniture Family

An Extended Family

The Windsor Contemporary Furniture Family continued to grow steadily during the 1950s, with additional pieces being developed to meet a broader range of household needs. From 1953 to 1956 the collection was publicised through large fold-out reference sheets. The first bound catalogue appeared in 1957, illustrated initially in sepia, with colour photographs of room settings added the following year. Similar brochures were produced annually until the end of the 1960s. It was not until the 1970s that the style and format changed.

Right from the start, a vital element in developing the Windsor Range had been to harness the potential of machines, although for Ercolani automation was not an end in itself, but simply a means of producing better quality designs. 'There is a constant striving for improvement in design and a determination that it is not the machine which will dictate the design but the design that governs the machine,' noted *The Cabinet Maker* in 1958.[1] Quite often the machines themselves needed redesigning in order to produce the components for a new model, so the design process was as much about improving the machines as about shaping the designs: 'If it is found that when a new prototype design has been approved and there is no machine on the market which will make all that it demands, then the company will set out to design and make its own.'[2]

As well as extending the overall scope of the collection, core designs in the Windsor Range were repeatedly modified over the years to improve particular aspects of their performance or appearance. This accorded with Ercolani's belief that design was essentially evolutionary. He regarded his work as part of a continuum: 'The whole evolution of art, as I see it, is by somebody doing better than has been done before,' he remarked. 'You cannot say, I have invented this ashtray, but you can make improvements to an ashtray.'[3] The Windsor chair had evolved organically over several hundred years. Ercolani's designs were triggered - and informed - by these archetypes, but in developing and expanding the Windsor Range, he created a new tradition of his own through a gradual process of experimentation and refinement.

Diversification of the Dining Chair

Up to 1954 the basic Windsor dining chair, as exemplified by the 4A Chair and the 139 Chair, had a bow back with six spindles. The 280 Contemporary Windsor Chair (1954) marked a significant departure with its curved horizontal seatback and diagonal criss-crossing sticks. Praised by *The Cabinet Maker* for their 'attractively interlaced backs' and 'spaced shapes', these chairs rank amongst Ercolani's most original designs.[4] As well as being visually arresting, the 'latticed and shaped stick back' had a 'natural springiness, which gives extra comfort, strength and reliability,' explained the company.[5] Because this chair was so innovative structurally, it could not be produced using existing machinery, so six months was spent designing and making a new boring machine in order to enable it to be put into production.[6] The original version was twice remodelled over the next three years. Although the lattice back remained a constant throughout, in the 306 Windsor Dining Chair (1955) the H-shaped stretcher was replaced by pairs of diagonal criss-crossing spindles. This feature was retained in the 376 Dining Chair (1957), but the fiddle-shaped seat was replaced by an oyster-shaped seat and its legs were more splayed.

The 287 Chair (1954), 'a sturdy all-purpose Windsor chair' with a wider bow and four attenuated diamond-shaped splats, was designed for 'beauty, strength and comfort.'[7] Produced with special hard-wearing lacquer or enamel finishes, as well as in natural or antique wax, the 287 Chair was a high performance heavy-duty model suitable for contract use, marketed with the Ercol Gold Seal. The same distinctive seatback, offering good lumbar support, was used on the low-slung 288 Nursing Chair (1954) and the 289 Nursing Rocking Chair (1954), both with an optional drawer underneath the seat.[8]

Top right	Bottom centre left	Bottom far right
376 Windsor Dining Chair, 1957	365 Quaker Dining Chair, 1957	305 Tub Easy Chair and 306 Windsor Dining Chair in Ercol Design Notebook, 1955

Bottom far left	Bottom centre right	
369A Goldsmith's Armchair, 1957	280 Contemporary Windsor Chair, 1954	

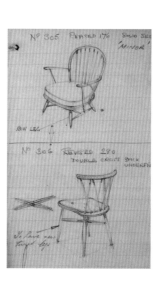

Top row (left to right)
333A Armchair; 333 Small Chair; 339 Rocking Chair, 1956

Bottom (left to right)
449A Bow Top Armchair, 1960; 287 Windsor Chair, 1954; 349 Love Seat, 1956

Ercol's growing mastery of the Windsor chair idiom was demonstrated in its 1956 collection, which promised: 'Chairs that welcome you with open arms, dining chairs to feast your eyes on, a love seat you will love at first sight, settees to settle down in, even a stool to put your feet up on.'[9] The curved horizontal seatback, first seen in the lattice-backed 280 Chair, was now adopted for the 333 Small Chair (1956), with its five vertical spindles and oyster-shaped seat. The chairs 'with open arms' were the 333A Armchair (1956) and the 339 Rocking Chair (1956), whose curved seatbacks swept round to the front supported by seven sticks, cradling the sitter. The pronounced diagonal angle of the arm support and the upward kink of the armrest added to the sculptural dynamism of these pieces.

As Ercol predicted, the 349 Love Seat (1956) quickly established itself as one of the company's most iconic designs. Epitomising the imaginative way in which the Windsor theme was extended, the Love Seat was a literal extension of the 333 Small Chair, its long curved seatback supported by 13 spindles, increased to 19 in a later variant, the 450 Love Seat (1960). This eye-catching feature, along with the sculpted quality of the double 'shaped out' seat, made it one of the most spectacular designs

in the range. As publicity photographs demonstrated, the Love Seat was multi-functional: it could either be used as bench seating at a dining table, as 'an occasional settee' in the living room or as a hall or landing seat. Two more classic Ercol dining chairs were added to the range the following year. The 365 Quaker Chair (1957) had a narrow back with a tall, slender tapering arched bow. The 369 Goldsmith's Chair (1957) was a high-backed chair with a wavy seatback. Both had oyster-shaped seats and both were produced in armchair versions as well. The 365A Quaker Armchair was displayed in the British Industries Pavilion at the Brussels Expo in 1958, specially selected by the Council of Industrial Design as an example of well-designed consumer goods. Significantly, Ercol was one of only five furniture companies chosen to exhibit, along with Gomme, Meredew, Gordon Russell and A. Younger.[10]

In September 1957 Ercol announced the launch of the 391 All Purpose Windsor Chair and the 392 Stacking Chair. Although principally intended for cafes and canteens, these designs entered the domestic range as well.[11] The 391 Chair was cheaper and more overtly utilitarian, with its square section seatback and trio of reinforcing spindles rising from the rear stretcher rather than the seat. This model retailed at 38s 6d, whereas the 392 Stacking Chair cost 47s 6d.

Above
450 Love Seat, 1960

Centre
Three views of 435
Goldsmith's Rocking
Chair, 1959

Far right
391 All Purpose Windsor
Chair, 1957

Opposite
Sanding a 391 All Purpose
Windsor Chair, c.1957-62

With its hourglass form and subtly contoured seatback, the 392 Chair was light, graceful and well-balanced. In fact, this design was so precisely engineered that it could be safely stacked to any height with no danger of toppling over, a feature highlighted in the firm's publicity: 'The Ercolion's ingenuity has produced a Windsor chair that stacks straight, not like the Leaning Tower of Pisa! As high as you like!'[12] A wheeled bogey (model 394) was also produced for moving large stacks of chairs. After completing stringent performance tests set by the Ministry of Education, the 392 Chair and a smaller version with a reinforced two tier seatback, the 440 Chair (1960), were specifically targeted at schools. The latter was subsequently produced in five graduated sizes as the 461, 462, 463, 464 and 465 Stacking Chairs (1963), each model colour-coded by means of a painted recessed disc on the rear of the seatback. Although specifically developed for the education market, these extra-strong chairs were also suitable for other commercial and institutional applications. They remained in production until 1970, but were eventually superseded by Robin Day's low-cost polypropylene shell school chairs, known as Series E (1971), manufactured by Hille.

The 401 Dining Chair (1958), also known as the Preformed Chair, was unique within Ercol's oeuvre for its use of moulded plywood (described as preformed at the time), rather than solid wood.[13] Yet, although it stands

out from the rest of the range, the curved plywood seat and seatback were veneered in elm to ensure that they conformed to the Windsor aesthetic, and were attached to the familiar Ercol underframe by two L-shaped bars made of steam-bent beech. Whilst emphasising the innovative manufacturing techniques used for this model, the company was anxious to reassure its customers that the 401 Chair embodied the same values as the rest of the collection:

> This chair marks a landmark in the development of furniture making. It is a marriage between the traditional Windsor under-frame – as developed by Ercol over the years – and the great technical potentiality inherent in preforming laminated wood to an exact shape. Hitherto laminations for preforming have had to be extremely thin in order to achieve the desired curved shapes. Now after intensive investigations the Ercol research team have developed a technique that makes possible the use of thick laminations. Thus, one of the outstanding characteristics of all Ercol furniture – the friendly feel of solid wood – is maintained.[14]

Right
Stack of 461 Stacking Chairs, 1963, in Ercol catalogue, 1966

Below
392 Stacking Chair, 1957

Below Left
461 to 465 Stacking Chairs, produced specifically for schools, 1963

'Stack straight as a die straight up to the sky,' rhymed the ERCOLion

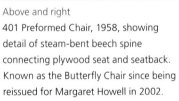

Above and right
401 Preformed Chair, 1958, showing
detail of steam-bent beech spine
connecting plywood seat and seatback.
Known as the Butterfly Chair since being
reissued for Margaret Howell in 2002.

With the launch of the 401 Chair, the evolution of the Windsor chair idiom was, to a large extent, complete. The 493 Dining Chair (1964), with its dynamic scalloped 'rungs', marked something of a departure, being more overtly decorative.[15] Another innovation later in the decade was the use of coloured finishes on the 557 Ladder Back Chair (1968) with its bright red, green, blue or orange stained frame. This trend appears to have been influenced by Habitat, which had been selling red-lacquered versions of Vico Magistretti's rush-seated Carimate Chair since 1964. The adoption of coloured finishes by Ercol in the late 1960s for various chairs in the Windsor Range reflected an attempt to appeal to the youth market. By this date the Windsor Range had been in production for more than two decades, so it would probably have seemed somewhat dated to the younger generation. By jazzing up the frames in bright pop colours, the chairs took on a more modern look, although in many ways this formula was alien to the 'true' spirit of the Windsor Range with its focus on the beauty of natural wood.

The Ercolion's New Suspenders

Easy chairs with loose cushions on a Windsor frame have come to epitomise Ercol, the first being the cable-sprung 176 Tub Easy Chair (1951). Yet, although it might seem natural to have extended the range in this direction, at the time this concept was completely untried: 'No one else would dream of creating an easy chair out of a Windsor chair,' Ercolani pointed out.[16] The challenge was how to combine the chair frame and the upholstery in a visually harmonious way to create comfortable cushioned seating that retained the Windsor chair aesthetic.

The striking colours and textures of Ercol's post-war upholstery fabrics complemented the warm tones of its beech chair frames, adding to the appeal of the furniture. Its 1955 Windsor Contemporary Furniture Reference Sheet alluded to 'a specially selected range of contemporary fabrics.' These were very much in evidence in the company's colour advertisements and catalogues throughout the 1950s and 60s. Some of Ercol's fabrics were custom-designed by Marianne Straub, a Swiss-born émigré textile designer

renowned for her subtle and imaginative weaves.[17] One of Ercol's major suppliers was the Stratford-on-Avon firm of Tibor, run by the Hungarian-born émigré designer Tibor Reich (1916-1996), renowned for his 'Deep Texture Weaves'.[18] The two firms worked closely together to ensure that Tibor's upholstery fabrics synchronised perfectly with Ercol's frames. In 1955 the Coventry retailer Owen Owen mounted an exhibition called *Adventure with Colour* juxtaposing Windsor furniture with Tibor fabrics.[19]

Windsor easy chairs fall into distinct categories: those with a back cushion as well as a seat cushion or those where the bow back was left exposed as a feature; and those with an open-framed sprung seat or a solid wooden seat, as in the 317 Grandfather Tub Chair (1955). The term 'Grandfather' denoted designs on a larger scale than normal, in this case a chair with a higher and wider back. Another closely related model, the 315 Grandfather Rocking Chair (1955) was praised by *Design* magazine as 'extraordinarily comfortable' and 'attractive from any angle.'[20] As Alex Gardner-Medwin noted: 'Much thought must have gone into the design for the chair to be so reasonably priced and still maintain good quality.' One of the novel features of these two chairs was that the bow was strengthened by a pair of supplementary spindles forking from a projecting support at the base of the frame. This ingenious device, derived from traditional Windsor chairs, provided structural reinforcement in a visually harmonious way.

The 203 Windsor Bergere Easy Chair and Settee (1953) – the first models on which this feature was adopted - were low-slung, with a deep seat, a high bow back and short splayed legs. These best-selling designs, which remained in production for many years, regularly appeared in advertisements. From 1956 onwards they were supplemented by the 341 Low Stool which, when abutted with the 203 Easy Chair, created a chaise longue. Although the 203 range was initially fitted with cable springs, by 1956 Ercol had switched to rubber webbing, a much lighter and more flexible system, referred to as 'The Ercolion's new suspenders'. This webbing, which had been developed by the Italian manufacturer Pirelli as an offshoot of its rubber tyres, consisted of lightweight rubber-coated fabric straps stretched across the frame. The same technique was used for the low-backed 334 Easy Chair and Settee (1956) and for all 'sprung' pieces in the Windsor range from this date onwards. Cushions, too, changed fundamentally during the mid 1950s, with down-filled and spring-filled cushions being replaced by latex foam rubber.

Although Pirelli webbing was adopted industry-wide, Ercol was one of the first firms in Britain to adopt this technology. Typically, Ercolani and his technicians customised the system to suit the specific requirements of his designs. Whereas other firms either tacked the webbing to the underside of the seat or wrapped it round the frame, on Ercol's chairs the straps were anchored in a groove cut into the frame, held in place by means of a dowel

Top
305 Windsor Tub Chair,
317 Grandfather Easy
Chair and 315 Grandfather
Rocking Chair, 1955, in
Ercol catalogue, 1968

Bottom (left to right)
315 Grandfather
Rocking Chair, 1955; 317
Grandfather Settee, 1956;
203 Bergere Easy Chair,
1953, and 341 Stool, 1956

Nº 334 SETTEE SHOWING FRAME

Pat. No. 800.828

Left (top to bottom)
554/2 Settee, 1968, with interwoven webbing; 334 Settee, 1956, with front to back webbing; 203 Bergere Easy Chair, 1953-6, with side-to-side webbing; self-anchoring device for securing webbing to frame

Opposite
203 Bergere Settee and Easy Chair, 341 Stool, 459 Occasional Table and 361 Trolley Bookcase in Ercol catalogue, 1966

Top right
Attaching webbing to a 355 Studio Couch, c.1965-7

slotted into the recess. The company was so proud of this system, which was both neat and secure, that it patented the design. Ercol's chair frames were often photographed without cushions in publicity images so that customers could admire the upholstery system itself. Before introducing a new technique such as this, rigorous testing was carried out. The webbing system developed for the 427 Easy Chair (1959), for example, was tested using a 12-stone robot sitter 87,064 times, the equivalent of eight sittings a day for 30 years.

Ercol's reputation for reliability, which had been fundamental to its ethos from its earliest days, was a vital tool in marketing the Windsor Range. The company was always on the lookout for improvements, which explains why the webbing configurations on certain long-lived models were altered over time. Initially the webbing ran widthways on chairs and front to back on settees. Later it was altered so that a mesh of webbing ran both lengthways and widthways for added strength. Adopting a belt and braces approach, Ercolani was particularly proud of the fact that his chairs incorporated more straps than those of other firms.[21]

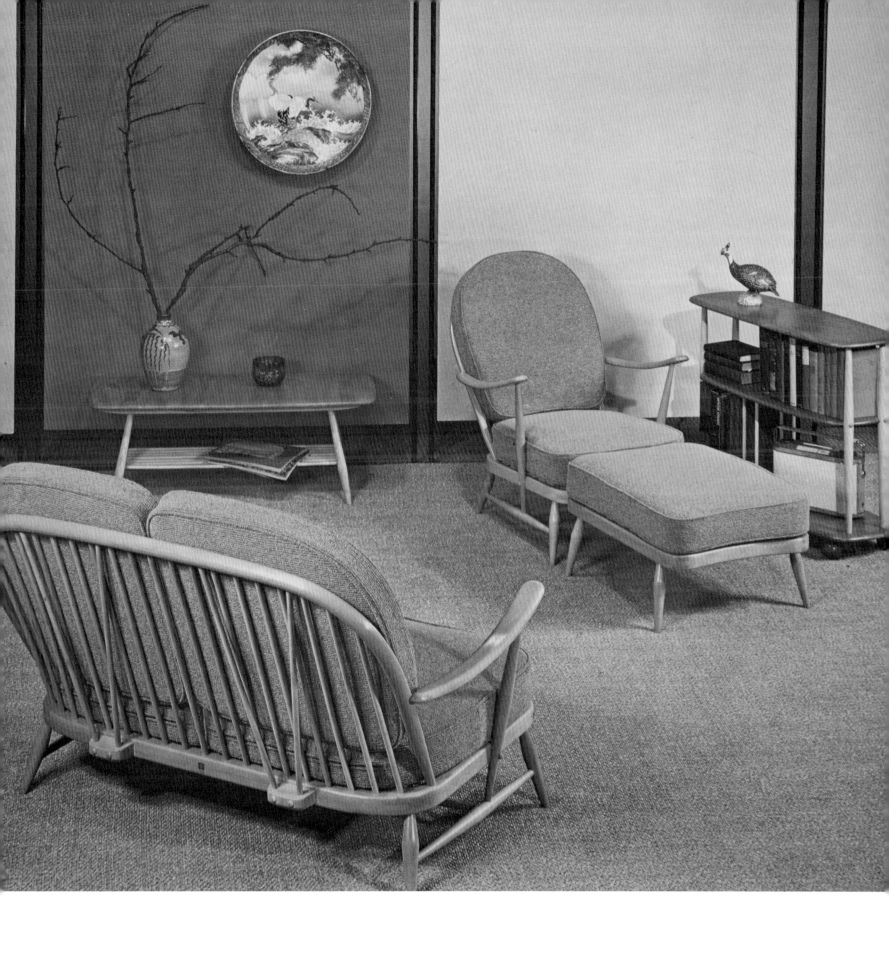

Opposite
355 Studio Couch with
back cushions, 1956

Above
355 Studio Couch showing
elm seatback, 1956

Right
482 Dressing Table, 414
Dressing Table Chair, 481
Wardrobe and 358 Beds in
Ercol catalogue, 1962

Webbing was a key feature of Ercol's 355 Studio Couch and 356-358 Beds, launched in July 1956, chosen in this instance specifically for it hygienic qualities and resilience. With their 'pleasing cradle-like frame of girder-like rigidity', the beds applied familiar Windsor characteristics – beech frames with steam-bent bows, spindles and splayed legs – in an unfamiliar context. 'Gay contemporary ticking' covered the Vitafoam mattresses, which were made from lightweight cavity-filled foam rubber.

The capacious 4-seater 355 Studio Couch was supremely practical, as well as being handsome and striking with its attractive solid elm seatback and low flared bow-shaped armrests. Back cushions were optional on this piece for those preferring to display the wood. The panel itself could be unscrewed to convert the couch into a bed, with the armrests doubling up as bed ends. 'If you are short of rooms but long on hospitality, consider my accommodating studio couch,' urged the Ercolion, who described this piece as 'couched in the same Windsor vernacular... heavenly to look upon and heaven to lie on.'[22]

The 364 Double Bow Easy Chair (1957) – a descendant of the traditional wing back chair and precursor of the present-day Evergreen Easy Chair - was also structurally groundbreaking. As its name suggests, the bow was bent in two directions, with the frame curving forwards as well as downwards at the sides. Each bow had to be steam-bent individually, a skilled operation involving two craftsmen who pulled the softened stave horizontally, then vertically, by hand. Several other variants were added over the next few years, including the 415 Tall Back Easy Chair (1958), the 477 Double Bow Low Back Easy Chair (1962) and the 478 Double Bow Tall Back Easy Chair (1962).[23] Speaking of the latter, the catalogue explained: 'In both chairs – tall back for the man of the house, a low back for madam – the back cushions are moulded to fit the double bow shape. Permanently curved to cradle your head as you relax.'[24]

The 427 Easy Chair (1959), which was designed by Lucian Ercolani Jnr, represented another interesting departure for Ercol, its beech frame being

Top
478 Tall Back Easy Chair,
355 Studio Couch, 456
Dropleaf Occasional Table,
and 477 Low Back Easy
Chair in Ercol catalogue,
1966

Centre and bottom left
427 Easy Chair with and
without seat cushions,
designed by Lucian Brett
Ercolani, 1959

Right
442 Easy Armchair and
443 Stool, designed by
Lucian Brett Ercolani, 1960

constructed from straight poles, rather than bent wood. With its intersecting horizontals and diagonals and its angled seatback supported by an extended back leg, this chair had a distinctly architectural flavour. Although it worked well as a standalone piece, being highly sculptural with interesting views from every angle, banks of chairs could be positioned side by side because of its rectilinear form. The square cushions were supported by rubber webbing stretched horizontally across the seat and seatback, with no cross rail at the front, a distinctive feature extolled by the Ercolion: 'This new sensation of "free floating sitting" brings deep, deep comfort never before possible in a chair so strong, so light weight and so compact in size.'[25]

The company was so proud of the 427 Chair that a technical drawing of the structure was featured in one of its advertisements, and the design itself was not only registered, but patented too.[26] 'Design for the comfort of the anatomy is an amalgam of science and aesthetics,' asserted the Ercolion, describing this chair as: 'A marriage of form and information. A means of support without obtrusive supporting means.'[27] A deep-seated armchair version - the 442 Bergere Easy Chair (1960) – was subsequently added to the range, along with a complementary ottoman, the 443 Stool (1960). When juxtaposed, these two pieces combined to create a sophisticated chaise longue.

Tables for Every Occasion

The first table in the Windsor Range was the prototype 150 Dining Table shown at *Britain Can Make It* in 1946. This was later put into production along with the circular 142 Occasional Table. Tabletops provided the ideal showcase for solid elm with its warm colouring and lively grain. The wood was repeatedly sanded during the machining, assembly and finishing processes so that it became incredibly smooth, taking on a silky lustre after the final wax polish was applied. Another distinctive feature of Windsor tables was that there were no sharp edges: square and rectangular tables had rounded corners and rims were softened with a graduated curved profile known as a thumb moulding.

The underframes, which were made of beech, sometimes incorporated ingenious devices, such as the rafter construction reinforcing the long rectangular 263 Dining Table (1953) and the sliding central leg and telescopic action of the under-rails on the 444 Extending Dining Table (1960), which incorporated storage space underneath for two extra leaves. Occasional tables were also made in hinged drop-flap versions, as in the low circular 308 Folding Occasional Table (1955). The long rectangular 456 Dropleaf Occasional Table (1961) had hinged flaps at either end, supported by sliding fold-out legs. The central section doubled up as a bench with removable cushions, which could be stored on the rack below. These suspended magazine racks, composed of rows of spindles, echoing the stick-backs of Windsor chairs, were another distinctive Ercol feature. On the 396 All Purpose Table (1957), part of a contract range for cafes and canteens, the rack was intended for parcels and gloves, 'a common feature which will be welcomed by women', the company claimed.[28]

Whereas most Ercol tables were circular, square or rectangular, the 354 Nest of Tables (1957) were described as 'oyster-shaped'. This term, which was also used for the new style of Windsor chair seats adopted in the mid 1950s, suggested that these tables evolved out of Ercol's chairs, although their three-legged structure was unique to this particular design. Trios of nesting coffee tables in graduated sizes were popular in Britain during the 1950s, although the majority were rectangular and they were often made from teak. The pebble shape of Ercol's tables reflected the prevailing fashion for organic forms, but in a subtle and understated way. The 354 Tables stand out for their design quality and craftsmanship, with their distinctive wedged-through splayed legs elegantly tapered towards the foot.

It was not until seven years later, with the launch of the 495 Nest of Five Tables (1964) with their dovetail-jointed box-like forms made in solid elm,

Top
213 Small Coffee Table, 1952

Second down
Sanding the rim of a table with a cylindrical sander, 1976

Third down
459 Occasional Coffee Table, 1961

Bottom
457 Tray Table, 1961

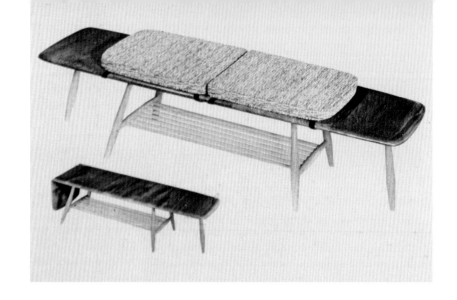

Top left
444 Slide Leg Extending
Table, 1960

Top right
456 Dropleaf Occasional
Table, 1961

Centre left
308 Folding Occasional
Table, 1955

Bottom left
354 Nest of Tables, 1957

that Ercol branched in a new direction. Rectilinear shapes were something of an anomaly in the Windsor Range aesthetic, however, the main trend during this period being to emphasise the organic qualities of the designs. An eye-catching new sculptural underframe, briefly adopted for tables and cabinets from 1967 onwards, marked a more radical departure, with legs replaced by a sculptural bone-like structure connected at the foot with an undulating bar. This highly unusual feature suggests the input of another designer, rather than Ercolani senior. It was seen in its most exaggerated form in a composite table promoted as Sixsome (1967), consisting of four 515 Segment Shape Occasional Tables (1967), encircling the rounded square 515 Quadrilateral Table (1967), surmounted by the 517 Circular Revolving Tray (1967). Because each part of the table was freestanding, the idea was that they could be used individually or as an ensemble. A novel concept developed in response to the trend for informal dining in the form of TV dinners and buffet suppers, Sixsome proved somewhat over elaborate and ultimately was not very successful.

Windsor Cabinets

Ercolani claimed to be the first manufacturer in history to produce cabinets with an elm carcase and beech legs, his first design being the 149 Sideboard exhibited at the Festival of Britain in 1951. Elm needed careful handling because it was not a structural wood and had a tendency to 'whip about' if used in the wrong way, hence the reason for combining it with beech.[29] As with Ercol's seats and tabletops, the elm boards used for its cabinets were made from several lengths of solid wood with dowel joints glued together in order to give the timber the necessary stability and strength. After Ercolani's initial stock of elm was exhausted, the company began buying up elm trees throughout the south of England in order to guarantee future supplies.

The 120 Sideboard (1946) and its successor, the 149 Sideboard (1951), were both something of a stylistic throwback, with echoes of the Arts and Crafts Movement in their panelled doors, bar-shaped handles and gate-latch style catch. Subsequent models were more clean-lined in form and consciously 'Contemporary' in styling, with square legs replaced by a new underpart with turned legs curling outwards at the foot in 1953. The 261 and 262 Sideboards, launched at the Furniture Exhibition at Earl's Court in 1953, made use of an imported tropical hardwood called agba.[30] This straw-coloured timber was used for the carcase, although the top was made from darker-coloured elm and the underpart in beech. Agba was also used by other firms, such as Heal's, Hille and Dunn's of Bromley, at this date. Its temporary adoption by Ercol suggests that elm may have been in short supply and that agba was easier and cheaper to obtain.

The 320 Sideboard (1955), which was a simpler version of the 261 Sideboard, had circular handles and flat drawer fronts. By this date the whole carcase was in elm and the beech legs had been straightened out, although they were still splayed.[31] Another new addition was the 330 Storage and Serving Cabinet (1955), a tall narrow sideboard with a top cupboard for storing crockery and glassware, its drop-flap front stable enough to be used for carving. 'The functional merits of the piece are as satisfying as its design qualities,' noted *The Cabinet Maker*, which reiterated Ercolani's claim that his cabinets were 'probably the only commercially-made pieces of furniture of solid elm.'[32] A perennial favourite, the 330 Cabinet was later remodelled as the 469 Serving Cabinet (1962), which was also promoted as a cocktail cabinet for living room use as well. 'My serving cabinet deserves a service medal,' proclaimed the Ercolion in 1963.[33]

Until 1956 sideboards were the only cabinets in the Windsor Range, but

following the termination of Ercol's chair-making contract with Harris Lebus, Ercolani decided to expand the firm's cabinet-making operations. A whole raft of new Windsor cabinets was launched in 1957, including the 366 and 367 Sideboards, the 368 Storage Unit and the 378 Serving Cabinet. The sideboards were in two widths and had drawers as well as cupboards, whereas the storage unit only had cupboards. Early sideboards were complemented by wall-hung plate racks. These were later supplemented by the 381 Panelled Dresser (1957), which was more clean-lined with solid backs.

Up to this point the drawers of Windsor cabinets had flat fronts, while cupboard doors were of frame construction with shallow recessed panels, both with circular handles. In 1958 sculpted oval handles were introduced on a range of bedroom furniture (model numbers 406 to 412), set over a concave ovoid recess, a standard feature from this date onwards. From 1961 the doors of Windsor cabinets were redesigned with a distinctive 'bulged' profile and mitred corners, created by using thick laminates of solid elm.[34] Drawers were also given a convex profile. The first cabinet to incorporate these new features was the 455 Sideboard (1961), which had three drawers in the centre flanked by cupboards on either side. This design has remained enduringly popular, continuing in production in its original form until 1994, and still manufactured in a revised version today as the 2073 Sideboard. New cabinets were periodically introduced during the 1960s with various configurations of cupboards and drawers, but the combination of convex fronts and oval handles remained a staple from 1961 onwards.

Standing apart from the work of other companies because of their use of elm, Ercol's Windsor cabinets were also remarkable for the fact that no plywood or chipboard was used. Because the whole cabinet was made of solid wood with neat dovetail joints, they were attractive enough to

Above left
120 Sideboard, 1946

Right
320 Sideboards in production, 1955, with agba carcase, beech underframe and elm top

Opposite
455 Sideboard, 1961

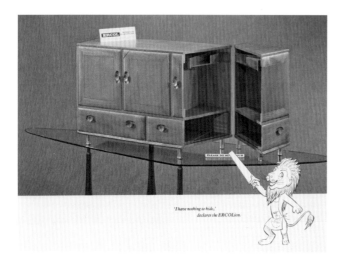

be viewed from all sides. Every detail of the design was carefully thought through, from the cutlery drawers in sideboards to the internal fitments in wardrobes. Their virtues were constantly praised by the Ercolion:

> Working in solid wood I am able to softly sculpture the edges and gentle curves of my furniture. My cabinet making is mathematically exact. The drawers slide and fit like a glove. My satin-smooth surfaces, exterior and interior, show the true beauty of wood grain gleaming with careful wax polishing. Look inside, outside or at the backs – the same high degree of finish is seen throughout.[35]

Ercolani was so proud of the craftsmanship embodied in his cabinets, which he felt was second to none, that he arranged for a piece to be sliced in two with a bandsaw and displayed at the Furniture Exhibition in January 1963. A photograph of this cabinet, shown in cross section, was illustrated in subsequent Ercol catalogues. Originally created to impress retailers with the quality of the company's materials and workmanship, it recalled the kind of showmanship displayed by Ercolani during his early years. A 30-minute film called *The Ercol Story* (1963), recording the process of manufacture from tree felling to final product, was also shown at this trade fair.[36]

Flexibility and Functionality

From 1957 onwards the Windsor Range was further expanded to include additional items for the living room, such as the 360 Desk Bureau (1957), a small portable writing cabinet with a drop-flap front, designed to sit on another item such as the 368 Storage Unit (1957) or the 379 Side Table (1957). Attention to detail was a feature running through all aspects of the Windsor Range. An interesting feature of this desk was that the top drawer was fitted with a secret lock accessed from inside the bureau. As this piece demonstrates, Windsor furniture was not just for show, it was intended for everyday use. As well as being handsome and beautifully crafted, it was also flexible and convenient to use.

Castors became increasingly common as an alternative to legs on Ercol's sideboards and cabinets, a practical device facilitating cleaning by making the furniture easier to move. These pieces, as well as the 361 Trolley Bookcase (1957) and the 458 Three Tier Trolley (1961), could be wheeled even when fully loaded. The 505 Trolley Table (1966) was a curious hybrid: with its two hinged flaps, it doubled up as a folding circular table, intended for informal dining.[37] Practical features such as these were highlighted by the Ercolion in his commentaries:

> There is often a duality of purpose about my designs that makes them specially useful in today's smaller rooms. For example, the sideboards, because they are mobile, and because the backs are finished as perfectly as the fronts can serve to dispense drinks, or move to table side for carving. Alternatively they can be used as room dividers or stand at right angles to a wall for informal room arrangements.[38]

Top left
469 Serving Cabinet, 442
Easy Armchair and 443
Stool in Ercol Catalogue,
1966

Bottom left
468 Sideboard sliced
in cross-section using
a bandsaw to show
construction

Centre left
455 Sideboard, 1961, in
Ercol catalogue, 1966

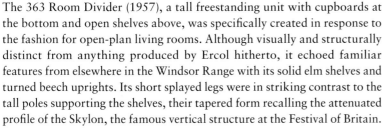

Top left
439 Drawer Fitment on
479 Writing Table, 414
Dressing Chair, 427 Easy
Chairs and 459 Occasional
Table in Ercol catalogue,
1966

Right (top to bottom)
361 Trolley Bookcase,
1957; 458 Three Tier
Trolley, 1961; 505 Trolley
Table with fold-out flaps,
1966

The 363 Room Divider (1957), a tall freestanding unit with cupboards at the bottom and open shelves above, was specifically created in response to the fashion for open-plan living rooms. Although visually and structurally distinct from anything produced by Ercol hitherto, it echoed familiar features from elsewhere in the Windsor Range with its solid elm shelves and turned beech uprights. Its short splayed legs were in striking contrast to the tall poles supporting the shelves, their tapered form recalling the attenuated profile of the Skylon, the famous vertical structure at the Festival of Britain.

Although beds had formed part of the Windsor Range since 1956, it was not until 1958 that Ercol launched a full range of bedroom furniture. The company's approach was characteristically independent-minded, its products being completely different to those of other more established firms specialising in this field. Particularly striking were the 409, 410 and 411 Cheval Units (1958), a trio of low-slung narrow dressing tables with tall slender mirrors, which could be arranged as an ensemble so that the mirrors provided views from various angles, an idea originally explored by Ercolani in the 1930s. The turned beech poles supporting the mirrors allied these pieces to the Windsor Range, as did the low bow seatback of the accompanying 414 Dressing Chair (1958). As with Ercol's sideboards, the backs of these bedroom cabinets were as carefully finished as the fronts. The Cheval Units, along with the 407 Wardrobe (1958) and the 405 Dressing Chest (1958), were all mounted on bronze-finished castors. Practicality was a primary consideration in the extra-large 431 Wardrobe (1959), which could be separated in half to make it easier to transport and install. Wardrobes came with a customised Ercol key stamped with the Ercolion motif.

Top right
358 Beds, 485 Cheval
Dressing Table, 414
Dressing Chair, 480
Hanging Wardrobe, 484
Dressing Chest in Ercol
catalogue, 1962

Left
363 Room Divider, 1957

Bottom right
480 Hanging Wardrobe,
1962

Building the Ercol Brand

During the 1920s and 30s Ercol had not sought to develop a public profile, relying on retailers to sell its products. All this changed after the war when the company began to promote its products directly to consumers under the Ercol brand name. Initially Ercolani was cautious about spending money on advertising, partly because he did not want the company to overreach itself financially, but also because he was wary of raising expectations and making promises that could not be fulfilled. Also, he wanted to ensure that the Windsor Range was copy-proof before advertising it in the national press. By the early 1950s, however, the Windsor Range was so closely bound up with the new identity of the company that it was worthwhile investing in promoting the Ercol brand.

Ercolani had always cultivated a close relationship with retailers but the war had disrupted normal patterns of trade. As sales director, Barry Ercolani played a vital role in Ercol's post-war marketing strategy, re-establishing links with furnishing stores and encouraging them to mount dedicated Ercol displays so that the distinctive character of the Windsor range could be appreciated. The company was wary of relying too heavily on their efforts to promote the Windsor Range, however, hence the decision to mount an independent advertising campaign so that Ercol could communicate directly with consumers. By familiarising the public with the Windsor Range through magazine coverage, consumers' appetites were whetted so that when they entered a shop they were immediately drawn to the Ercol display.

Teaming up with the advertising agency Alfred Pemberton proved a wise decision as they were very successful in establishing the Ercol brand and building up such a loyal and appreciative customer base. Pemberton's were so keen to secure the account when they approached Ercolani in 1947 that they offered to undertake the work initially for as little as £2,000. It was they who brought the Ercolion to life and at their initiative that the reincarnated Ercolion took centre stage in Ercol's publicity, a decisive ploy in capturing the public's imagination and communicating the unique character of the Windsor Range.

The growth in Ercol's advertising budget during the 1950s and 60s paralleled the expansion of the Windsor Range. In 1951, when the first modest collection was launched, £11,000 was spent on advertising. In 1953 the company began to place full-colour advertisements in magazines such as *House & Garden*. By 1955 expenditure had doubled to £22,500 per annum, although this was still relatively modest as the company's turnover had risen to £1,000,000. By the following year, demand for Windsor furniture was so great that customers were obliged to wait up to a year to receive their orders. Until production could be increased, therefore, Ercol decided that it was unwise to increase advertising. It was only after the factory was extended that a major national advertising campaign was mounted. By 1959, advertising expenditure had risen to £100,000, increasing to £150,000 by 1965. Again, this was directly related to turnover, which tripled during this period, rising to £1,250,000 in 1959 and reaching £3,000,000 by 1967.[39] These figures provide clear evidence of the phenomenal commercial success of the Windsor Range and the effectiveness of the company's marketing.

Top left
The Ercolion in his pyjamas, Ercol catalogue, 1962

Top right
'Everything is so ERCOLovely' advertisement, *House & Garden*, 1956

Bottom right
334 Easy Chair and Settee, 1956, in Ercol catalogue, 1966

The Ercolion Roars

Whilst emphasising qualities such as continuity, flexibility and reliability, Ercol sustained interest in the Windsor Range by regularly adding new pieces. When the 1958 collection was presented to the press at a special lunch hosted by Ercolani at the Hungaria Restaurant in London, it was described by *The Cabinet Maker* as 'a welcome hors d'oeuvre' to the annual Furniture Exhibition at Earl's Court:

> It attracts all the leading journalists who write on furnishings, and they always fall under the spell of Mr. Ercolani's characteristic craftsman's enthusiasm for his designs and yet the captivatingly informal and inconsequential way in which he talks about and demonstrates the finer points of his furniture. That air of "I don't want to sell you anything but just show what we have done" atmosphere which he creates so successfully provides all the information required without the use of superlatives.[40]

The Ercolion proved extremely valuable in nurturing the company's relationship with the public. A lively and engaging character, closely based on Ercolani himself, both in appearance and manner, he always had something amusing and interesting to say, whether enthusing about a new model or explaining the practical benefits of a technical feature. Puns, alliteration and word play featured large in the Ercolion's vocabulary. In a 1953 advertisement entitled 'The Ercolion woos the ladies', for example, he extolled the virtues of the 248 Windsor Fireside Chair in poetic verse: 'O women in your hours of ease, uncertain, coy and hard to please, you needn't be chairy of entrusting your hours of ease to my latest fire-side chair.'[41] In 1954 he wittily expostulated on the merits of the 203 Bergere Easy Chair and Settee: 'There are no follies about my Bergere suite... Taking but little room, it has room enough on those extra long, deep foam rubber seat cushions for the lankiest individual to loll, lounge or lie back in blissful comfort.'[42]

As a marketing device, the Ercolion was remarkably flexible, literally so as he could adopt a variety of persona and had a penchant for dressing up. In a booklet called *What the Press says about Ercol Furniture*, the Ercolion introduced a series of articles from newspapers and magazines, reappearing on each page in a different guise with an appropriate bon mot. As well as playing a prominent role in advertisements, he acted as master of ceremonies in Ercol's catalogues, fronting the introductory preamble and popping up at strategic points throughout the publication.

During the early days of Furniture Industries Limited, it was probably Ercolani himself who wrote the commentaries in the firm's catalogues, as they carried his idiosyncratic stamp. After Pemberton's came on board, they prepared Ercol's advertising copy, although the ideas and tone of voice were still closely allied with Ercolani. The big difference now was that the message was pitched directly at the public, rather than purely to the trade. As well as interiors magazines such as *House & Garden*, *House Beautiful* and *Ideal Home*, advertisements were placed in the colour supplements of newspapers such as *The Observer* and *The Sunday Times* during the 1960s. They were also actively targeted at young couples setting up home through specialist magazines such as *Getting Married* and *Brides*.

Although the Windsor Range was presented as stylish and modern through images of room settings in glorious Technicolour, consumers were reminded that standards of craftsmanship at Ercol harked back to another age. Underpinning the glossy pictures and the playful commentary was a didactic message about the merits of solid wood furniture, communicated through the friendly persona of the Ercolion. Had Ercol furniture proved unreliable or flimsy, this marketing strategy would have backfired, but because it was so well-made and the materials were of such high quality, the furniture reinforced the positive message in the firm's publicity.

The unique selling point of the Windsor Range was that it looked and

felt so different to other furniture on the market. Right from the start, it stood out from its competitors and the short-lived fashions of the day. Although marketed as 'Windsor Contemporary' during the early 1950s, because of its roots in the vernacular traditions of the Windsor chair, it reached out beyond its own time and has not dated in the way as other less distinguished post-war furniture. This is why it continues to appeal to consumers and collectors today.

Speaking of the effectiveness of the company's post-war marketing strategy, Barry Ercolani stressed the importance of 'the implied guarantee':

> For the previous forty years, 90 per cent of furniture had been made of plywood and veneers. The fact that we were using elm in a different way meant that we had to tell people what we were doing; we used advertising to inform. Nowadays if I stop Mrs Jones in the street and ask her what she can tell me about Ercol, she knows it's solid-wood furniture... The result of all this is that we don't really sell our furniture. We ask the retailers to believe in us, to believe in our furniture... With most things today you work back from the marketing to the product. Here, we work outward from the product.[43]

It was the dual combination of Ercol's aesthetic and structural distinctiveness, and its proven reputation for quality and reliability, that made its advertisements so effective. They reinforced what the public increasingly knew to be true, that the Windsor Range was made to last and would not go out of a fashion in a few years' time. The fact that it was so soundly constructed was a key factor in its success at the time and is still central to its continuing appeal today. It has stood the test of time: it looked good then and it still looks good now.

Expansion and Succession

Because of growing demand for the Windsor Range, the Ercol factory was repeatedly extended from the mid 1950s onwards. Early post-war additions included a new cabinet assembly shop and office block, built on the north side of the works on land purchased from Gomme's. Output doubled between 1955 and 1961 as a result of this expansion. By 1963 production had doubled again, with a further 100 per cent increase in capacity over the next two years.[44] By this date the factory occupied a 12-acre site, with the buildings extending to around a third of a mile in length. Inside the works there was over a mile of fixed rollers, with pallets being used to pass components and furniture from one work stage to the next on a one-on, one-off basis. Upholstery work was still carried out at the old Walter Skull factory. This made good sense because the fabrics and foam could be kept in a clean environment, away from the sawdust in the main works. In order to ensure sufficient supplies of wood, the company stored large quantities of timber at the High Wycombe factory. Timber was also stored and cut on Ercol's behalf by various other mills in the area. In 1975 the company acquired an additional timber yard and sawmill at Latimer, near Amersham, where logs were cut and planks were air-dried.

In addition to the physical expansion of the factory and the corresponding increase in the workforce, mechanisation had a huge impact on the firm's productivity. By 1959 the company employed 500 staff, an increase of 48 per cent since 1938. During that 20 year period the factory had increased in size by 41 per cent, but output had grown by an astonishing 900 per cent. As *The Cabinet Maker* observed in 1958: 'It somehow seems completely contradictory that a firm whose furniture has about it so much traditional feeling is able to say that it is probably the most mechanised in the country.'[45] By this date the factory was so efficient that Ercol was producing 2,000 pieces of furniture a day, with a new chair being completed every ten

seconds.[46] By 1961 Ercol's workforce had reached 700 people, rising to around 800 by 1968, with an annual turnover of £3,000,000, making it one of the largest and most productive furniture factories in the country, along with Lebus and G-Plan.

Ercolani's motivations in improving efficiency and increasing production were different to those of other companies, as he was not spurred by the desire to make profit for profit's sake. His aim was to make good quality, affordable furniture without compromising on standards. The pricing was worked out very carefully, with some pieces that were easier and cheaper to manufacture subsidising others that were more complex and expensive to make. As the company admitted in 1963:

> So keen are costings that each kitchen chair contributes less than a penny to the company profits. Even so, the fact that large quantities of chairs can be manufactured and marketed economically helps to subsidise the production of cabinet goods which by themselves do not bring in sufficient revenue to pay for the quality and craftsmanship that goes into each and every piece.[47]

Given the scale of manufacturing, overseeing day-to-day production and ensuring that the works was operating to maximum efficiency was an extremely demanding task. This side of the business was handled by Lucian Ercolani Jnr. Introducing new designs involved careful planning and considerable investment. Each model required a new set of jigs, for example, and the machines used to shape the components often had to be specially adapted. Once the machining and assembly processes had been formulated, work studies were carried out to assess the optimum time for each stage of the manufacturing process. 'Every job is broken down to individual operations, and each operation in turn is studied carefully to reduce movement and handling to a minimum,' noted one commentator.[48] Complex pieces, such as Windsor sideboards, might involve as many as 400 separate operations. This information was used to calculate rates of pay and to work out the cost of the final piece. Developing a prototype for a new design was so expensive that, generally, at least 50,000 pieces had to be sold in order to cover the initial development costs.[49]

In 1955 *New Homes* magazine published an article about Ercol called 'Modern furniture manufacture', which highlighted the significance of machines in enabling the company to keep its prices down while maintaining high standards:

> The furniture itself bears the stamp of the craftsman of the near-gone "hand-made" days - and yet on inspection one observes that the precision of the joinery repeated over and over again could not have been achieved by hands alone. No measuring rules are used; each component must fit exactly into a series of jigs assembled to a hair-breadth accuracy. Ingenious machinery, mostly designed and built up in the factory and working at very high speed, takes the rough wood and produces a chair in next to no time.[50]

Ercolani and his sons not only took great pride in the efficiency of the factory in terms of productivity, but in the skills of the workforce and the responsible way in which the works were run. The moral righteousness and ethical principles underpinning their enterprise are clearly apparent in a statement in the company's 1966 catalogue:

Top
Aerial view of extended Ercol factory, c.1965

Centre
Ercol's new offices, next to original factory on right, c.1960

Bottom
Finishing shop, c.1965-7 with 369 Goldsmith's Dining Chairs (left), 376 Windsor Dining Chairs (centre) and 450 Love Seat in spray booth (right)

Opposite
Ercol employee using a pad sander on seats of 391 All Purpose Windsor Chairs, c.1957-62

Notice the absence of sawdust and shavings. Notice the sense of order and the smooth flow of parts along the well thought out assembly lines as chairs, tables and sideboards take shape. Everywhere you see machines for sawing, planing, cutting, boring, shaping, bending and smoothing – all speeding up the job, but there is nothing soulless or mechanical about the production. Everywhere the individual touch is in evidence. A new generation of craftsmen has grown up with respect for modern methods and modern tools.[51]

Building on the solid foundations of their father's enterprise, it was Lucian and Barry's far-sighted approach to management that ensured the company remained so extraordinarily successful. However, even with the expanded factory, Ercol struggled to meet demand during the mid 1960s. At Barry's initiative, therefore, the company took drastic action by offering preferential terms to 500 of its 4,000 retailers, prioritising those which generated the highest sales and guaranteeing them shorter delivery times. A system of 'planned ordering' was also introduced so that the factory could plan its production schedule well in advance. Computerisation brought further efficiencies in sales, production planning and stock control from 1965 onwards. The investment costs were considerable (almost £200,000 was spent on the new computer system) but the organisational benefits were significant.

Although Lucian and Barry had taken over from their father as joint managing directors by 1961, the Old Man continued to play an active role as chairman. In 1964, on the occasion of his OBE, Ercolani was praised by his friend Edward Pinto for his 'remarkable energy skill and enthusiasm' and for his 'inspired leadership, which has raised others with him.' *The*

Top left
Prototype Windsor chair
with a high squared
bow, c.1957-60 (not
manufactured)

Top right
Lucian R. Ercolani and
his wife Eva outside
Buckingham Palace after
receiving his OBE in 1964,
with their sons Barry (left)
and Lucian Jnr (right)

Bottom left
412 Chest of Drawers,
1958

Cabinet Maker also noted approvingly that: 'Mr Ercolani has made his own special niche in the furniture trade and it is the combination of his qualities as both a designer and manufacturer which have enabled him to set and maintain such a high standard.'[52]

Ercolani himself, although modest about his personal achievements, was immensely proud of having built up the company from nothing and having financed its growth from profits. The fact that it was a family firm was incredibly important to him and he resisted any suggestion that Ercol should become a public company. When he was approached by a city investor in 1965, the proposal was given short shrift: 'We like our industry and have made lifelong sacrifices to build our Company and Factory to what it is now – one of the most advanced in the country – with men who like our work and like us, and we have no wish or intention that any shareholding pass out of our control.'[53] Even at the age of 80, Ercolani was still a force to be reckoned with, as Paul Ferris recognised in 1968: 'His hold on the business has diminished as he has handed over responsibility to his sons, but his influence remains powerful, especially in design. Nothing much escapes him; he watches the daily sales-figures like a hawk, and every new design must be approved by him.'[54]

Tradition and Modernity

With its unusual blend of tradition and modernity, the Windsor Range stood apart from mainstream trends during the 1950s and 60s, be it reproduction furniture, hard-edged Modernism or youth-orientated Pop design. While this did not hinder its saleability, it confused the design cognoscenti as they were unsure whether or not to approve. This explains why, although the 4A Chair had been enthusiastically endorsed by the Council of Industrial Design at *Britain Can Make It*, the Windsor Range received scant recognition from the design establishment later on. One particularly striking omission was that, in spite of (or perhaps because of) its commercial success, none of Ercolani's designs ever received a Council of Industrial Design Award, a startling (but presumably deliberate) oversight.

Although pieces from the Windsor Range continued to appear in *Design* magazine spasmodically during the 1950s, Ercol was not sanctioned in the same way as more overtly Modernist firms, such as Hille and Race. The fundamental incongruity between these two aesthetics was highlighted in a survey of bedroom furniture in *Design* in 1959, where Ercol's 412 Chest of Drawers (1958) in solid elm was illustrated on the same page as

John and Sylvia Reid's sleek steel-framed, Formica-topped C124 Dressing Table (1958) for Stag.[55] The fact that Windsor furniture was made of solid wood, rather than obviously modern materials such as plywood, steel or plastics, meant that it bucked prevailing technological trends. 'Certainly other materials may be lighter or stronger,' Ercolani admitted. 'Look at plastics, and plywood. Both marvellous materials. But for furniture – for beauty, for richness, for warmth – in my mind nothing can compare with solid wood.'[56]

The problem with the Windsor Range as a whole (from the COID's somewhat narrow perspective) seems to have been the lingering suspicion that, because it was rooted in the vernacular, it was somehow anti-modern. Yet, as Ercolani rightly argued, the Windsor Range transcended its historical origins: 'Here is a chair which has been good enough in the past in one idiom. I am going to give it to you in a new idiom, with a new quality. Now what offence am I giving the world by that?'[57] Whereas the consciously architectural 427 Easy Chair (1959), with its geometrically 'correct' structure, was selected for the Design Index (the COID's list of approved products), the 391 All Purpose Windsor Chair (1958) was not considered Modernist in the metropolitan sense.[58] Nevertheless, it was deemed appropriate for a rural retreat and was proposed as dining furniture for a weekend cottage by *Design* magazine in 1961.[59]

In reality, the only 'straight' vernacular design produced by Ercol was the 472 Double Bow Fireside Chair (1962) – later known as the Chairmaker's Chair - which, as Ercolani explained at the time of its launch, was based on an antique Windsor chair:

My new chair was inspired by an old one that I bought 40 years ago for £35. The old chair is badly warped because when it was made craftsmen did not know how to condition wood, but it is still a comfortable chair. I have wanted to use its basic design for many years but only recently have we had the machines able to make it better than the old craftsmen. We took over 40 photographs and made over 700 drawings before we discovered how we could pleasantly modernise it. We wanted to fill today's requirements at a price anyone could pay.[60]

Handsome in appearance, generous in dimension, yet light in weight, the 472 Chair was such a satisfying design that its merits were acknowledged by the Furniture Makers's Guild, which awarded it a Guild Mark in 1962.[61]

Top left
391 All Purpose Windsor
Chairs and 395 Table, 1957

Top right
472 Chairmaker's Chair
and 473 Chairmaker's
Rocking Chair, 1962, in
Ercol catalogue, 1969

Bottom right
499 Windsor Settee, 1964

Above
338 Fireside Chair, 1956

Opposite
Windsor tables and chairs
in Ercol catalogue, 1970

Ercolani himself was so pleased with the result - particularly the 'flying arms' which encircle the chair in one clean sweep and curve upwards at the front - that he created several other variants, including the 473 Chairmaker's Rocking Chair (1962). Two kidney shaped three-seater sofas, the 499 Windsor Settee (1964) and the 501 Windsor Double Bow Bergere Settee (1965), were aptly characterised as a 'conversation pieces' because their curved form encouraged sociability. [62] Whereas the 501 settee had shaped back cushions, the 499 Settee had an exposed bow and a distinctive 'hooped' underframe, described as 'horn-like' at the time. Practical as well as decorative, this convex structure provided extra strength for the long span of the seat. As these pieces demonstrate, although the Windsor Range drew on recognisable historical idioms, it displayed considerable ingenuity in its design and construction. Traditional Windsor chairs were just a starting point. Once Ercolani had mastered the technical challenge of producing them industrially, he applied the same engineering principles to other designs that had no historical precedent.

Contemporary Critique

Although most of the criticism levelled at the Windsor Range by the design establishment arose from the fact that it appeared to be historically derivative, conversely, some critics objected to modish 'Contemporary' features such as the splayed legs on Ercol's tables and chairs. By the late 1950s these had come to be regarded as somewhat vulgar because they were antithetical to the 'plumb lines' of orthodox Modernist design. Yet, as Ercolani pointed out, there were compelling structural and economic reasons for splayed legs: as well as being stronger, the furniture was also cheaper to produce. It was the

splayed legs that gave his chairs such a sprightly quality: they were literally light on their feet. The 'aggressive' angle of the leg, combined with its tapered form, injected movement into the designs. 'A chair is a moveable piece of wood,' he observed; 'they must be good-looking for their own sake.'[63]

The fact that the Windsor Range was so successful commercially was also regarded with some suspicion by the design establishment, the assumption being that good design and popular taste rarely go hand-in-hand. Furthermore, because the company carried on producing the same corpus of designs over many years, this was interpreted as a sign of creative stagnation. The public recognised the Windsor Range as a design classic, however, so they did not want it to change. The reason it remained in production for so long, therefore, was not because the company had run out of ideas but simply due to the strength of popular demand.

Ercolani himself, being over 60 when the expanded Windsor Range was launched, did not fit the bill as a young post-war designer, in the way that others, such as Terence Conran, Robert Heritage and Robin Day, clearly did. The fact that he was also an industrialist was not in his favour either. It was mistakenly assumed that in-house designers were inferior to freelance and consultant designers, and that little of merit was likely to emerge from a company's own design studio, certainly not designs by the managing directors of large firms. In view of all these prejudices, it was hardly surprise that Ercolani should end up feeling aggrieved: 'I feel the design people have never given me credit for what I've done,' he lamented in 1968.[64] Yet, the truth was that most people instinctively liked the Windsor Range. Quintessentially English, it struck a chord in the nation's psyche and was cherished in hundreds of thousands of homes.

The cool reaction of the design establishment was ironic in many ways because it was during the post-war period that the British public fell head over heels in love with Scandinavian design. Danish furniture became incredibly popular during the 1950s and 1960s and was imported in bulk. In fact, it was so influential that several British manufacturers, including Kandya and Gomme, enlisted the services of Danish designers to give their collections an authentically Scandinavian twist.[65] The appeal of Danish furniture lay in its sound design and fine craftsmanship. The same was true of Ercol, yet for some irrational reason, the Danes were considered more progressive. Paradoxically, outside Britain, it was the Scandinavians who were most appreciative of the Windsor chair tradition. Whereas Ercol had few direct competitors in the UK initially, Windsor chair variants by various Danish and Swedish firms were sold by Heal's during the 1950s.

The crucial point about the Windsor Range was that it was both traditional and 'Contemporary' at the same time. Ercolani arrived at his concept of modernity by re-establishing a link with tradition, contradictory though this might sound. There was no denying its historical origins; they were readily apparent in the designs themselves and enshrined within its name. Yet, as Ercolani stressed, the Windsor Range formed part of a continuum: as well as celebrating the past, it looked to the future. In this respect it stood apart from other 'Contemporary' furniture of the 1950s, much of which, with hindsight, was rather mannered and self-consciously or superficially modern. 'How very mistaken are those people who seek for modernity at all costs,' he declared.[66] The longevity of the Windsor Range was due to the strength of Ercolani's original concept: while experimenting with archetypal forms, he adapted them to modern manufacturing methods and the requirements of modern living.

Ultimately, the fact the Windsor Range received meagre official approbation from the British design establishment during its heyday is of little significance. Amongst consumers, Ercol's popularity continued unabated throughout the 1950s and 1960s: 'I haven't had to ask anyone if they like my furniture for 20 years,' reflected Ercolani in 1968. 'I've just made it and they've bought it.'[67] The Windsor Range also received the enthusiastic endorsement of the Queen when she visited High Wycombe in April 1962. She was reported to be 'thrilled to bits' by the ceremonial arch created in her honour, consisting largely of Windsor Range chairs, including 392 Stacking Chairs and low-backed 414 Dressing Table Chairs.[68] While it could be argued that commercial success and royal approval are no guarantee of aesthetic merit, in Ercol's case, quality, originality and popularity went hand in glove.

A Family Affair

The word 'family' crops up repeatedly in relation to Ercol, hardly surprising given that the Ercolani family have always played a central role in the running of the firm. During the 1950s and 60s the company's core collections – Windsor Contemporary and Old Colonial – were presented as two distinct furniture families, marketed in parallel. Although the two ranges had their own character, they were closely related in terms of shapes, one might even say 'in-bred'. While unlikely to be combined in the same home, they were 'cousins' nevertheless.

But the Ercol story is not just about the Ercolani family and the Ercol furniture family, it is about the people who created that furniture and who continue to make it today. Many of the workforce were (and still are)

WELCOME TO OUR QUEEN

employed by the company for their entire careers. Family members often worked along side each other within the company and quite a few were second or third generation Ercol workers, following in the steps of their parents and grandparents. Although the company is not quite as incestuous as it used to be, there is still something very personal about the way Ercol is run, which is highly unusual in this day and age.

Because Ercolani created the company literally from scratch, during the early days he recruited all his staff. Even later on as the workforce swelled, he spent such a lot of time at the works that he knew many of his staff by name. 'There seems to be no bossism about Mr Ercolani,' noted *The Observer* in 1959. 'I can walk among my men and feel a oneness,' Ercolani confirmed.[69] The Ercol Silver Band, which used to perform in the factory canteen every Wednesday tea break, helped to foster a sense of community, even when the company had grown very large. Ercolani himself had been a keen trombonist in his youth when he was a member of the Salvation Army Band, hence his enthusiasm for this ensemble. The Ercol band played an important role at special events, such as the remembrance services commemorating Ercol employees who had died during the two World Wars, and long service awards when staff who had worked at the company for 21 years had their names inscribed on a board.

For many years the most important day of the year in the Ercol calendar was the annual works outing to the seaside, usually to Bournemouth or Margate. Instituted in 1963, this tradition lasted until the 1990s. At their peak in the late 1960s, the scale of these events was staggering, as it involved spouses, children and retired staff as well as current employees. These outings took months of planning and required significant outlay by the company, but from Ercolani's point of view it was the ideal way of thanking his staff for all their hard work over the previous year. A reunion and a well-earned holiday, they brought together workers from the past, present and future - including the Silver Band - for a memorable day out.[70]

For the 1968 works outing, 2,000 people travelled to Bournemouth on three specially chartered trains and were then taken on a boat trip around Poole Harbour. Ercolani's health was failing by this date – he celebrated his 80th birthday that year - so his son, Lucian Jnr, acted as master of ceremonies in his father's absence. Ercolani and his wife sent a telegram saying, 'Our thoughts are with you especially on this your great yearly day. We hope and pray you are enjoying a lovely day and all the fun you have looked forward to.' A telegram despatched in reply was signed 'with much love from the Ercol family, all 2000 of us.'

Chapter 6:
The Romance of Old Colonial

Opposite
Old Colonial furniture,
Ercol catalogue, 1958

Below
Ercol price list, January
1956

Furniture with a Human Story

Although the Windsor Range dominated Ercol's output during the 1950s and 60s and was its most successful and high-profile collection at this date, the company produced another range called Old Colonial throughout the post-war period. Marketed in tandem with the Windsor Range, but more backward-looking in character, Old Colonial was originally conceived during the interwar years when reproduction furniture was the order of the day. Inspired by 17th century English oak furniture, its dark brown 'antique wax' finish and carved details were in stark contrast to the light honey tones and clean lines of the Windsor Range.

Old Colonial pre-dated the Windsor Range by almost a decade, so it was literally conceived during another age. In order to understand the rationale behind Old Colonial, therefore, it is necessary to wind the clock back to 1937 when it was first created. Although Furniture Industries Limited got off to a good start during the 1920s, Ercolani had been struggling to sustain the company since the onset the Depression during the early 1930s. The concept for Old Colonial came to him in a flash one day when he was waiting to be served at the local pharmacy, wondering why that business was doing so well that its customers were forced to queue up, while he was having to make such strenuous efforts to secure orders for his furniture. The answer, he realised, was to develop a popular, commercially successful line that would ease the strain on the company's finances.

In a publicity brochure called *Furniture with a Human Story*, Old Colonial was described as oak furniture 'imbued with the glamour and romance of that period when sturdy Britons settled across the seas.'[1] However, although its name alluded to early American settlers, the designs drew on native English furniture traditions: 'Many of these pioneers were skilled in woodwork... and took a personal pride in continuing the style of furniture which they had always known in their Homeland,' Ercolani explained.[2] Although his prose was somewhat fanciful with its allusions to

Sir Walter Raleigh, the Pilgrim Fathers and the Mayflower, Old Colonial reflected his admiration for the plain, solid, unpretentious oak furniture of the 17th century, particularly the Cromwellian era when furniture was cleaned up and shorn of the 'idolatrous embellishments' associated with the preceding royalist period.[3]

Ercolani's aim with Old Colonial was to express 'English-born traditions in the best English style.'[4] Stylistically it was closely related to an earlier collection produced by the Walter Skull branch of Furniture Industries Limited from 1932, marketed as *Oak Down the Ages*. Old Colonial was a simpler variant, better suited to larger scale production, which could be manufactured and sold more cheaply. Whereas a sideboard from the Skull range cost £6 17s 9d, for example, an equivalent Old Colonial sideboard was only £5 10s. Dining chairs were also considerably cheaper, costing between 20s and 27s in the Skull range, but as little as 16s in Old Colonial.

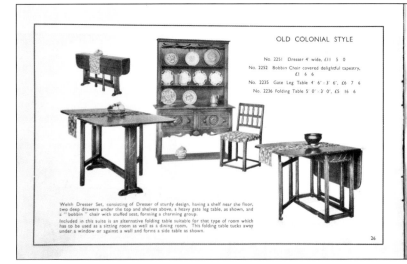

Above and right
Old Colonial dining room
furniture and upholstered
seating, *Furniture of Today*
catalogue, 1937

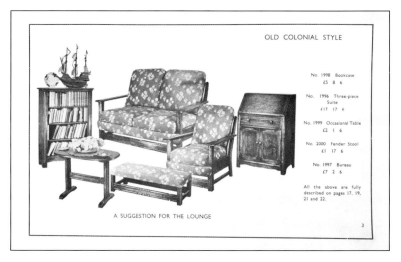

Elizabethan Simplified

When Old Colonial was first produced it was made from dark stained oak, with 'tooled and worn off surfaces' roughened with a spoke-shaver to make look the furniture look old. The reason for developing this range, according to the brochure, was that antique furniture was a luxury, whereas Old Colonial offered a practical and affordable substitute for the man in the street: a moderately-priced range with 'authentic detail', which could be collected piece by piece.[5]

Old Colonial was not reproduction furniture as such, however, as it was consciously designed to meet the needs of modern consumers: 'Elizabethan simplified and more in keeping with what to-day we call "fitness for purpose",' was how Ercolani characterised it at the time.[6] Whilst emulating 17th century idioms, the designs were scaled down and adapted to suit the size and needs of mid 20th century domestic interiors. On a personal level, Old Colonial embodied Ercolani's hopes and aspirations at this critical moment in time: 'Each piece expresses the designer's sincerity, and whether you buy a single chair or a complete suite, you will find built into it an ageless charm of which you will never tire.'[7]

The first collection was designed at breakneck speed following Ercolani's initial brainwave. As soon as the drawings were finished, they were copied and sent out to the firm's salesmen by courier. The first range consisted of a trestle table, dining chairs, a sideboard and a corner cupboard. Cost-wise it was very competitively priced at £20 for a dining suite. Ercolani was so determined to make Old Colonial a success that he telephoned all the West End retailers personally to tell them about the new collection, securing £5,000 worth of orders in a single afternoon, with a further £10,000 taken the following week. As the range proved immediately popular, it was soon expanded to include a wider selection of dining room furniture, as well as easy chairs, settees, bureaus, bookcases and bedroom suites. Although production was halted following the outbreak of World War II, Old Colonial played a key role in restoring the company's fortunes during the late 1930s, a lesson Ercolani never forgot.

Revival of Old Colonial

The commercial success of Old Colonial explains why Ercolani chose to reintroduce it again after the war - even though it was now somewhat outmoded - because it was something he felt he could depend on. Although by this date he was increasingly preoccupied with the Windsor Range, Old Colonial was his insurance policy in case his new Windsor Contemporary designs failed to take off. Initially Ercolani hedged his bets. In 1950 Old Colonial was presented as the company's principal collection in trade advertisements. Following the Festival of Britain, however, the Windsor Range took precedence in terms of publicity.

In the firm's November 1951 catalogue, the two ranges were presented on equal terms. A drawing showed the Ercolion watering a tree with a chair suspended on the main trunk and two branches growing up on either side, one labelled 'Old Colonial', the other 'Windsor Contemporary'. '"Behold" said the Ercolion, "the Ercol family tree, which produces some very fine furniture. There are two main branches. They are called Old Colonial and Windsor, and one of the most pleasant things about them is that the members of each family live very happily together.'[8] This policy of dual promotion continued for the next two decades, with half of each catalogue devoted to the Windsor Range and half to Old Colonial. Retailers could choose whether to stock one range or both, depending on the tastes of their clientele.

No. 420/421
Carved Buffet-Sideboard (on left)
LENGTH 4' 9½"
DEPTH 1' 10¼"
OVERALL HEIGHT 4' 6½"
Old Colonial Antique Waxed Finish
A sturdy, solidly built buffet, finely carved and of imposing proportions and made entirley of solid wood. The two cupboards enclose a half-width shelf running right through. The large drawers offer plenty of room for linen, table mats and cutlery. The top section can be both cocktail cabinet and wine cellar: and it is high enough to take bottles as well as glasses. The lower section may be bought as a separate sideboard.

No. 282 *Sideboard* and
No. 422 *Dresser Top*
LENGTH 4' 9½" DEPTH 1' 7½"
OVERALL HEIGHT 5' 6½"
(to top of dresser)
Old Colonial Antique Waxed Finish
A commodious sideboard and dresser top with four drawers and two cupboards —each fitted with a full depth shelf. The top drawer contains a sliding pull-out cutlery tray. The sideboard top and all shelves of the dresser itself are grooved to hold plates securely.

No. 331/258
Panelled Dresser
LENGTH 4' 0½"
DEPTH 1' 5½"
HEIGHT (TO TOP OF DRESSER)
4' 11¼"
Old Colonial Antique Waxed Finish
Two cupboards and two drawers, one of which is fitted with sliding lift-out cutlery tray. The two cupboards are fitted with long shelf. The shelves of the dresser top are grooved for plates.

No. 268 *Plate Rack*
OVERALL WIDTH 38"
„ HEIGHT 19½"
Old Colonial Antique Waxed Finish
For use either with any of the sideboards shown or separately. Fitted with metal plates for screwing to the wall.

No. 331 *Sideboard*
LENGTH 4' 0½"
DEPTH 1' 5½"
HEIGHT 2' 9"
Old Colonial Waxed Finish
Two cupboards and two drawers, one of which is fitted with sliding lift-out cutlery tray. The two cupboards are fitted with long shelf for easy convenience. Both the sideboard and the hanging plate rack can, of course, be purchased separately.

Old Colonial designs illustrated in the November 1951 catalogue included the 153 and 181 Refectory Tables and the 145 Gateleg Table, the latter described as 'inspired by an old Cromwellian model.' Dining chairs were produced in a range of vernacular designs, including the 104 Ladderback Chair, the 154 Fretback Chair and the 159 Yorkshire Chair, the latter with a decorative seatback 'inspired by a unique chair of the Elizabethan period in York Cathedral'. There were four different sideboards, all with panelled doors, with optional dresser and canted buffet back attachments. Interestingly, whereas the latter fell into the Non-Utility category, being more decorative than functional, and were therefore liable to 35% purchase tax, the sideboards themselves met Utility requirements (as did most of the other pieces in the collection) and were therefore tax free.[9]

Cross Fertilisation and Segregation

One of the curious aspects of the post-war version of Old Colonial was that, alongside the overtly historical pieces derived from its pre-war designs, the collection incorporated some of the newly developed shapes from the Windsor Range. Whereas the period designs continued to be produced in oak initially, the Windsor pieces were made from beech and elm, as in the Windsor Range proper, but with a dark 'antique wax' finish so that they complemented the rest of the Old Colonial range. As a result, the new

'Contemporary' shapes took on the same archaic character as the period designs. Speaking of the Old Colonial version of the 176 Windsor Tub Easy Chair (1951), for example, *The Cabinet Maker* remarked: 'When finished dark it assumes an almost traditional aspect.'[10]

Several of the early post-war Wing Chairs and Easy Chairs from the Windsor Range were also co-opted into Old Colonial, but other designs were specific to one collection or the other. The 210 Bergere Easy Chair (1953), with its low arched back and cabriole legs, was exclusive to Old Colonial, for example. The choice of upholstery also distinguished Old Colonial seating and affected how the range was perceived. The fabrics associated with this collection were deliberately old-fashioned, including printed floral chintzes and traditional jacquard-woven textiles with fringing and piping, redolent of the Edwardian era, in marked contrast to the brightly coloured textured fabrics used for the Windsor Range.

Some Windsor shapes were 'colonialised' by embellishing them with pseudo-historical decorative elements. With their shaped arms and pierced splats, the 243 Small Chair and 250 Tub Chair (1953) were described in a publicity leaflet as 'Windsor (Period inspired) Fleur de Lys dining and tub chairs combining antique charm and modern comfort'. As its shape number indicates, the 279 'Period inspired Windsor chair' (1954) was designed in close proximity to the 280 Lattice Back Dining Chair (1954),

No. 387 *Dropleaf Dining Table*
SIZE OPEN 4′ 6″ × 2′ 5½″
SIZE CLOSED 2′ 0″ × 2′ 5½″. HEIGHT 2′ 4½″
Old Colonial Antique Waxed Finish
A simple period inspired table for the smaller room. The leaves are supported on strong sliding metal arms. This table will seat six people when opened and the size can be increased still further by the use of the No. 265 End Table. (See small illustration on extreme right of this page.)

No. 434 *Draw-leaf Refectory Table*
LENGTH OPEN 7′ 0″
LENGTH CLOSED 4′ 6″
WIDTH 2′ 9″ HEIGHT 2′ 5½″
Old Colonial Antique Waxed Finish
A new Refectory table of substantial size and weight with a solid oak top incorporating a draw-leaf centre section. Designed to seat up to six people when closed and up to ten when fully opened. The extra-strong trestles are handsomely moulded from 2-inch-thick timbers.

No. 155 *Refectory Table*
LENGTH 5′ 0″ WIDTH 2′ 6″
HEIGHT 2′ 4½″
Old Colonial Antique Waxed Finish
Heavy underframe and solid top; designed to seat six people.
Note: The 265 Extension Table illustrated right can be used to increase the seating accommodation to eight, and also can be used with No. 387 Dropleaf Table.

No. 377 *Dropleaf Dining Table*
SIZE OPEN 4′ 1″ × 3′ 8½″
SIZE CLOSED 2′ 0″ × 3′ 8½″ HEIGHT 2′ 4½″
Old Colonial Antique Waxed Finish
A round shaped Dropleaf Table with strong sliding metal arms to support the leaves. Designed to seat six people.

No. 419 *Fixed Top Refectory Table*
LENGTH 6′ 0″ WIDTH 2′ 7½″ HEIGHT 2′ 4½″
Old Colonial Antique Waxed Finish
A substantial Refectory Table with a solid oak fixed top. The extra-strong trestles are moulded from 2-inch-thick timbers and the long stretcher rail is wedged to give absolute rigidity. Designed to seat up to eight people.

No. 153 *Draw-leaf Table*
LENGTH 5′ 9″ EXTENDED, 3′ 9″ CLOSED
WIDTH 2′ 4″ HEIGHT 2′ 5½″
Old Colonial Antique Waxed Finish
Refectory Table with heavy underframe and sliding pull-out leaves; can seat six people when closed, and eight when fully opened.

Top
Old Colonial tables, Ercol catalogue, 1958

Bottom left
Old Colonial furniture, Ercol catalogue, 1958

Bottom right
375 Period Inspired Windsor Dining Chair, 1957, later variant of 279 Chair, 1954

No. 416
Tall Panel-back Chair
No. 416A
Tall Panel-back Armchair
Old Colonial Antique Waxed Finish

An imposing tall panel-backed Chair and matching Armchair. A strap-on cushion fits over the polished, solid wood seat slats. The cushion cases are easily removed for cleaning.

No. 417
Tall Spindle-back Chair
No. 417A
Tall Spindle-back Armchair
Old Colonial Antique Waxed Finish

A tall spindle-back Dining Chair and matching Armchair. Based on a traditional Yorkshire design combining elegance with strength. A strap-on cushion fits over the polished, solid wood seat slats. The cushion cases are easily removed for cleaning.

No. 281 *Small Chair*
No. 281A *Armchair*
Old Colonial Antique Waxed Finish
Tall ladder-back Chair and matching Armchair based on a Cromwellian design. The seats are webbed and upholstered.

No. 291 *Small Chair*
No. 291A *Armchair*
Old Colonial Antique Waxed Finish
A larger panelled back-heavy Dining Chair and matching Armchair with carved top rail. The loose seats are webbed and upholstered.

No. 292 *Small Chair*
No. 292A *Armchair*
Old Colonial Antique Waxed Finish
A larger heavy period Dining Chair and Armchair of Yorkshire inspiration. The top rails are finely carved, and the seats are webbed and upholstered.

a key design from the Windsor Range. Both chairs had similar horizontal curved seatbacks, but the 279 Chair had three carved decorative splats with a decidedly Spanish flavour, as opposed to the clean-lined criss-crossing spindles of the 280 Chair.

Apart from its dark stain, it was ornamental details such as these that distinguished Old Colonial designs. On the 496 Ladder Back Dining Chair (1964), for example, the 'rungs' were scalloped rather than straight, while the dynamic curved seatback of the 493 Dining Chair (1964) conjured up bats with outstretched wings. Although the 493 was also assimilated into the Windsor Range, its decorative form meant that it sat more comfortably in the Old Colonial collection. Interestingly, in spite of these archaic features, these pieces harnessed advanced manufacturing techniques, Ercol being one of the first companies to exploit a new wood bending process developed at the Forest Products Research Laboratory, enabling timber to be bent whilst cold, then set by radio frequency heating, without the risk of fracturing. As the wood could be cut to shape before being bent, this made the process cheaper than steam bending. The timber was also greatly strengthened as a result.[11]

Top
Old Colonial dining chairs, Ercol catalogue, 1958

Bottom right
Old Colonial dining room furniture, including 496 Ladder Back Dining Chairs, 1964

The Romance of Old Colonial

Because of the element of crossover between the shapes, Old Colonial designs were illustrated in sepia in the firm's early reference sheets, whereas the Windsor Range was illustrated in black and white. Photographs of room settings also highlighted the fundamental differences between the two ranges. The flowery fabrics and dark frames of Old Colonial gave this range a more antiquated character. Although the company had initially suggested that the two collections might be combined within an interior, the contrasting aesthetic of the segregated groupings in these room settings suggested the opposite. In general, Old Colonial remained more static over the years – as befitted its conservative character – while the Windsor Range was more innovative, with regular injections of new designs.

In 1957, exactly 20 years after the launch of Old Colonial, Ercol produced its first major post-war catalogue. Alluding to the merits of the original concept, whilst stressing recent improvements, the Ercolion asserted: 'Today my Old Colonial range has all its predecessors' virtues of strength and individuality, and it possesses to an even greater degree the charm and mellow beauty associated with the 17th century historical period.'[12] By this date, a large number of Windsor Range shapes had been incorporated into Old Colonial, including some of the most overtly 'Contemporary' pieces such as the 355 Studio Couch (1957) and the 362 Bookcase (1957). However, alongside these modern forms were several self-consciously traditional pieces, such as the 416 Panel-back Chair and the 417 Tall Spindle-back Chair (1958), the latter a taller variant of the earlier 159 Yorkshire Chair (1951).

Over the years the origins of Old Colonial, as recounted by the Ercolion, became increasingly romanticised. In a section of the 1965 catalogue called 'The Romance of Old Colonial Furniture', Ercolani's trip to the US in 1923 was pinpointed as a key source of inspiration. 'It was there, at the Metropolitan Museum of Art, New York, I first saw these solid and satisfying designs. Looking at them and admiring the rugged honesty of their craftsmanship, I thought how fitting it would be to recreate in England a range of furniture with the same simplicity and aptness for purpose, derived and developed from such distinguished ancestors.'[13] Given the similarity between this account and the story related in Ercolani's memoirs concerning the genesis of the Windsor Range, it suggests an element of confusion or wishful thinking, hardly surprising given the fact that more than 40 years had elapsed.

By this date, however, the Windsor Range far outstripped Old Colonial on the British market in terms of sales, although in Europe, where English furniture was associated with traditional designs, the situation was reversed. During the 1970s, following the reaction against Modernism and the rise of the country house look, Old Colonial took on a new lease of commercial life, both in Britain and abroad. When Ercol expanded its exports into Canada, Australia and the Far East, for example, Old Colonial was its chief asset and accounted for the bulk of sales. Old Colonial remained enduringly popular amongst Ercol's more conservative clientele for many years. Traditional designs such as the Swan Chair, a Windsor chair with a swan motif carved in the central splat, have continued in production up to the present day.

No. 370 *Windsor Dining Chair*
No. 370A *Windsor Dining Armchair*
Old Colonial Antique Waxed Finish
Similar in design to the 371 and 371A but without the fleur-de-lis motif back slat. Notice the beautifully shaped and widely spread legs with the underframe close to the oyster-shaped seat. The foam filled cushion is fixed by straps and press-studs, and the cushion covers are detachable for easy dry cleaning.

No. 371 *Windsor Dining Chair*
No. 371A *Windsor Dining Armchair*
Old Colonial Antique Waxed Finish
Notice the beautifully shaped and widely spread legs with the underframe close to the oyster-shaped seat. The foam filled cushion is fixed by straps and press studs, and the cushion covers are detachable for easy dry cleaning.

No. 375 *Period Inspired Windsor Dining Chair*
Old Colonial Antique Waxed Finish
A Dining Chair with finely shaped back slats of Spanish inspiration and graceful fleur-de-lis motifs. Particularly noteworthy is the oyster-shaped seat and the position of the underframe. The foam filled seat cushion is fixed with straps and press-studs and the cushion case is detachable for easy dry cleaning.

No. 365 *Quaker Back Windsor Dining Small Chair*
No. 365A *Quaker Back Windsor Dining Armchair*
Old Colonial Antique Waxed Finish
An extremely comfortable high-back version of the traditional Windsor Chair. Rounded oyster-shaped seat with foam filled seat cushion fixed to the frame with straps and press-studs. Covers are detachable for easy dry cleaning.

No. 369 *Goldsmith's Windsor Dining Chair*
No. 369A *Goldsmith's Windsor Dining Armchair*
Old Colonial Antique Waxed Finish
A development of the traditional Goldsmith's Chair The seat is oyster-shaped and the foam filled cushion is fixed with straps and press-studs. Covers are detachable for easy dry cleaning.

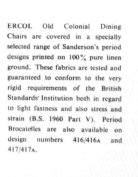

ERCOL Old Colonial Dining Chairs are covered in a specially selected range of Sanderson's period designs printed on 100% pure linen ground. These fabrics are tested and guaranteed to conform to the very rigid requirements of the British Standards Institution both in regard to light fastness and also stress and strain (B.S. 1960 Part V). Period Brocatelles are also available on design numbers 416/416A and 417/417A.

The Conundrum of Old Colonial

In spite of its commercial success and longevity, it could be argued that Old Colonial was somewhat lacking in authenticity by comparison with the Windsor Range. By obscuring the natural colour and grain of the wood with such a dark stain and by implying that it was made from oak, Old Colonial furniture, although equally well made, was not quite what it appeared on the surface. Another significant (albeit more unobtrusive) difference between the two ranges was that until the early 1960s the backs and drawer bottoms of Old Colonial cabinets were made of plywood, whereas in the Windsor Range they had always been made of solid wood. In 1963, however, Ercol announced that it was changing its policy and bringing Old Colonial into line with the Windsor Range in order to ensure consistency between the two collections.[14]

Yet, for all Ercolani's arguments about 'fitness for purpose', Old Colonial did not sit comfortably alongside the Windsor Range, either aesthetically or philosophically. In retrospect, it is hard to understand how he could square the two collections as they seemed to be pulling in different directions. The fact that Ercol continued producing Old Colonial during the 1950s and 60s, even after the Windsor Range had proved to be so successful, undoubtedly undermined Ercol's credibility with the design establishment. Because Old Colonial enjoyed a new wave of popularity in the 1970s, this affected Ercol's public image, making the company seem more conservative than it had previously been during the preceding decades. As a result, the true significance of Ercolani's pioneering achievements with the Windsor Range became somewhat obscured.

Interestingly, although Ercolani had often created period designs during his early career as this was the norm in the industry at the time, his attitude to reproduction furniture became much more ambivalent in later life and he criticised it for 'cheating the eye with something that didn't exist.' In a candid interview with Paul Ferris in 1968, he acknowledged that copying objects from the past was essentially sterile as it stifled the spark of creativity.[15] However, in interviews with the press Ercolani justified the collection in the following terms, saying:

> What we are trying to do is to put ourselves in the place of a craftsman living in Cromwell's time. What would that craftsman have done if he had lived as long as we have? We are allowing the experience of those extra 300 years to help us to do a job today probably a little better even than that man, had he lived long enough, would have done.[16]

Chapter 7:
Ercol after Ercolani

Opposite
Windsor Range,
Ercol Catalogue, 1972

Changing of the Guard

Lucian Ercolani celebrated his 80th birthday in 1968. Although increasingly fragile, he continued as chairman, latterly working mainly from home. His final years were spent writing his memoirs, which were published a year before his death at the age of 88 in 1976. Ercolani's last major achievement as a designer was the furniture he created for the Worshipful Company of Furniture Makers in 1972, an organisation he had joined twenty years earlier when it was known as the Furniture Makers Guild. His three ceremonial chairs for the Master, Senior Warden and Junior Warden were presented as a personal gift, having previously served as Master himself in 1957. Made from elm, a timber indelibly associated with Ercolani, the chairs were produced by two of Ercol's finest craftsmen, cabinet maker E.G. Cann and carver A.C. Gray. The Master's chair was adorned with a carved relief panel of the Livery Company's crest, with carved foliage representing oak, elm and beech and three panels depicting furniture making tools.

Following Ercolani's death, he was succeeded as chairman by his eldest son Lucian, who had been joint managing director with his brother Barry throughout the 1960s. Although his sons were very different in character, Ercolani recognised facets of himself in them both: 'I see in Lucian my steady side, my inventive side, the side of me that is sound common sense and reliability,' he observed. 'Barry is the volatile me, the poet, the dreamer, the emotional one.'[1] Having inculcated the same values in his sons, Ercolani ensured that the ethos he had worked so hard to establish would be perpetuated in the future. 'Our business is a way of life,' confirmed Lucian Jnr in 1962. 'If you work for the Old Man you live life his way. You don't just design, make or sell his furniture for 10 hours a day. You have first to dream dreams, then make them come true – as we all try to do.'[2]

Whilst steering the company in new directions, Lucian and Barry provided vital links with the past through their many years of experience of working alongside their father. Their approach, which was evolutionary rather than revolutionary, was to build on the firm's existing strengths, while expanding the collection and exploring new markets. As the company stated in its 1986 catalogue:

The brothers – and the team they've built to guide Ercol Furniture Ltd - believe in working quietly, conscientiously towards an ideal. Lucian and Barry Ercolani have achieved something quite remarkable; a company whose products are different because they've refused to compromise in the face of a constant temptation to use cheaper, less durable materials or inferior techniques… The two men have distinctly different skills, which may explain why they dovetail so well. Barry, the lover of words, the intuitive thinker, has developed a strong rapport with Ercol's stockists, both at home and abroad. Lucian, more at home with the actual craft of furniture making, has a vivid understanding of the value of design.[3]

Top left
Master's Chair for
Worshipful Company
of Furniture Makers,
designed by Lucian R.
Ercolani, 1972

Top right
Lucian R. Ercolani in
Master's Chair, 1972

Bottom right
873 Windsor Chair, 1985,
also known as the Latimer
Chair

Following a remarkable period of sustained growth and creative stability during the 1950s and 60s, elements of change began to appear at Ercol during the early 1970s, although there was no dramatic policy shift, as it was recognised that design continuity and longevity were vital ingredients in the success of the company's products. Continuity and longevity were also crucial aspects in the strength of the workforce. Many employees started out as apprentices and remained at the company throughout their careers, often following in the footsteps of a parent or sibling. Ercol had built up huge expertise in design and manufacturing, particularly since the war. This provided the bedrock of its continuing success during the 1970s. By 1973 its turnover had reached £4.5 million, double that of a decade earlier.

In spite of the oil crisis of 1974-5 and the ensuing recession, Ercol managed to buck prevailing trends and remained one of the most successful and profitable furniture companies in the UK. In 1975 it employed around 790 people, and even a decade later in 1986 its workforce still numbered 750. During the 1970s the demand for Ercol's products was so great that the company did not have to try very hard to sell its furniture. Stores were allocated £10,000 worth of furniture every month and there were long waiting lists. During the 3-day week in 1974, the standard delivery time was 18 months.

New Recruits

'The 1970s was a great period for Ercol,' confirms Lucia Ercolani (b.1948), who joined the company in April 1973 and worked alongside her father, Barry, for many years, accompanying him on sales trips abroad. 'Tom Dean was works manager at this date,' she recalls. 'It was a very tight ship.'[4] Having been forced to abandon her original career as a ballet dancer through injury, Lucia had then worked as a fashion model. She later teamed up with a photographer who did room sets for *House & Garden* and this, in turn, led to her job at Ercol in sales and marketing. Up to that point the company's public relations had been handled externally, but in 1973 it was decided to employ someone directly so Lucia was invited to take this on.

Although it was a great privilege to work for the family firm, it could be tough for the third generation, admits Lucia, sums up her grandfather's approach as autocracy with kindness. 'When I joined it was very male-orientated,' she recalls. 'Initially I wasn't allowed on the factory floor!' She describes her father as an extraordinary man with many talents (including poetry) and a real gift for selling: 'He spoke beautifully and was very quick, like a theatre producer. He was also very good at copy writing and was always very imaginative in what he wrote. His philosophy was to market the people behind the designs.'[5]

Above left

Portrait of Lucian Brett
Ercolani (left) and Barry
Ercolani (right) by David
Poole, 1990

Right

(top) Tom Dean, managing director of
Ercol Furniture from 1986-97; (centre)
Lucia Ercolani; (bottom) Don Pedel (left)
and Edward Tadros (right) at Ercol's Silver
Jubilee Exhibition, Hyde Park, 1977

Lucia and Barry's success in courting the British media and in promoting Ercol abroad had direct benefits in terms of sales. Each Christmas Ercol held a big press reception in London, for example, and every spring the company hosted an Open House where retailers and journalists were invited to visit the factory. These events, which began in 1973, proved so successful that Ercol's neighbour, G-Plan, soon followed its lead. Lucia's remit also included press photography. Because of her previous magazine experience, she tried to tackle this creatively as possible and come up with fresh ideas that would appeal to the media. Drawing on her connections in the ballet world, for example, dancers from the Ballet Rambert were invited to pose on Ercol's chairs, which, needless to say, proved a big hit with the press.

Another new recruit in September 1973 was Lucia's cousin, Edward Tadros (b.1949), the son of Roma Tadros (1919-2004), Lucian R. Ercolani's daughter. The Tadros family lived in Bournemouth, which was the Old Man's favourite holiday destination, so it was during these visits that Edward got to know his grandfather. After attending Bryanston School, Edward studied furniture design at Kingston School of Art, a good grounding for his future career. His first 18 months at Ercol were spent working in different parts of the factory, learning about the manufacturing process first hand from beginning to end. After this he joined the sales department and spent time travelling around the country visiting Ercol's retailers and mounting special displays. He then returned to the factory and, after a stint as assistant works manager, became works director, with responsibility for the whole production cycle from timber conversion to inspection and packing. In 1993, 20 years after joining the company, Tadros was appointed as chairman after his Uncle Lucian stood down. Since the retirement of Tom Dean as managing director in 1997, Tadros has alternated between the overseeing role of chairman and the executive role of managing director, sometimes doing both jobs at the same time.[6]

When he first started work at Ercol, Edward would be regularly summoned to visit his grandfather at home. Although Ercolani was notoriously demanding, they got on well and Edward has lasting respect for what his grandfather achieved: 'The Old Man brought a lot of practical ideas to manufacturing. Materials were very scarce during and after the war, so the Windsor Range was driven by the need to use materials in the most economic way. He was committed to using machines as much as possible so that craftsmen were able to make the best use of their time. A craftsman's time is one of the most precious resources; it's crucial not to squander it.'[7] This drive for efficiency in the use of materials and labour is still fundamental to Ercol today. Edward's pragmatism is perhaps the

435 Goldsmith Rocking Chair
428 Quaker Rocking Chair
452 Rocking Chair

470 Windsor Tub Rocking Chair

most obvious characteristic inherited from his grandfather. Like him, he is keenly aware of the need for the company to adapt to changing economic circumstances and market conditions in order to survive.

One reason why the transition from one generation to the next has been relatively smooth at Ercol is because the company's shares are largely owned by family trusts. Even if a family member does not work for the company, they still benefit financially, although share dividends are relatively modest so that profits can be reinvested in the company. 'The real plus side of a family business is its ability to be flexible,' stresses Edward. 'You can focus on the success of a business. You don't have to meet dividend deadlines or meet city expectations for a profits deadline.'[8]

New Image

One of the most visible signs of change at Ercol was the adoption of a new corporate identity after the company moved its advertising account from Pemberton's to Masius Wynne-Williams in 1970. After more than two decades of valuable service, the Ercolion was 'retired', a symbolic moment in the company's history as this character had been so closely associated with the company's founder. Rather than focusing on the personality of an individual, Ercol's new corporate identity drew attention to the materials from which the furniture was made.

Whereas in the past Ercol had relied on the witty banter of the Ercolion to educate its customers, the company now communicated its ideas through other means, including specially commissioned artwork, photographs and films extolling the strength and beauty of solid wood. Its 1973 catalogue was profusely illustrated with stunning photographs of beech and elm trees in their full splendour. As Ercol pointed out in a promotional film called *Living Wood* (1999): 'Victoria was Queen when the beech trees were planted that are now delivered as timber to the Ercol yards, and the elm we use is even older.' Yet, while emphasising the heritage of its timber, Ercol reassured customers that felling mature trees was not destructive, but was part of the natural cycle: 'Do not be sad that trees like this are felled: trees have a crowning maturity, like all living things, after which they decay.'[9]

Above and right
995 Campden Dropleaf
Table, 1993, showing
detail of leg

With hindsight, in view of the impending decimation of Britain's elm tree population by Dutch elm disease (an unforeseen catastrophe that unfolded from the mid 1970s), Ercol's new corporate identity based on the silhouette of a tree was somewhat ironic. At the time, though, the company's commitment to solid wood in general, and its allegiance to elm in particular, were vital in differentiating its products from those of other firms. 'Elm is a tree native to most countries of temperate climate, but it grows most profusely in this country, so as to call it a native English tree,' observed Ercolani in 1973, adding poignantly (and presciently) that: 'Our lovely countryside would seem bare without those stately and attractive elm trees, full of foliage and colour.'[10]

At this date Ercol had one of the largest kilning plants in Europe, with 32 steam kilns, each with a capacity of 1000 cubic ft. The kilning of each batch of elm took between 10-14 days. The quantities involved were vast, with 500,000 sq ft of elm and 250,000 sq ft of beech being processed in 1973. 'Both beech and elm go through a two-part seasoning process,' explained the company. 'First, timber stands out in the open air, one year per inch thickness. After that, every single cubic inch of wood goes through kilns that are controlled to laboratory standards of accuracy. This seasoning process is one of the reasons for the remarkable stability of Ercol furniture.'[11]

Hitherto, Ercol had relied almost exclusively on British timber, but the spread of Dutch elm disease was so rapid that, by 1980, the company was obliged to start sourcing elm from the US. Although some elm continued to be drawn from native stocks until as late as 1988 (the Blenheim Estate near Oxford being one of the company's local sources), by this date the company was forced to admit that Dutch elm disease had 'changed the face of the country, some would say a continent.'[12] In a promotional film called *For the Love of Wood* (1987), the company still managed to put a brave face on things. This film, which explained the manufacturing processes through the words of its employees, reaffirmed that the quality and individuality of Ercol's furniture arose directly from its use of solid wood. Because each tree was different in terms of structure, colour and grain, no two pieces were the same. Great skill was required, not only in identifying which trees should be felled, but at each stage of the production process, from sawing the planks, to kilning the timber and matching the grain.

Ercol's calm handling of the Dutch elm disease crisis was symptomatic of its level-headed approach. Instead of abandoning elm, which would have been the easiest option, the company made strenuous efforts to identify reliable alternative sources. By 1990 it was buying in most of its elm from North America. In order to ensure quality and consistency, the company

teamed up with a group of foresters and sawmill owners in Menahga and
Bagley in Minnesota. 'We weren't looking for suppliers, we were looking for
partners,' noted Tom Dean, who would fly over to the US every six months
to check on the timber.[13] 'We can't have any failures in our products because
of our reputation for quality,' he emphasised.[14] This alliance has proved
long-lasting and continues to the present day. The same company, Renneberg
Hardwoods, still supplies Ercol with all its elm. Significantly, although some
of its furniture is now made in ash and oak, Ercol continues to produce
key designs from the Windsor Range in their original form: beech and elm.

Don Pedel

Ercolani's long-time colleague Tom Redrup, who had joined the company
in 1928, remained head of design until 1975 and continued working for
Ercol until 1982, which explains why there was such remarkable consistency
throughout the post-war period. He was succeeded by Don Pedel (1933-
1993), who had joined Ercol in 1954 after studying at High Wycombe
School of Art. Pedel had been personally recruited by Ercolani Snr and he
was also very close to Lucian Jnr, so it was natural that he should take over
from Redrup as head of design.

The Windsor Range was at the height of its popularity during the 1950s
and 1960s so Pedel's early years were devoted to developing the core range.
Whilst recognising that the company must move with the times, Pedel
steeped himself in the heritage from which the Windsor Range was drawn:

As a furniture designer, the pieces you create must reflect the changing values
of the people you make them for. So in that time, our designs have changed, our
people have changed, even the way we make furniture has changed, but we've
never broken with our past traditions. We've always kept this "overlap", this
passing on of ideas and craft and understanding from one person to the next.[15]

As Pedel recognised, teamwork was central to the Ercol design studio, and an understanding and empathy for wood was vital in creating appropriate designs:

> We don't start with some enormous brief that states the market needs this, that or the other. An idea comes to you, and you offer it to your colleagues, then to the jig-shop for prototypes, and slowly, slowly it develops from there. To design you have to know your material. You must have a feel for timber, literally know how timber works. A piece of furniture should have some magic ingredient, something that you fall in love with but our designs must have an enduring quality to them, a harmony of line and detail, with facets that the owner can discover over the years.[16]

Striking out in the Seventies

Ercol had always had a contract dimension, but this was actively marketed from 1968 onwards through its Contract Furniture Catalogue. Although most of the designs derived from the core Windsor Range, some were specifically developed for the contract market, such as the high-backed 608 Kitchen Chair (1970), with its curved horizontal seatback and six

Modula

spindles, the outer sticks thicker in the centre and tapering towards the top and bottom. Made of beech and elm, it was produced with a white enamel finish as well as natural wood, complemented by a plain, rectangular table with a utilitarian plastic laminate top.

A collection of upholstered seating and tables called Modula (1970), designed as a flexible rectilinear system so they could be banked together, was intended for either contract or domestic use. Although made of beech and elm, Modula had a more Modernist aesthetic than the Windsor Range. With its simple structure and straight turned legs and uprights, it was less complicated to manufacture and therefore cheaper to produce. In 1971, for example, the 203 Windsor Bergere Easy Chair cost £39.60, whereas the 601 Modula Easy Chair cost £23.55, more than 40% less.

Although the Windsor Range remained central to Ercol's identity during the 1970s, its supremacy gradually began to diminish over the course of the decade, while Old Colonial grew in popularity due to the fashion for period design. This shift was already apparent by 1971 when, for the first time, Old Colonial occupied twice as many pages in the catalogue as the Windsor Range. The introduction of Mural – a modular system of cupboards and bookcases made from elm, which could be extended along a wall - marked a significant turning point in 1970. An offshoot of Old Colonial, Mural was conservative in character with its dark finish and traditional styling. It was also much larger in scale than previous designs, described in the catalogue as: 'Truly furniture in the grand manner... to be cherished and admired.'[17] Initiated by Lucian Jnr and designed by Don Pedel, Mural was highly controversial when it was first developed. Ercolani Snr strongly disapproved of this design, which he felt was out of character with Ercol's image and principles, being pseudo-historical and partly veneered. Nevertheless, Mural went ahead in spite of his objections and proved very successful commercially, remaining in production for many years.[18]

Changing fashions were also reflected in two subsequent ranges, which confirmed that Ercol was making a conscious attempt to diversify into new areas. Pine Line (1971), a range of pine furniture designed by Don Pedel, was a notable departure as the company had not previously used this timber: 'The Ercol Pine Line brings you the glory of solid pine; a warm wood, kind to the touch, worked and finished with a craftsmanship that can seldom be matched today,' proclaimed the catalogue. Although lighter than Old Colonial, the designs were similarly traditional, including Arts and Crafts style ladderback chairs, refectory tables, Welsh dressers and rustic chests of drawers. The William Morris style floral chintzes used for upholstery on the accompanying easy chairs and settees highlighted the nostalgic character of this range. In addition to natural pine, a dark Pickled Pine finish was introduced in 1981.

Top left
Pine Line, 1971, in Ercol
Catalogue, 1972

Top right
Soft Touch easy chairs
and settees, 1971, in Ercol
Catalogue, 1972

Bottom right
717 Wychwood Easy Chair,
1975

By this date the market for pine furniture had become increasingly competitive, and although Pine Line was much better made than most other furniture of this type, ultimately Ercol struggled to compete on price. The 635 Pine Dresser, for example, cost around £100 in 1972, a considerable investment at the time. Being made of softwood rather than hardwood, unlike the rest of Ercol's collection, the timber was more difficult for the company to handle from a technical point of view, although in the end the main reason for discontinuing Pine Line was because the company's other ranges were doing so well, particularly Old Colonial.

The Soft Touch Range of armchairs and settees, introduced from 1971 onwards, also signified a change of direction for Ercol. Unlike the easy chairs in the Windsor Range, the frames were fully upholstered, the 'show wood' element being largely limited to a trim. The upholstery was also much chunkier, made of thick foam, further emphasised by deep buttoning. This trend towards more mainstream upholstery designs proved relatively short-lived. With the launch of the 717 Wychwood Easy Chair (1975), Ercol returned to a more familiar aesthetic. Here, the solid elm frame supporting the slung seat was more obviously in keeping with the company's heritage. Stylistically too, although redolent of the 1970s, it perpetuated the values of classic Ercol.

Export Expansion

During the 1950s Ercol had concentrated primarily on the domestic British market, demand in this field being insatiable since the war. In 1965 Barry Ercolani led a trade delegation to Japan organised by the British National Export Council. As a result of this visit, the company established a partnership with a chain of Japanese department stores called Takashimaya.[19] This marked a turning point for Ercol which, in recent years, had been making a concerted effort to expand its export sales.

The export drive was spearheaded by Barry, who served on the British Overseas Trade Advisory Council and helped to set up British Weeks in various European cities. These events could be very productive. Ercol's sales in the Dutch store, Vroom & Dreesman, tripled after a special display was mounted during British Week in Amsterdam in May 1965.[20] The company also established good trade links in Switzerland, Germany and France, producing multilingual publicity leaflets emblazoned with the Union Jack. In November 1965 *The Cabinet Maker* noted:

> Ercol is high in the furniture export league. It estimates that by the end of this year its annual sales to Europe will have reached £400,000. In eight years its exports to Switzerland alone have been built up to £100,000 annually. It did business with practically every country on the Continent, including Denmark, where in the past two years its sales of Old Colonial furniture amounted to a significant £20,000.[21]

Ercol also expanded in various Commonwealth countries. In 1965 it established links with three of Canada's most important retail houses.[22] In Australia, which became Ercol's single largest export market, the company received extensive press coverage, selling through David Jones and the

Top left
The Ercolion promoting exports of Ercol furniture, c.1965

Top right
371 Windsor Dining Chair and 371A Armchair, 1957, in Ercol catalogue, 1973

Bottom right
Old Colonial Dresser in Ercol catalogue, 1973

Top left
455D Windsor Sideboard,
823 Ladderback Chair, 821
Saville Table, 810 Windsor
Bookcase, 1982

Bottom left
835 Evergreen Easy Chair
and 839 Old Colonial
Television and Video
Cabinet, 1983

Top right
766 Harmony Bergere
Settee and Easy Chairs and
459 Occasional Table in
Ercol catalogue, 1980

Myer Corporation, one of the largest stores in the southern hemisphere. The company also developed lucrative trade links in the Middle East - Bahrain was a good export market for a while - and in other parts of the Far East, notably Hong Kong and Singapore. By 1976 Ercol was selling to 33 countries and exports accounted for 30% of its sales (over £2,000,000 of its annual turnover). Barry's success in this field led to his OBE for services to export in 1978.

As with other British furniture companies selling their products abroad, the main emphasis was on traditional designs because, from a foreign perspective, this was perceived to be the UK's strength. At this date Ercol made little attempt to market the light-coloured Windsor Range in Europe and Japan, therefore, concentrating almost exclusively on dark-stained Old Colonial instead. Although exports were vital in enabling Ercol to weather the recession, by the late 1980s Ercol's products were out of step with the European market and exports sharply declined. Cheap imports, particularly from the Far East, also began to affect its market both at home and abroad. Although the company has managed to reverse this decline and has increased its exports again in recent years, competition from lower-price furniture produced in China and Eastern Europe represents one of the biggest challenges facing Ercol today.

Ercol in the Eighties

British domestic consumers remained Ercol's core market but, as fuel, labour and materials costs rose, the company was obliged to raise its prices, which narrowed its customer base. This affected the company's approach to marketing. While there had always been an emphasis on quality and reliability, these aspects were now stressed even more strenuously in order to justify higher prices. The value of tradition and heritage was also given

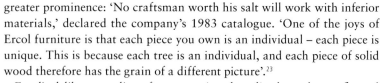

greater prominence: 'No craftsman worth his salt will work with inferior materials,' declared the company's 1983 catalogue. 'One of the joys of Ercol furniture is that each piece you own is an individual – each piece is unique. This is because each tree is an individual, and each piece of solid wood therefore has the grain of a different picture'.[23]

Ercol's deliberate policy of not pursuing short-lived trends was flagged up as a virtue in the company's 1987 catalogue, by which date the Windsor Range was over 40 years old:

> Remember the chrome and glass look of the seventies? The lurid "pop art" colours and shapes of furniture in the late sixties? Or even the fifties wirework and colour balls style of furniture, inspired by the molecular models of the new "atomic age"? They all had their day… It's taken the human body millions of years to evolve to its present shape – a shape that doesn't take too kindly to perching on chrome bars or slumping near floor-level on shapeless lumps of foam… Then, too, there is the question of materials. Metals and their alloys can be stamped or drawn into shape; plastics and foams and polyesters all take the shape of their moulds. But the material Ercol have chosen to work with is solid wood, partly for its beauty, partly for its warmth, and above all for man's affinity with it as a living substance.[24]

The core Windsor chair range remained fairly stable during the 1980s, but different types of upholstered seating and cabinets were developed to meet new requirements. With Harmony Bergere (1980), a range of Windsor-style upholstered easy chairs and settees with bow and stick backs, later renamed Jubilee (1981), Ercol returned to its roots. Created by Don Pedel,

a notable feature of this design was that the seatback curved round at the sides in the form of a double bow. The arms were also created from a bow and stick structure. Jubilee was a real tour de force, with its 'sweeping, sinuous curve of beech that blends three different planes into a single sweep of solid wood.'[25] The slightly squarer form of this design meant that the seating, although not exactly modular, could be banked in rows or right angled groups.

The 835 Evergreen Easy Chair (1983) - a descendant of the 364 Double Bow Easy Chair (1957) - proved true to its name and has remained in production with minor alterations right up to the present day.[26] As with Jubilee, the bow is steam-bent on two axes, first horizontally and then vertically, a highly-skilled manual operation involving two craftsmen. The bends were achieved with the aid of special flexible strapping using a high-specification material originally developed by NASA, which is stronger than steel.

With Silver Mist (1988), an unusual range of dining room furniture that was much more overtly organic and expressive than the rest of Ercol's collection, Pedel struck out in a different direction. Made of ash, the fluted effects on the seatbacks and cabinet doors were created by abutting numerous separate strips of wood.

Mike Pengelly

Another important member of the design team from 1966 until his retirement in 2001 was Mike Pengelly (b.1945), who had joined the company after studying furniture design at Rycotewood College and Wycombe College. Pengelly had briefly worked for the High Wycombe firm of Henry Stone & Son before being recruited by Ercol. Following his initial interview with Lucian Jnr, he was invited to meet the Old Man, 'a humbling experience', he recalls. 'The Old Man was very forceful, a hard taskmaster, but he had real belief and vision. You couldn't work with Ercolani and not be affected by him. His conviction rubbed off on you.'[27]

Pengelly's first two years at the company were spent unlearning everything he had been taught at college, and immersing himself in the manufacturing practices and design ethos that were specific to Ercol. Until the late 1970s he was mainly employed on drafting work and small projects, but he later began contributing designs in his own right. With Saville (1985), a highly successful collection of upholstered ladderback seating, he finally got the opportunity to make his mark. It was largely at Pengelly's initiative that the cabinetmaking side of the Windsor Range was expanded. An extensive range of wall storage units was developed, designed in conjunction with Don Pedel, including glazed storage cabinets and low units for television and hi-fi equipment, produced in three finishes: Natural (light), Traditional (dark) and Golden Dawn (a warm medium tone).[28]

Pengelly's aptly named Renaissance Settee and Armchair (1993) helped to sustain the company during a difficult period over the next few years and is still in production today. Although made of ash rather than beech, its solid bentwood frame was clearly Windsor-inspired. The multiple subtly curved slats supporting the arms and seatback are bent in groups using radio frequency heaters using air-dried timber rather than kiln-dried wood.[29]

Craft and Industry

Ever since its foundation in 1920, Ercol has attempted to strike a balance between nurturing craft skills and harnessing technology. This recognition of the value of individuals and the benefits of investing in their development has been reflected in Ercol's approach to training. Until recently, in-house apprenticeships were the standard method through which school leavers acquired the necessary skills to work in the factory. In 1975 the company trained between 15 and 25 apprentices annually, more than any other furniture manufacturer in the south of England.[30] Ercol's apprenticeships, which were described as 'unfashionably thorough' in 1986, were very carefully structured, covering all aspects of furniture manufacture. The first year was spent gaining experience in different sections of the factory, from wood machining and assembly to polishing and upholstery. Apprentices would then begin to specialise in their chosen field, while attending courses on day release at Wycombe College (later Buckinghamshire College), which had a large training section catering to the needs of the local furniture industry. After three years, an apprentice would progress to the next level and become a journeyman, obtaining various City and Guilds qualifications along the way. After completing their apprenticeship, staff were encouraged to continue their training, sometimes via livery scholarships from the Worshipful Company of Furniture Makers.

Ercol's apprenticeship scheme has since been phased out in its original form, partly as a result of staff reductions, but also because of changes in working practices, particularly the increasing use of CNC machines, which have simplified and streamlined the manufacturing process. Major changes in the education system have also radically altered how vocational training is provided, so that school leavers are now more likely to enrol in full-time further or higher education. The furniture training facilities at

Bottom left
Windsor cabinets in Ercol catalogue, 1993

Bottom right
Renaissance Easy Chair, designed by Mike Pengelly, 1993

Buckinghamshire College were later moved to Rycotewood College at Thame and have since been transferred to Oxford and Cherwell Valley College (part of the National School of Furniture), which now trains Ercol's apprentices on its behalf. Training is still actively fostered by the company, which currently has two apprentices, but the primary focus now is on management training, with workers from the shop floor being actively encouraged to diversify into other areas and obtain qualifications in factory management.

As highlighted above, the most significant development affecting furniture manufacturing over the last three decades has been increasing automation. The first computer numerically controlled routers, known as CNC machines, were introduced at Ercol in 1985. Multi-station shapers were adopted initially, although these proved somewhat restrictive as they relied on a pool of standard shape cutters and profiles, thereby limiting the scope of the designs. CNC machines have become increasingly sophisticated over the years and now offer much greater flexibility. Each machine is fitted with between three and eight different cutting heads, which are programmed to cut the wood to the desired shape. The operator can switch between different heads, depending on which component is being made.

CNC machines are now the standard cutting tools in the factory and have revolutionised manufacturing. CNC machine operators must have an understanding of wood, however, otherwise they will produce faulty parts. As Edward Tadros noted in 1992, craftsmanship is still highly valued at Ercol, and the advantage of using machines is that it frees up the time of the craftsman:

> Look around our workshop today and you'll see that we're using new technology alongside the best of traditional craft techniques. New technology is helping us to create shapes and forms in solid wood that simply were not possible before – and it's worth pointing out that the self-same technology is also helping us to make furniture with more accuracy, greater quality and better use of time and material. But new technology for Ercol isn't like putting a new robot on some car assembly line. Solid wood is unique and ever-varying, so between the machine and the wood you must always have the vital element of skilled human judgement.[31]

Top right
Ercol apprentice under tuition, 1993

Bottom left and centre
930 Saville Easy Chair and Settee, designed by Mike Pengelly, 1989, in Ercol catalogue, 1993

Bottom right
Ercol employee at the control panel of a Rye CNC machine, 1976

Top left
chairs commemorating
Barry Ercolani (1920-1992)
in All Saints Church, High
Wycombe made by Ercol
to compliment the choir
stalls designed by the
High Wycombe Furniture
School.

Bottom left
Ercol 50th anniversary
bronze medal featuring
Lucian R. Ercolani, 1970

Ercol in the Nineties

The early 1990s was a troubled period for Ercol, which, like many other British manufacturers, was badly affected by a global economic downturn. In order to ensure its survival, the company was obliged to take drastic action. Around 250 of its 650 staff were laid off in 1991, a devastating blow for Ercol and all the individuals concerned, many of whom had long service records. Staffing levels have continued to decline since then so the Ercol of today is a much leaner operation than in the Old Man's day. The recession had a significant impact on Ercol's pension fund, which was changed from a final salary scheme to a defined contribution scheme in 1993.

The 1990s was a time of change in other respects as well. Barry Ercolani retired in 1990 and died in 1992. Lucian Jnr was succeeded as chairman by Edward Tadros in 1993, although he never officially retired and continued as a director until his death in 2010, retaining the unofficial title of president. Tadros also took on the role of managing director in 1997, following the retirement of the company's long-serving managing director Tom Dean. Lucia Ercolani became a director from 1998, but stood down following her retirement in 2006, having worked for Ercol for 33 years.

Dutch elm disease was a huge blow for Ercol during the 1970s and 80s, yet somehow the company managed to weather the storm. Following Lucian Ercolani's death in 1976, Ercol could quite easily have folded, had it not passed into the capable hands of his sons and, in due course, his grandson. Virtually all the other furniture companies in and around High Wycombe have closed during the intervening years, including big names such as G-Plan and Parker Knoll. The UK's once huge and profitable furniture industry is now a shadow of its former self, which makes Ercol's survival all the more significant and remarkable.

Chapter 8:
Ercol Today

Opposite and above
Ercol's new factory at
Princes Risborough,
designed by Horden
Cherry Lee, 2002

New Factory – New Beginning

2002 marked the start of a new era for Ercol. After 82 years on its original site at High Wycombe, the company moved eight miles down the road to a new state-of-the-art factory at Princes Risborough. Some of the buildings at the old works dated back to the 1920s, so by this date they were rather antiquated and not well-suited to modern manufacturing equipment, such as CNC machines. Ercol's steam kilns became defunct following the decision to process its timber abroad, rather than at the factory. Due to reductions in space requirements, it no longer needed such a huge building. These were the main reasons for its relocation, along with a desire to modernise and upgrade its facilities.

As a result of rising property values, it made sense for Ercol Holdings Ltd (Ercol Furniture's parent company) to sell the High Wycombe site for housing and reinvest the capital in a new purpose-designed, well-equipped, energy efficient factory that suited the reduced scale of the firm's manufacturing operations.[1] The site at Princes Risborough had a special resonance for Ercol as this was the former home of the Forest Products Research Laboratory, where Lucian Ercolani had conducted his ground-breaking early experiments with steam kilns in the mid 1940s when he was developing the Windsor Range.

Throughout its history, Ercol has always pursued an independent path, rather than following others' leads. This is why it survives today when so many other furniture firms have folded. This spirit of independence is evident in its impressive new factory, designed by the leading architectural practice Horden Cherry Lee, a landmark building measuring 160,000 sq ft and costing £11 million, of a style and quality more commonly associated with university campuses than business parks. Characterised by the architects as a pavilion in a park, the factory was designed to frame views of the surrounding woodland.[2] Rectilinear in form, its white-painted, steel frame construction is Modernist in style, evoking the robust but elegant aesthetic of Mies van der Rohe. Rather than being sheathed in cladding, as most factories tend to be, the building is largely transparent (literally as well as metaphorically), with glass curtain walling for the north-west-facing offices and showroom at the front.

As well as looking stunning, the factory provides good working conditions and was designed to be environmentally friendly. Noise emissions were significantly reduced by using noise absorbent panels and creating an acoustic envelope within the building for the noisy dust extraction plant. Heating is provided by a huge purpose-made biomass boiler, fuelled by scraps of wood and sawdust extracted from the plant. The flooring in

the showroom and restaurant is made from solid maple, using timber supplied by Ercol's long-term partner Renneberg Hardwoods in the US. The building won a Sustainable Business Award for the South East in 2003. It also won awards from the RIBA (Royal Institute of British Architects in the South East), CABE (Commission for Architecture and the Built Environment) and the Civic Trust. 'We are very proud of our building,' remarked Edward Tadros, Ercol's chairman and managing director, following the official opening by Princess Anne on 23 October 2002. 'We were determined not to build a shed. This huge investment will enable us to compete in a global market, capitalise on our skills base and innovate new product lines.'[3]

Many employees had been used to walking to work at the old factory, so the move to Princes Risborough was a big change for them, but the new building is right next to the train station and there are good bus links, so it is easy to commute from High Wycombe. The building has proved popular with employees, its large, airy, open plan interior being very different in character to the cave-like spaces in the old works. Natural light is maximised throughout the factory, with extensive solar-controlled glazing in the offices and showroom and a 120 metre long, 3.7 metre high window in the production area. 'We have higher ceilings, nice views and we don't feel as isolated as we did,' remarked wood machinist Roy Graves. 'I now have trees in front of me, which is lovely and they are a reminder of the material we work with.'[4]

The relocation took place between July and September 2002, with the machines and the shop floor being transferred first, then the office staff. In order to minimise disruption, removal work began during the factory's annual two-week summer shut down. This used to be vital for maintenance, although it has since been phased out as it is no longer essential at the new factory. A new system of flexible working has also been introduced so that the company's manufacturing cycle ties in with the fluctuating patterns of consumer demand over the course of the year. In 'low weeks' the staff only work three days, but in 'high weeks' (at times of peak demand) it rises to 43 hours per week. It all balances out over the course of the year.

Ercol's operations director, Ian Peers, has the challenging task of working all this out. He joined the company as production manager in 2005, at the same time as Nick Garratt, who took over from Edward Tadros as managing director in 2010, having previously been head of sales and operations. As Garratt has an engineering background, on a day-to-day level they tend to focus on their particular area of experience so their roles are complementary. Tadros has since reverted to the role of chairman, enabling him to focus more on design and sales. A pragmatist who takes great pride in the achievements of his grandfather, he realises that the company needs to evolve in order to survive. 'It's no good just being an efficient manufacturer,' he admits. 'You need to make an effort to reach consumers, so that the brand name is strong in the consumer's mind. Building and sustaining a relationship with retailers is vital. You need to be proactive to make the relationship work.'[5]

Manufacturing Flexibility

Whereas in the past, continuity and solidity were central tenets in Ercol's identity, in recent years the company has evolved into a leaner and more flexible enterprise. Running a manufacturing company in the 21st century is challenging and unpredictable, as Ercol discovered to its cost shortly after the relocation. The terrorist attack in the US in September 2001 triggered a global economic downturn, prompting Ercol's sales to drop by 3.7% to £18.66 million. When the company relocated to Princes Risborough in 2002, its workforce stood at 400, but as a result of the recession, short-time working was introduced and 95 staff were shed over the next two years. 'It is a great pity as we think everyone has worked so hard to get the bricks in the right place and we have just been tripped up for the moment by the economic conditions,' reflected Tadros in May 2003. 'We moved here to keep our very skilled workforce and we are determined and committed to staying here in business in the future.'[6]

The British and overseas markets are both highly competitive, but the UK market has become particularly price sensitive over the last two decades. In order to compete in the middle range of the market, therefore, Ercol has diversified its ranges and broadened its pricing structure in recent years.

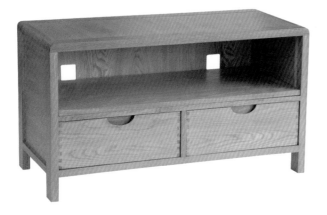

Opposite top
Wooden components
being bent on a press
by Thomas Zielinski,
2012

Opposite bottom
1395 Bosco Television
Unit, 2011

Left
1913 Evergreen Easy
Chair with new
upholstery in 2013

Because of the high cost of manufacturing in the UK, realistically the only way of reducing prices is to transfer some production abroad. Before its relocation, Ercol manufactured all its furniture at its High Wycombe factory, but since then the company has accepted the need for partial outsourcing. Some of its furniture is now made at factories in other countries (currently around 30%), although Ercol remains committed to manufacturing in Britain. As Edward Tadros stresses, this is a positive move as it enables the company to tailor its products to the demands of the market:

> The company needs a broader manufacturing base, so we're aiming for a mixed model. In the past we had control over the whole manufacturing and selling process, right through from growing the trees to advertising and selling through retailers, but now we buy in our timber and outsource some production, so we're sharing the process with various other countries. The work done overseas has never been at the expense of the work here. We're in the fortunate position that the work in the UK and the work overseas have mutually enhanced the overall performance of the company.[7]

Globalisation has also affected material supply networks. Many of the raw materials and components that used to be sourced in the UK are now imported. Ercol still has direct connections with Renneberg Hardwoods, its trusted wood supplier in Minnesota, which continues to provide most of its oak and elm, but the factory no longer converts its own timber. This is now purchased pre-cut and seasoned, with ash and beech now sourced mainly from Italy.

China is now an important manufacturing hub for Ercol furniture. Bosco (2011), a recent collection of oak dining furniture with distinctive curved radius corners and finger joints, is produced there. Other pieces are made in various parts of Europe: Savona bedroom furniture is made in Turkey, for example, while the Gina Recliner is currently produced in Slovenia. The chairs for the Artisan (2006) and Mantua (2008) dining ranges, made in oak and ash respectively, are produced by a specialist chair manufacturer in Udine in the Veneto, the chair-making area of Italy. All the pieces from the Windsor Range are still produced at Princes Risborough, however, as are many of the pieces sold through independent UK retailers, such as the cane-sided Bergere Sofa and Armchair, and an upholstered seating range with 'show wood' solid ash legs called Ravenna.

Another example of Ercol's flexible approach to manufacturing is in the field of upholstery. Whereas cloth used to be cut by hand using cardboard templates, this process is now fully automated using a high-speed computerised cutting machine to increase productivity and ensure minimum waste of fabric. Cushions are produced by specialist suppliers. The largest and most complicated, such as those used for the Evergreen Armchair, used to be cut from a single block of foam. This practice was rather wasteful as it meant that the off-cuts were thrown away, so cushions are now formed by gluing several pieces of multi-density foam. The foam itself has also changed a lot over the years. As well as being more fire retardant, it is much more eco-friendly.

Old and New Markets

As Ercol discovered in the 1950s, by encouraging retailers to display its furniture sympathetically and by educating their staff about the merits of the product, higher sales were more likely to result. Ercol's annual Open House events, inaugurated in 1973, where shop managers, buyers and press are invited to the factory, are still an important marketing tool, although fewer people are able to attend these days than in the past. Independent stores, such as Heal's in London, Hopewells in Nottingham and Ponsfords in Sheffield, remain an important outlet for Ercol and are still greatly valued by the company, but because of changes in the buying habits of consumers over the last 30 years, there are fewer shops of this kind. Today it is large groups such as Barker & Stonehouse, Stokers, Sterling and Furniture Village that dominate the market and are Ercol's most significant clients. Ercol has recently forged a successful new alliance with The White Company, which has stores nationwide.

Top right
Devon Bed, produced
by Ercol for The White
Company, 2013

Bottom left
Chiltern Display Cabinet,
produced by Ercol for John
Lewis, 2010

Although Ercol had supplied furniture to the John Lewis Partnership for many years, its association with this large and powerful department store group has been renewed and expanded over the last four years and now accounts for a significant proportion of Ercol's turnover. What makes this relationship special is that the company produces custom-designed ranges that are exclusive to John Lewis, notably the Chiltern Range (2010). Recognising the input of different stakeholders, the alliance is very collaborative, with new models being developed by Ercol's in-house designers to a specific brief from John Lewis in order to meet the latter's requirements

The Chiltern Range incorporates variants of classic Ercolani designs from the 1950s, capitalising on the fashion for retro design and renewed public interest in the Windsor Range. The Chiltern Chair, for example, is an updated version of the 376 Chair (1957) with its distinctive lattice back. These criss-crossing spindles provide a leitmotif for the Chiltern Range as a whole and have also been incorporated into other pieces, including a bench, display cabinet, coffee table and bed. The Chiltern Range also includes a dining table and nest of tables which echo designs from the Windsor Range, although they differ from the original collection in being made of oak or black and white lacquered ash and beech. Because of John Lewis's insistence on lower prices, production of these ranges is outsourced to China and Croatia.

In the 1970s exports accounted for about a third of Ercol's turnover, but by 2001 this had dropped to around 5%. As part of its current strategy for growth, the company is gradually re-building its international profile. Its largest overseas market is currently in Japan, where it sells through the chain of fashion and interiors shops run by the British fashion designer Margaret Howell and has recently established a new distribution contract with a company called Daniel. Ercol also exports to Hong Kong, Singapore and Australia and is currently investigating potential new markets in Northern Europe and the US.

One way of opening up new markets and establishing contacts is through trade fairs, an area in which Edward Tadros takes a lead role. The advantage of trade fairs is that they act as a magnet for national and international buyers, as well as providing a means of communicating directly with the public. In recent years, as well as exhibiting at Tent during the London Design Festival, Ercol has participated in the Milan Furniture Fair and the International Contemporary Furniture Fair in New York.

Ercol Originals

Margaret Howell had long admired the post-war designs of Lucian Ercolani, and it was she who initiated the re-launch of a group of classic Windsor Range designs in 2002. Initially these reissues were sold exclusively through her shops, but they have since been marketed more widely under the name Ercol Originals. The first designs to be reproduced were the 392 Stacking Chair (1957) and the 401 Preformed Dining Chair (1958), marketed today as the Butterfly Chair. Like all the reissues, they are produced at the High Wycombe factory and are made as closely as possible to the original designs in terms of shape and materials. The seat of the Butterfly Chair is made from elm or walnut-veneered moulded plywood, for example, and the spine of the chair is fabricated from pre-bent laminated beech. The seat is screwed and glued to the underframe by means of two oval wooden plates.

The robust construction of both these chairs makes them well-suited to contract use and because they can also be finished in different colours, they can be customised to the colour schemes of specific interiors. In 2011 the 392 Stacking Chair was produced in white and green for an ethical fast food restaurant called Pod Food in Shoreditch, while dark-stained versions were specified for the more traditional interiors of restaurants and cafes at Edinburgh Castle and Stirling Castle. The Butterfly Chair has also proved popular in bars and restaurants, including a trendy kitchen bar in

Opposite
Stack of 392 Stacking
Chairs, 1957, reissued for
Margaret Howell, 2002

Top left
401 Butterfly Chair, 1958,
reissued for Margaret
Howell, 2002, shown here
with stained finish

Top right
Aston Wright, leading
hand for cabinet and table
assembly, sanding a table
from the reissued 354 Nest
of Tables, 2012

Bottom left
401 Butterfly Chairs in
Las Iguanas restaurant,
Westfield Shopping Centre,
Stratford, 2011

Paris called Mojo. It has also been used to furnish several branches of the Brazilian-themed restaurant group, Las Iguanas, in Cambridge and London over the last few years.

Following the success of these two chairs, other classic Windsor designs have been put back into production as part of the Ercol Originals collection, including the 450 Love Seat, the 382 Dining Table (marketed as the Plank Table), the 911 Chairmaker's Chair and the 912 Chairmaker's Rocking Chair (variants of the 472 Double Bow Chair and 473 Rocking Chair). New additions in 2010 included the legendary 355 Studio Couch and the 354 Nest of Tables (often referred to as Pebble). The latest pieces to be added to the range are the 206 Windsor Bergere Armchair and 207 Stool, both re-launched in 2012.

All these pieces are produced in their original materials with beech frames and elm tops or seats. Contemporary variants have also been created, such as a startling version of the Love Seat half spray-painted in bright blue. In April 2013 the Studio Couch was exhibited at the Milan Furniture Fair upholstered in an eye-catching printed fabric called Blotch by the radical textile design duo, Timorous Beasties. The 206 Armchair has been produced in dynamic printed fabrics designed by Tamasyn Gambell and vibrant weaves by Bute. Ercol also continues to collaborate with Margaret Howell, producing a customised version of the 392 Stacking Chair with black legs and frame exclusively for her company in 2012.

Alongside these reissues, the company continues to produce selected items from its ever-evolving Windsor Range. The designs currently in production are direct descendants of Ercolani's original designs, which have been modified and updated over the years. Familiar pieces such as the 1875 Quaker Chair, the 1876 Swan Chair and the 1877 Windsor Chair are all clearly derived from early post-war designs, the latter a variant of the original 4A Utility Kitchen Chair. Solid elm Windsor cabinets are also still going strong. The 2073 Sideboard, with its two doors and three drawers, is another offspring from Ercolani's original line.

Some pieces in the Windsor Range are now produced in ash or a combination of ash and beech, such as the beech-framed 1459 Coffee Table with its slatted magazine rack suspended under an ash top. The 1665 Bar Stool (2012), originally created for Ercol's draughtsmen at their drawing boards, also combines an ash seat with beech legs. This design was put into production as part of Ercol Originals after vintage pieces displayed on the company's stand at a trade fair generated a wave of interest. The timeless appeal of the Windsor Range is confirmed by its enduring popularity with architects. Quaker Chairs and 1665 Bar Stools were recently chosen for a stylish new coffee shop in Uxbridge called Harris + Hoole, opened in 2013.

As well as appealing to interior designers, the Ercol Originals range has attracted a new generation of domestic consumers with an affinity for post-war design. A favourite with magazine stylists, these pieces frequently appear in room sets in magazines and have also been used as retro props on television shows. 'The furniture stays the same but the marketing evolves,' observes Edward Tadros. The cult status of Ercol Originals was confirmed in 2009 when *Wallpaper* magazine organised an installation in the courtyard of the Victoria and Albert Museum featuring two dramatic criss-crossing arches of 392 Stacking Chairs. The sculpture, which was devised by maverick Italian-born furniture designer Martino Gamper, was one of the highlights of the London Design Festival. Its impact was further intensified by the fact that the chairs in one of the arches were sprayed in a variety of rainbow colours. Ironically, the chairs had to be adapted in order to produce the necessary curvature on the arch because the design of the chair is so precisely engineered that it stacks upright to any height without tilting.

Opposite
355 Studio Couch, 1956,
reissued 2010

Below
392 Stacking Chair, 1957,
reissued for Margaret
Howell, 2002

Top left
Stack of Windsor bows for
1875 Quaker Chair

Top right
Ercol Draughtsman's Stool,
c.1959

Bottom left
1665 Bar Stools, 2012

Design Responsiveness

From 1997 to 2005, the Dutch-born designer Floris van den Broecke (b.1945) was employed as the company's design director, having previously been professor of furniture at the Royal College of Art from 1985 to 1997. At his instigation, new pieces were commissioned from three leading freelance designers, Terence Woodgate, Antonio Citterio and Fred Scott, but although these designs were exhibited at 100% Design in 2003, none entered production in the end as they were not considered quite right for Ercol. Better suited to the image of the company was the Gina Recliner (2004), an extremely comfortable adjustable chair with a solid ash frame and moulded foam upholstery, designed by Ingemar Jonsson and Cathy Pot. Named after the Italian actress Gina Lollobrigida due to its curvy shape, it was advertised under the slogan: 'It's every chair you've ever wanted.'

Since van den Broecke's departure, Ercol has employed a variety of design strategies. In response to changing fashions and the impact of globalisation, the company has become more outward-looking and pluralistic, pursuing several initiatives concurrently on different fronts. After actively collaborating with freelance designers for several years, the company has now returned to the tried and tested practice of developing most of its designs in-house. Working closely with the production team at the factory, the design team was headed by Ruth Wassermann until September 2013, and latterly consisted of two designers (Lisa Sandall and Dylan Freeth) and three production engineers.[8] The company's design policy is to broaden and update its product range in order to ensure Ercol moves with the times in terms of styling and price, adopting a more structured approach to product development based on market research at trade fairs and discussions with retailers. Furniture design is more fashion-based than in the past, so the range needs to be constantly refreshed.[9]

Left
Gina Recliner, designed by Ingemar Jonsson and Cathy Pot, 2004

Overleaf
Double arch created from 392 Stacking Chairs, installation designed by Martino Gamper at the Victoria and Albert Museum, 2009

Top left
2270 Artisan Lamp Table
and 2269 Artisan Coffee
Table, designed by James
Ryan, 2006

Centre left
2266 Artisan Cabinet,
designed by James Ryan,
2006

Bottom
2383 Mantua Dining table,
designed by James Ryan,
2008

Pinto (2011), a range of painted elm furniture, illustrates the type of designs now being developed by Ercol in response to current trends. Its subtle matt finish is designed to allow the grain to show through. The Pinto dining range was supplemented by a collection of bedroom furniture in 2012. The success of Pinto has paved the way for Ercol's alliance with The White Company, a firm specialising exclusively in white furniture and furnishings. In 2012 Ercol produced white versions of pieces from the Ercol Originals range. It has since developed a range of white bedroom furniture called Devon (2013) exclusively for The White Company, made from oak and light-coloured birch, incorporating stylistic detailing associated with the Windsor Range, such as bedheads composed of spindles.

Most of the freelance designers that Ercol has worked with in recent years have a particular association with the English vernacular tradition of designing in wood. James Ryan, who designed the popular Artisan (2006) and Mantua (2008) furniture ranges, originally trained as a craftsman furniture maker and is now chief designer at the Edward Barnsley Workshop, which has direct links back to the Arts and Crafts Movement. Sir Terence Conran (b.1930) also has a long-standing love affair with wood,

Top
Barton Stacking Tables, designed by Terence Conran, 2012

Centre right
Barton Armoire, designed by Terence Conran, 2012

Bottom
Barton Coffee Table, designed by Terence Conran, 2012

Above
2334 Treviso Desk,
designed by Matthew
Hilton, 2010

Top Left
Matthew Hilton in a
Windsor chair produced
by Matthew Hilton Ltd
(prototype by Ercol)

Opposite
1520 Holland Park Chair,
Russell Pinch, 2012

Bottom right
Russell Pinch and Oona
Bannon, the husband -
and - wife duo known
as Pinch

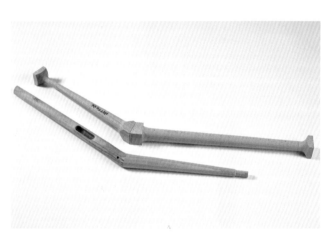

Above
Angled finger joint, developed for
the Holland Park Chair (opposite), a
technically ingenious, extra-strong joint
connecting the rear legs to the seatback
uprights. Made from beech, the timber
is dried, cut, turned, mortise-drilled,
glued and sanded.

having been closely connected since the mid 1980s with a company called Benchmark specialising in high-quality cabinetmaking, based on his estate in Berkshire. Conran's Barton Range (2012), a range of plain clean-lined modern furniture made of American oak, developed in conjunction with Ercol's design team, grew out of a project for the Conran Shop. In addition to an armoire, sideboard, media cabinet, shelving unit and dining table, it featured a small stacking occasional table incorporating a distinctively Ercolian feature in the form of an inverted V-shaped bentwood leg.

Matthew Hilton (b.1957) began designing furniture for SCP in 1986 and has since established his own brand, Matthew Hilton Ltd, to manufacture and market his own designs in 2007. His Treviso Desk (2010) for Ercol - an attractive modest-sized oak desk designed for computer use - has

proved highly successful and was awarded a Design Guild Mark from the Worshipful Company of Furniture Makers in 2010.

Russell Pinch (b.1973), who created many designs for the Conran Shop before establishing his own small company, Pinch, also has a special affinity with wood. His Holland Park Chair (2012) for Ercol, a robust dining chair with an unusual angled joint connecting the back leg and seatback, originally created for Holland Park School in London, is produced in two versions, with or without arms. Whereas the Treviso Desk appeals primarily to the domestic market and is sold through retailers such as John Lewis, the Holland Park Chair was developed for the contract market, although it is equally suitable for domestic use and was recently added to the Ercol Originals range. Already it is proving popular with commercial clients in the

catering field. In 2012 a customised version was installed in a new London restaurant called the Perkin Reveller near the Tower of London, emblazoned with Chaucer's shield. The Holland Park Chair was also recently chosen for the River Cottage Canteen in Bristol, a new restaurant run by chef and broadcaster Hugh Fearnley-Whittingstall, opened in 2013.

The crucial point for Ercol, whether collaborating with an external designer or developing a new range in-house, is that the furniture should express the company's identity in a positive and unambiguous way. There is no point in producing eye-catching, aspirational contemporary designs that might have originated from other firms. In order to ensure the company's survival, Ercol's products must be realistic commercially, geared towards an existing customer group or a predetermined target market. Where specialist expertise is needed, Ercol enlists the help of freelance designers. For the Paladina range of bedroom furniture, for example, Ercol commissioned Tim Fenby, who had previously collaborated with the bedding firms Ducal and Silentnight. More recently, sofa specialist Ian Archer was invited to design the Svelto Sofa (2013), part of a range of stylish oak living room furniture created by the Ercol design team, also including coffee tables and stacking units with unusual off-centre shelves.

Survival of the Fittest

Lucian R. Ercolani ran the company with a mixture of idealism and pragmatism. These dual virtues have been upheld by his successors, and are still at the core of Ercol's ethos today. Thanks to the commitment of the Ercolani family and the dedication and elasticity of its workforce, Ercol has proved extraordinarily resilient. Having weathered the turbulent 1990s, it has reinvented itself in a more efficient and flexible form since the Millennium and currently produces about £13 million worth of furniture annually. 'Our aim is to export more and to spread our sales over more countries than at present,' explains Edward Tadros. 'In the past Ercol has always met the challenges it has faced. That's why the company has survived when so many other British companies have disappeared.'[10]

Ercol has undergone a remarkable resurgence in terms of public profile over the last decade, largely due the exposure it has received through the Ercol Originals range. Because the company is still family-run and because the Windsor Range has enjoyed such remarkable longevity, the notion of tradition has a genuine resonance at Ercol.

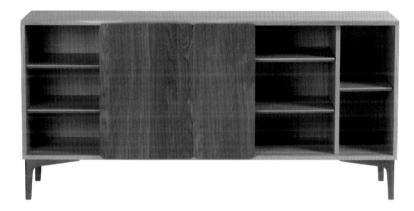

Top right
Svelto Coffee Table designed by Lisa Sandall, 2013

Left
Svelto Sideboard, designed by Ruth Wassermann, 2013

Bottom
Svelto Sofa, designed by Ian Archer, 2013

In recent years the company has evolved, of necessity, into a rather different commercial and manufacturing entity than it was during the Old Man's day, but it still retains its founder's vision at its core.

The Ercolani family's involvement in Ercol looks set to continue for many years to come. Edward's sister, Vicky Tadros (b.1959), who originally studied ceramics at West Surrey College of Art and Design at Farnham, has worked for Ercol for the last 19 years. After running her own knitwear company and then working as export manager at Sue Stowell Wallpapers and Fabrics, Vicky moved to Milan, where she handled imports of British wallpapers and textiles for a company called English Home Design. Following a stint at Colefax and Fowler, she joined Ercol in 1994, where she is responsible for selecting upholstery fabrics, arranging showroom displays and overseeing catalogues, brochures and other graphics.

Edward's son, Henry Tadros (b.1987), has also recently joined the company as a graduate trainee after studying at the School of Oriental and African Studies in London. Following in his father's footsteps, his induction has involved spending time working in each section of the company, before focusing on sales. Lucian Ercolani would be proud of the fact that his great grandson has opted to perpetuate the family dynasty. He would also be quietly gratified that the Windsor Range – his single greatest achievement – is enjoying a new lease of life.

Top left
Vicky Tadros, 2012

Top right
Henry Tadros, 2012

Opposite
Multicoloured pieces from the Ercol Originals Range, 2012: (clockwise from top left) 392 Stacking Chairs, 450 Love Seat, 1665 Bar Stool, 401 Butterfly Chair and 354 Nest of Tables

Bottom right
Seven wood colour finishes currently available, 2013

Appendix 1

Ercol Factory Today – Furniture in the Making

Part 1 – Assembling a Quaker Dining Chair

The 1875 Quaker Dining Chair is one of Ercol's classic Windsor chair designs. Created by Lucian R. Ercolani in 1957, it has remained in continuous production right up to the present day with only slight modifications. This sequence of photographs records the key stages in assembling the chair using a set of machined parts. The original 365 Quaker Chair had a beech frame and an elm seat, but this version is made in ash. The leading hand in chair assembly at Ercol is Nick Hanham. The furniture maker featured below is journeyman Steve Rolfe.

1.

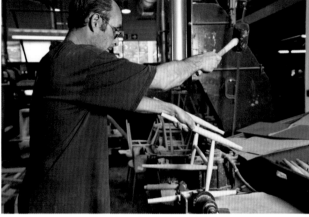

2.

3.

4.

5.

6.

1. Inserting glue in holes drilled in the legs for the stretcher.

2. Having assembled the underframe (known as the spider), the legs are clamped and the joints are knocked in with a mallet.

3. The legs of the inverted underframe are pushed into holes drilled through the seat. The legs are knocked in with a hammer to push them through the holes.

4. A small wedge is tapped into a slot in the top end of the leg projecting through the seat, thereby securing the joint.

5. The tops of the protruding legs are removed using a pad sander.

6. The rim of the seat is smoothed with a bobbin sander.

7.

8.

9.

10.

11.

12.

7. The base is clamped and glue is inserted in holes drilled in the seat for the bow and spindles.

8. The spindles are positioned in the holes.

9. The bow is carefully manoeuvred into position over the spindles and slotted onto the seat, using glue to fix the joints.

10. The chair is then inverted and placed in another clamp.

11. Pressure is applied from below to push the ends of the bow through the holes in the seat. The tension of the spindles is carefully adjusted in the process.

12. Wedges are inserted in slots in the projecting ends of the bow in order to secure the joints. The protruding sections are then sawn by hand and sanded smooth.

13. (overleaf) Journeyman Steve Rolfe with the assembled chair.

1.

2.

3.

4.

1. View of factory floor showing machinery and sawdust extraction equipment.

2. Timber store.

3. Master craftsman Steve Dover in the jig shop, where prototypes are made and jigs are produced.

4. CNC machine cutting chair seats.

5. Detail of CNC machine adzing the 'shaped out' forms of chair seats.

5.

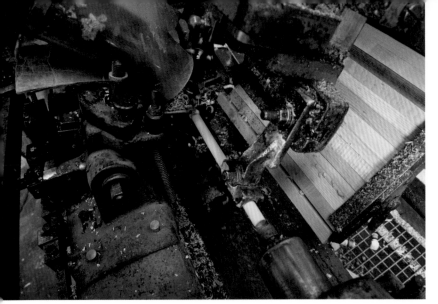

6.

7.

8.

9.

6. Automatic lathe, which turns squares of timber into spindles.

7. Leading hand Robert Taylor and Thomas Zielinski bending a stave in a jig after the timber has been softened in a steam retort.

8. To create a double bow, the beech square is pulled forwards, then downwards, a highly skilled operation.

9. After the metal braces have been clamped in position, the unit will be baked in a drying oven to cure the wood.

10. Bending several pieces of wood together using a press, operated by hydraulic rams to either side of the jig. The wheel operates a clamp to keep the timber centralised in the jig.

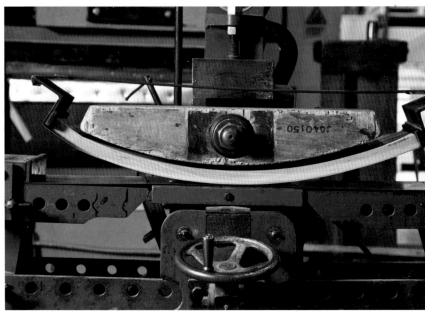

10.

11.

12.

13.

14.

11. Thomas Zielinski placing machined timber in a radio-frequency press, used to shape components with shallow bends by using heat to dry the wood from the inside.

12. A hydraulic press used to bend multiple Windsor chair bows. The sides of the bending press are pushed up by hydraulic rams, which press steamed beech squares into shape against the central former.

13. Trevor Tims sanding the bow of an Evergreen Easy Chair.

14. The stave is pressed against a revolving drum sander; the bow is spun round so that the whole surface is smoothed.

15. Table ends shaped on a CNC machine, stacked up in front of bobbin sanders in the machine shop.

15.

16.

17.

18.

19.

16. Shaping ash table ends on a CNC machine.

17. Stack of chair seats and partly assembled chairs.

18. Stacks of drawers in cabinet assembly area.

19. Bill Rayner adjusting a drawer stop while assembling a Windsor cabinet.

20. Fitting an oval handle over an ovoid recess on a drawer, a distinctive Ercol feature.

20.

21.

22.

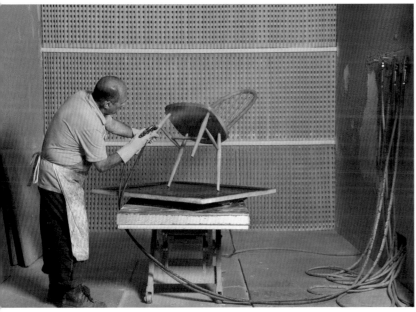

23.

24.

21. Fitting an elm door on a Windsor sideboard.

22. Keith Wilson polishing a Mantua Table to bring out the pattern in the grain after applying a coloured stain.

23. Eddie Hedley spraying water-based semi-matt lacquer on a Quaker Chair.

24. Completed Swan Chairs on mobile trays.

25. Roy Tew attaching rubber webbing to the frame of a 355 Studio Couch.

25.

26.

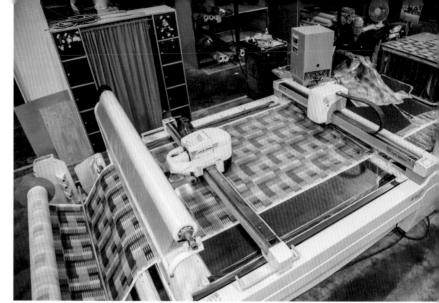

27.

28.

29.

26. The interwoven webbing is anchored in the frame, the tension being carefully adjusted in the process.

27. Peter Stuart removing a piece of cloth cut by a computer-controlled Lectra fabric cutting machine.

28. Linda Shrimpton making cushion cases in the upholstery department.

29. Jeremy Brown inserting foam cushions in cushion cases.

30. Ercol's offices with showroom below.

31. (Opposite) Quaker Chair passing through a drying tunnel on a conveyor belt to dry the lacquer. The drying is achieved by a carefully controlled balance of heat and air flow as the chair moves through the tunnel at a controlled speed.

30.

Design Notebooks, 1954-56

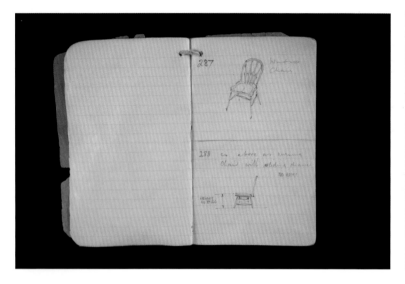

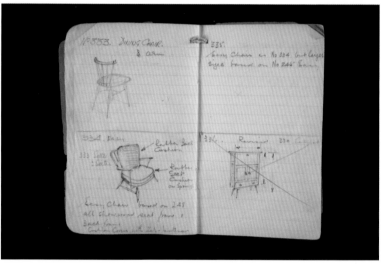

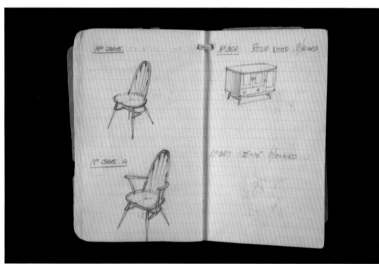

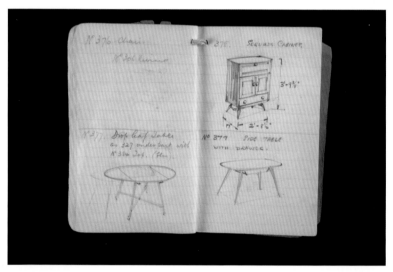

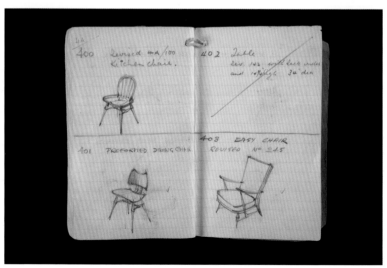

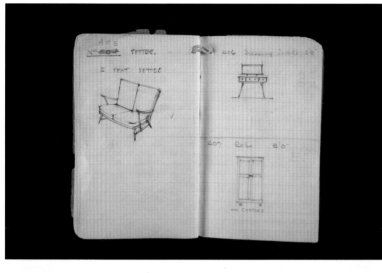

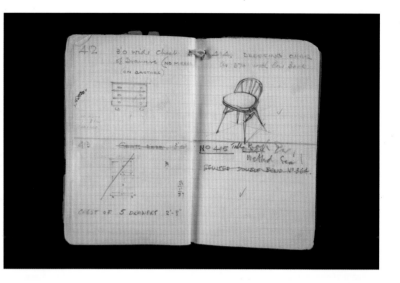

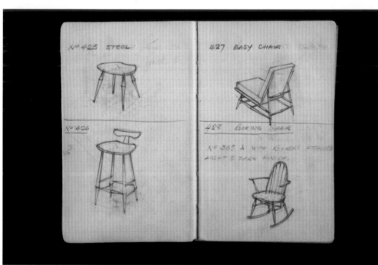

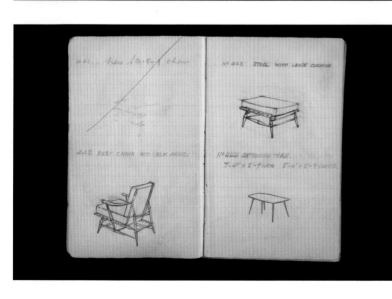

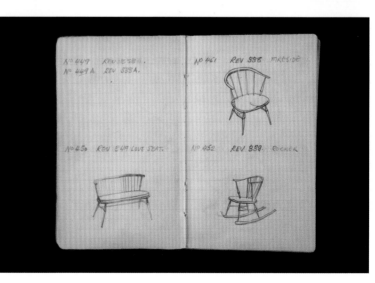

IDENTIFICATION SHEET SIDE 1 – EAS

USE THIS DRAWING IDENTIFICATION SHEET TOGETHER WITH THE WEBBING AND CUSHION

203 CHAIR HAS TEN BACK STICKS CURVED ARMS	27" 68.5	24½" 62 TEN BACK STICKS CURVED ARMS	
203	**252** WITH BACK SLAT **3S 2S**	**204** **3S 2S**	**870 PRINCESS** **3S 2S** **501** **3S** **609**

TENSION SPRING PLATFORM REVERSIBLE SEAT CUSHION

* 835 SEAT – 23½" 59.5
* 913 SEAT – 24½" 62
CURVED ARM

36" 91.5

40½" 103

CURV

176 — **835-913 EVERGREEN** — **914 SPRING TIME** **2S** — **478** BUTTONED BACK. — **478** PIPED BACK Not available

SOLID SEATS

SEAT CUSHION NOT REVERSIBLE

305 **307** WITH SLAT — **472** — **911 948** with swan slat. — **317** **318** WITH SLAT — **451** 451* 13½" – 34 — **567** **566** WITHOUT

WITH BACK FLAPS

CHAIR WITHOUT ARMS = 671
CHAIR WITHOUT ARM PADS = 672

CHAIR WITHOUT PADS = 675

685 — **684** **3S 2S** — **427** — **442** — **403** **2S** **399**

LADDER BACK

SPINDLE BACK SCROLL ARM

FLAT ARM

932 CLOISTER — **881 YORKMINSTER 3S2S** — **350** only complete cushions available **2S** — **445** — **615** **3S 2S**

UPHOLSTERED BA

CURVED ARM

952 SALISBURY 3S2S — **248** cushions not available — **294** cushions not available **2S** — **245** cushions not available — **244**

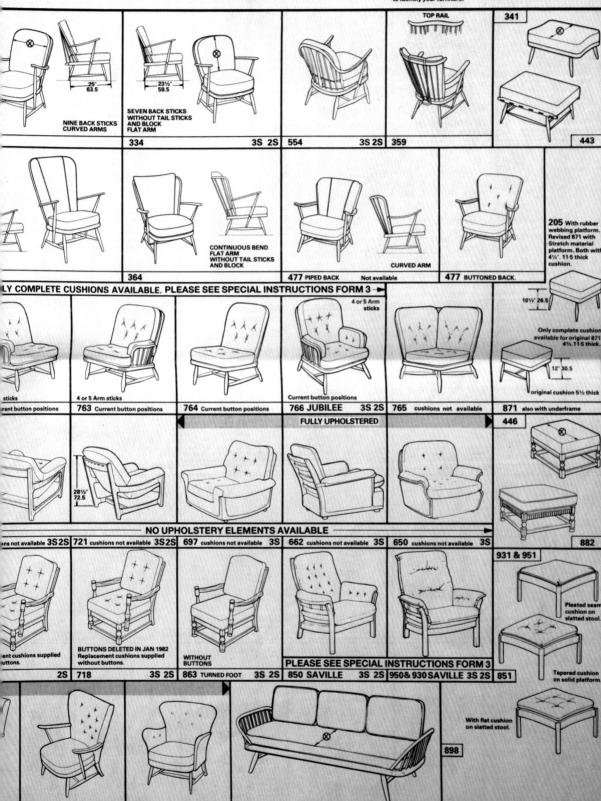

NINE BACK STICKS CURVED ARMS — 25" / 63.5 — **334**

SEVEN BACK STICKS WITHOUT TAIL STICKS AND BLOCK FLAT ARM — 23½" / 59.5 — **3S 2S**

554 3S 2S

359

TOP RAIL

341 / **443**

CONTINUOUS BEND FLAT ARM WITHOUT TAIL STICKS AND BLOCK — **364**

477 PIPED BACK   Not available

CURVED ARM — **477** BUTTONED BACK

205 With rubber webbing platform. Revised 871 with Stretch material platform. Both with 4½". 11·5 thick cushion.

ONLY COMPLETE CUSHIONS AVAILABLE. PLEASE SEE SPECIAL INSTRUCTIONS FORM 3 →

...ns sticks   Current button positions

4 or 5 Arm sticks   **763** Current button positions

764 Current button positions

4 or 5 Arm sticks   Current button positions   **766 JUBILEE** 3S 2S

765 cushions not available

10½" 26.5
Only complete cushion available for original 871 4½". 11·5 thick.
12" 30.5
original cushion 5½ thick

871 also with underframe

FULLY UPHOLSTERED

446

28½ / 72.5

NO UPHOLSTERY ELEMENTS AVAILABLE

...ons not available 3S 2S   **721** cushions not available 3S 2S   **697** cushions not available 3S   **662** cushions not available 3S   **650** cushions not available 3S   **882**

931 & 951
Pleated seam cushion on slatted stool.

...nt cushions supplied ...uttons. 2S

718 BUTTONS DELETED IN JAN 1982 Replacement cushions supplied without buttons. 3S 2S

863 TURNED FOOT 3S 2S   WITHOUT BUTTONS

850 SAVILLE 3S 2S   **PLEASE SEE SPECIAL INSTRUCTIONS FORM 3**

950 & 930 SAVILLE 3S 2S   **851**

Tapered cushion on solid platform.

With flat cushion on slatted stool.

898

2S **312** cushions not available 2S   **236** cushions not available   **355**

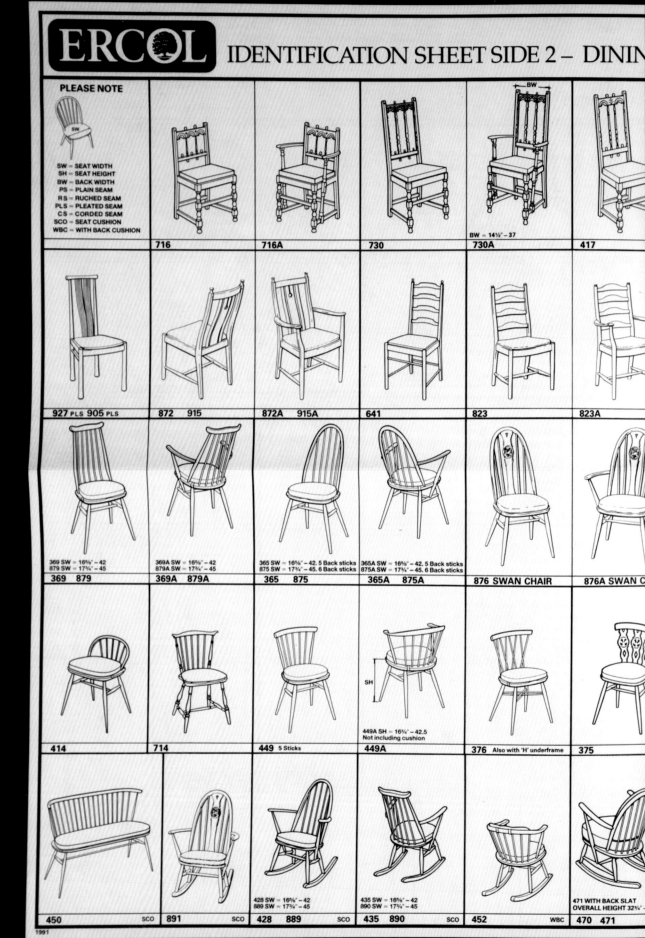

PLEASE NOTE

SW = SEAT WIDTH
SH = SEAT HEIGHT
BW = BACK WIDTH
PS = PLAIN SEAM
R S = RUCHED SEAM
PLS = PLEATED SEAM
CS = CORDED SEAM
SCO = SEAT CUSHION
WBC = WITH BACK CUSHION

716

716A

730

BW = 14½" – 37

730A

417

927 PLS 905 PLS

872 915

872A 915A

641

823

823A

369 SW = 16⅝" – 42
879 SW = 17¾" – 45

369

879

369A SW = 16⅝" – 42
879A SW = 17¾" – 45

369A 879A

365 SW = 16⅝" – 42. 5 Back sticks
875 SW = 17¾" – 45. 6 Back sticks

365 875

365A SW = 16⅝" – 42. 5 Back sticks
875A SW = 17¾" – 45. 6 Back sticks

365A 875A

876 SWAN CHAIR

876A SWAN C

414

714

449 5 Sticks

449A SH = 16¾" – 42.5
Not including cushion

449A

376 Also with 'H' underframe

375

450   SCO

891   SCO

428 SW = 16⅝" – 42
889 SW = 17¾" – 45

428 889   SCO

435 SW = 16⅝" – 42
890 SW = 17¾" – 45

435 890   SCO

452   WBC

471 WITH BACK SLAT
OVERALL HEIGHT 32¾"

470 471

1991

BW

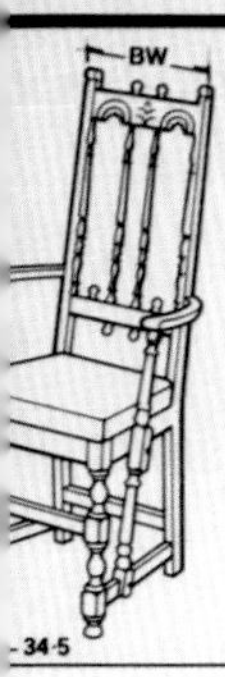

34·5

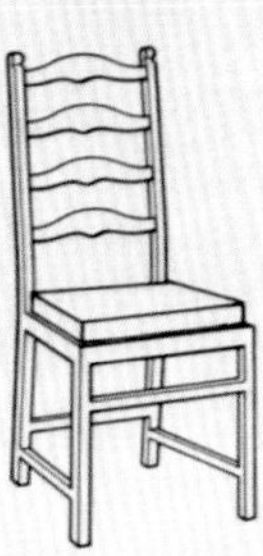

715

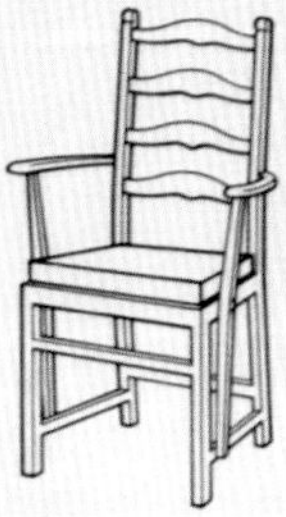

715A

416 PANELLED BACK

416A PANELLED BACK

706

CUSHIONS NOT AVAILABLE

OVERALL HEIGHT 391 Ht 2'7" – 79
OVERALL HEIGHT 608 Ht 3'0½" – 93

ticks

391 608

400

243 WITH BACK SLAT
Cushions supplied with straps.
Studs supplied.

139 243

243A Cushions supplied with straps. Studs supplied.

139A 243A

'H' UNDERFRAME AND BACK SLAT

514

6⅝" – 42
7¾" – 45

878

371A SW = 16⅝" – 42
878A SW = 17¾" – 45

371A 878A

370 SW = 16⅝" – 42
877 SW = 17¾" – 45

370 877

370A SW = 16⅝" – 42
877A SW = 17¾" – 45

370A 877A

873 Has 'H' underframe
909 – CRINOLINE UNDERFRAME

873 909

909A

496A

557

557A

559A

493A

BACK SLAT
HEIGHT 37" – 94

316

WBC

available WBC
473 – 'H' UNDERFRAME
912 – CRINOLINE UNDERFRAME

473 912 949 with swan slat

956 WHEATSHEAF CS

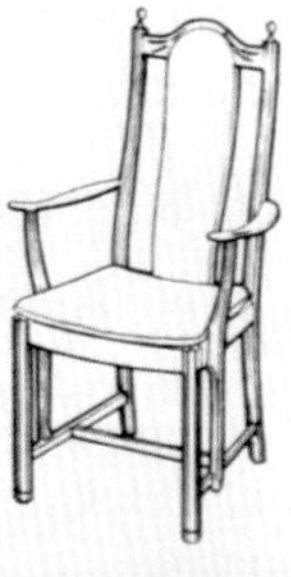

956A WHEATSHEAF CS

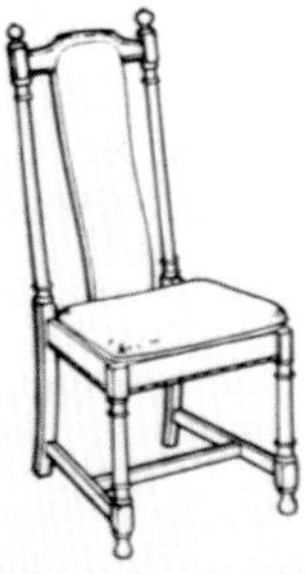

944 CS

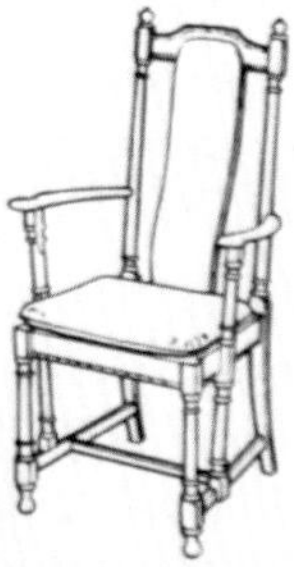

944A CS

Appendix 3

Ercol Labels and Marks

A selection of labels, marks and colour charts, intended as an aid for identification and dating.

1. CC41: Impressed Utility mark stamped on rear of seat. Denotes pieces such as the 4A Chair produced under the Government's Utility Furniture Scheme, c.1945-52. The CC41 logo originally referred to Civilian Clothing 1941, but was also adopted for Utility furniture in 1943.

2. B.O.T. PRICE-CONTROL-MARK: Board of Trade price control label printed on paper glued to underside of seat. Denotes maximum price that could be charged by retailers for tax-free Utility furniture, c.1945-52.

3. The RELIABILITY Mark / Please quote Design No / F.I.Ltd HW (Furniture Industries Limited, High Wycombe): Rectangular cream paper label glued to underside of seat, featuring Ercol recumbent lion logo, printed in black with orange border, c.1951-57. Enabled customers and retailers to identify design numbers of specific models. Predated change of name from Furniture Industries Limited to Ercol in 1958.

4. THIS IS AN ERCOL PRODUCTION: Small blue printed metallic paper label featuring Ercol recumbent lion logo, glued to the rear of seat on some post-war designs such as the 391 Chair, c.1954-7.

5. MADE IN ENGLAND: Small blue printed metallic paper label featuring Ercol recumbent lion logo, glued to the rear of seat, probably introduced c.1957. This was the most commonly used label on Windsor Range furniture from the late 1950s to the mid 1970s.

6. REG DESIGN No 884892: Ink-stamped design registration number for 392 Stacking Chair, registered May/June 1957.

7. REG DESIGN No 884923: Ink-stamped design registration number for 391 All Purpose Windsor Chair, registered May/June 1957. For other registered design numbers, see Appendix 4.

8. BS KH 1960 2056 / BS AF 1960 2056 / BS DD 1960 2056: Impressed British Standard Kite Mark stamped into the wood on the underside of seat, denoting designs that met quality standards established by the British Standards Institution.

9. APPROVED TO BRITISH STANDARD BS 3030: Impressed British Standard Kite Mark stamped into the wood on underside of seat, denoting designs that met quality standards introduced by the British Standards Institution.

10. ERCOL: Metal alloy key for wardrobes featuring embossed Ercolion, introduced c.1958.

11. Colour-coded painted recessed discs on rear of seatbacks on 461 to 465 Chairs, 1963. Denoting five different sizes of stacking chairs for schools: Green = 461 Chair (ht. 30½in). Blue = 462 Chair (ht.28½in). Red = 463 Chair (ht.25¾in). Yellow = 464 Chair (ht.23¼in). White = 465 Chair (ht.21in)

12. MADE IN HIGH WYCOMBE BUCKINGHAMSHIRE ENGLAND 472: Gold paper label printed in brown with Ercol recumbent lion logo and design number (eg. 472), introduced for a short period, c.1977-8.

13. MADE IN HIGH WYCOMBE BUCKINGHAMSHIRE ENGLAND 730 1979: Gold paper label printed in brown with Ercol recumbent lion logo, incorporating design number (eg. 730) and year of production, 1979-80.

14. MADE IN HIGH WYCOMBE BUCKINGHAMSHIRE ENGLAND: Gold paper label printed in brown with Ercol recumbent lion logo, no design number or date, 1981 – 1995.

15. Tree badge: Inset metal alloy disc with embossed oak tree logo, initially produced with silver finish, c.1996, later produced with gold finish.

16. ERCOL badge: Inset metal alloy disc with embossed capitalised ERCOL logo, introduced c.2002.

17. ercol badge: Inset metal alloy disc with embossed lower case ercol logo, introduced c.2006, currently in use, 2013.

18. MADE IN ENGLAND / MARGARET HOWELL / REISSUE: Brown stamped mark with Ercol recumbent lion logo, denoting reissued Ercol Originals designs produced for retailer Margaret Howell, c.2002 to present.

19. MADE IN ENGLAND / 2012 / PERKIN REVELLER: Brown stamped mark denoting Holland Park Chairs made for the London restaurant Perkin Reveller, including year of production, 2012.

1.
11.
2.
12.
3.
13.
4.
14.
5.
15.
6.
16.
7.
8.
9.
10.

Notes

- Most designs were originated by Lucian R. Ercolani and developed by Ercol Design Studio.
- Design numbers and names of designs are as recorded in company archives.
- Dates are first and last recorded production dates, based on price lists, catalogues, trade journals and advertisements.
- Dimensions are included when available, mainly in imperial, as recorded in Ercol catalogues.
- Descriptive notes focus on features that help to identify specific pieces. Unless otherwise indicated, the following general points apply:
    - Chairs with solid seats have a beech frame and an elm seat, usually with a loose pallet cushion. Pallet cushions were initially fixed to the frame by ties, but were later secured by straps and press-studs on the underside of the seat from c.1957.
    - Upholstered seating has a beech frame. Coil-sprung seat cushions were replaced by latex foam cushions from 1953. Seat cushions were supported by tension cable springs until 1955; Pirelli rubber webbing was introduced in 1956.
    - Tables have a beech frame with an elm top.
    - Cabinet are made of solid elm, mounted on a beech underframe or castors. Flat-fronted doors and drawers with circular handles were the norm until 1960: convex profile doors and drawers with oval handles over ovoid recess were introduced in 1961.
    - All Windsor Range pieces were finished in natural wax. Windsor shapes incorporated into the Old Colonial Range were given a dark stained finish known as antique wax.
- Designs specific to the Old Colonial Range, including Windsor-related designs with decorative features, are not included in the following list.

4A Windsor Utility Kitchen Chair, 1945-53
Designed by Utility Furniture Panel, 1943, design amended by Lucian R. Ercolani, 1944-5
Bow seatback, 6 spindles, fiddle-shaped elm seat

100 Windsor Chair, 1954-57
Variant of 4A: bow seatback, 5 spindles, fiddle-shaped elm seat

114 Small Easy Chair, 1950
Square-framed beech seatback, 10 spindles, seat cushion on tension springs

120 Sideboard, 1946
Beech frame and carcase, 2 doors with 4 recessed panels and gate-style catch, 2 internal drawers w.48in

121 Table, 1946
Beech frame and top, straight-sided top with curved ends w.54in, dp.24in

139 Small Chair, 1949-56
Variant of 4A: bow seatback, 6 spindles, D-shaped elm seat

139A Armchair, 1949-56
Variant of 4A: bow seatback, 6 spindles, curved arms on diagonal supports, D-shaped elm seat

140 Fireside Chair, 1951-56
Bow seatback, 5 spindles, curved arms on diagonal supports, D-shaped elm seat
ht.28in, w.24in

141 Rocking Chair, 1951-55
Bow seatback, 5 spindles, curved arms on diagonal supports, rockers, D-shaped elm seat ht.28½in, w.24in

142 Occasional Table, 1951-70
Circular elm top
ht.17½in, d.29¼in

149 Sideboard, 1951-52
Variant of 120: beech legs, elm carcase, 2 doors with 2 recessed panels and gate-style catch, 2 drawers with circular handles w.48in

150 Trestle Table, 1951-52
Variant of 121; beech legs, straight-sided elm top with curved ends
w.54in, dp.27in

151 Plate Rack / Bookshelves, 1951-54
Beech frame, open back, 3 shelves
w.41½in

169 Easy Chair, 1950-52
Upholstered square seatback, curved arms on diagonal supports, seat cushion on tension springs
ht.34in, w.29in, dp.35in

176 Tub Easy Chair, 1951-52
Bow seatback, 7 spindles, curved arms on diagonal supports, seat cushion on tension springs
ht.31½in, w.26in

177 Side Table, 1951-52
Extension to 150 Table: 3 legs, rectangular elm top
ht.29in, w.27in, dp.19½in

189 Wing Easy Chair, 1951-52
Upholstered wing seatback and rolled arms, seat cushion on tension springs
ht.34in, w.31in

190 Wing Easy Chair, 1951-52
Upholstered square seatback and rolled arms, seat cushion on tension springs

191 Wing Easy Chair, 1951-52
Upholstered wing seatback with buttoned arms, seat cushion on tension springs
ht.34in, w.29in

192 Wing Easy Chair, 1951-52
Upholstered square seatback with buttoned arms, seat cushion on tension springs

**203 Windsor Bergere Easy Chair
and Settee, 1953-83**
Bow seatback with forked struts, 8 spindles on
203 Chair, curved arms on diagonal supports,
seat cushion on tension springs (1953-55) or
rubber webbing (1956 onwards)
ht.30½in, dp.35in, w. of 203 chair 27½in, w. of
2-seater settee 52in, w. of 3-seater settee 69¾in
Later variants: 204, 1983-1992; 205, 1986
onwards; 206 Easy Chair reissued 2012

213 Small Coffee Table, 1952-74
Rounded rectangular elm top
ht.17in, w.27in, dp.16½in

219 Fireside Chair, 1952
Variant of 169: upholstered square seatback,
curved arms on diagonal supports, seat cushion
on tension springs
ht.32in, w.25½in, dp.26in

228 Dropleaf Table, 1953-55
Rounded rectangular dropleaf elm top
ht.29in, w.54in, dp.29in

236 Upholstered Arm Easy Chair, 1953-59
Wing seatback with buttoned upholstery, curved
front legs, seat cushion on tension springs or
rubber webbing
ht.32in, w.28½in, dp.29in

245 Open Arm Easy Chair, 1953-57
Variant of 169: upholstered square seatback,
curved arms on diagonal supports, seat cushion
on tension springs
ht.34in, dp.34in, w.27in

248 Windsor Easy Chair, 1953-70
Variant of 219: upholstered square seatback,
curved arms on diagonal supports, seat cushion
on tension springs or rubber webbing
ht.31½in, w.26in, dp.26in

249 Windsor Tub Chair, 1953-54
Variant of 176: bow seatback, 7 spindles, curved
front legs, seat cushion on tension springs
ht.31in, w.25½in, dp.26in

261 Sideboard, 1953-54
Variant of 149: agba carcase, elm top, curved
beech legs, 2 cupboards with 4 wavy recessed
panels and gate-style catch, 2 drawers above
ht.21in, w.48in, dp.18in

262 Sideboard, 1953
Agba carcase, elm top, beech underframe with
antique wax finish, 2 cupboards with 2 recessed
panels, 2 drawers above, circular handles
ht.35in, w.51in, dp.19½in

263 Fixed Top Dining Table, 1953-56
Rounded rectangular elm top, beech underframe
with rafter construction
ht.29in, l.54in, w.28in

265 Extension Dining Table, 1953-67
Extension to 228, 263, 382 and 383 Tables: 3
legs, curved rectangular elm top
ht.29in, l.18in, w.27in

266 Occasional Table, 1953-54
Variant of 142: circular elm top, curved legs
ht.17in, d.30in

267 Occasional Table, 1953-54
Rounded rectangular elm top, curved beech legs
ht.17in, l.27in, w.16½in

268 Hanging Plate Rack, 1953-c.1994
Shaped ends, 2 grooved shelves
ht.19½in, w.38in

280 Contemporary Windsor Chair, 1954
Curved horizontal seatback, 4 pairs of
crisscrossing spindles, H-shaped stretcher, fiddle-
shaped elm seat

285 Sideboard, 1954
Variant of 262: agba carcase, elm top, curved
beech legs, 2 cupboards with 2 recessed
panels and bar handles, 2 drawers above
with circular handles
ht.35in, w.51in, dp.19½in

287 Windsor Chair, 1954
Bow seatback, 4 diamond-shaped splats, f
iddle-shaped elm seat

288 Nursing Chair, 1954
Bow seatback, 4 diamond-shaped splats,
optional drawer under fiddle-shaped elm seat

289 Nursing Rocking Chair, 1954
Bow seatback, 4 diamond-shaped splats,
optional drawer under fiddle-shaped
elm seat, rockers

295 Wing Easy Chair and Settee, 1955-57
Variant of 245: upholstered wing seatback,
curved arms on diagonal supports, seat cushion
on tension springs
ht.34½in, dp.34in, w. of chair 27¼in, w. of
settee 51½in

304 Dropleaf Dining Table, 1955-56
Oval dropleaf elm top
ht.28in, w.45in, w.40½in

305 Tub Chair, 1955-c.1985
Variant of 249: bow seatback, 7 spindles, curved
arms on diagonal supports, D-shaped elm seat,
optional back cushion
ht.31½in, w.27½in, dp.26in

306 Windsor Dining Chair, 1955-70
Variant of 280: curved horizontal seatback,
4 pairs of crisscrossing spindles, double cross-
stick stretcher, fiddle-shaped elm seat
ht.31½in, w.16½in, dp.19in

308 Folding Occasional Table, 1955-72
Circular dropleaf elm top, sliding leg
ht.16in, d.24in

**312 Wing Easy Chair, 1955-57, and Settee,
1957**
Variant of 236: tall wing seatback with buttoned
upholstery, curved arms on diagonal supports,
seat cushion on tension springs
ht.36½in, w. of chair 29½in, dp. of chair 32½in,
w. of settee 54in, dp. of settee 33in

315 Grandfather Rocking Chair, 1955-c.1995
Tall bow seatback with forked struts, 10 spindles,
rockers, oyster-shaped elm seat, optional back
cushion
ht.37½in, w.29½in, dp.31in

317 Grandfather Tub Chair, 1955-c.1995
Tall bow seatback with forked struts, 10 spindles,
oyster-shaped elm seat, optional back cushion
ht.37½in, w.29½in, dp.29in

317 Grandfather Settee, 1956
Tall bow seatback with 2 pairs of forked struts,
20 spindles, double shaped-out elm seat,
optional back cushions
ht.37½in, w.55in, dp.29in

320 Sideboard, 1955
Variant of 261: agba carcase, elm top, beech
underframe, 2 cupboards with 2 recessed panels
and gate-style catch, 2 drawers above with
circular handles
ht.33in, w.48in, dp.18in

324 Nursing Chair, 1955-56
Variant of 288: bow seatback, 6 spindles,
optional drawer under D-shaped elm seat

325 Nursing Rocking Chair, 1955-56
Variant of 288: bow seatback, 6 spindles,
optional drawer under D-shaped elm seat,
rockers

328 Sideboard, 1955-56
Beech underframe, elm carcase, 2 tall central doors, 2 small side doors, both with 2 drawers above, circular handles
ht.34½in, w.51½in, dp.19½in

330 Serving Cabinet, 1955-56
Beech underframe, elm carcase, panelled door on left, 4 drawers on right, drop-flap cupboard above, circular handles
ht.46in, w.38½in, dp.18in

333 Small Chair, 1956-70
Curved horizontal seatback, 5 spindles, oyster-shaped elm seat
ht.30¼in, w.16, dp.19in

333A Armchair, 1956-70
Curved horizontal seatback with upturned arms, 7 spindles, oyster-shaped elm seat
ht.30in, w.21in, dp.20in

334 Easy Chair and Settee, 1956-85
Low bow seatback, 7 spindles on chair, 16 spindles on settee, curved arms on diagonal supports, seat cushions on rubber webbing
ht.30in, dp.28¾in, w. of chair 27¼in, w. of 2-seater settee 51½in, w. of 3-seater settee 67¾in

335 Easy Chair, 1956-82
High bow seatback, 7 spindles, curved arms on diagonal supports, seat cushions on rubber webbing
ht.34½in, w.27¼in, dp.31¼in

338 Fireside Chair, 1956-59
Variant of 333A: curved horizontal seatback with upturned arms, 7 spindles, oyster-shaped elm seat, seat and back cushions
ht.30in, w.21½in, dp.21¾in

339 Rocking Chair, 1956-59
Variant of 333A: curved horizontal seatback with upturned arms, 7 spindles, rockers, oyster-shaped elm seat, seat and back cushions
ht.30in, w.21½in

341 Stool, 1956-c.1985
Complements 203 and 501 Easy Chairs: straight-sided frame with convex ends, seat cushion on rubber webbing
ht.13½in, w.20in, dp.27½in
Later variants: 205 Extension Stool, c.1987-95; 1205 Stool, currently in production, 2013 (ht.41cm, w.54cm, dp.54cm)

349 Love Seat, 1956-59
Curved horizontal seatback, 13 spindles, double shaped-out elm seat
ht.30in, w.49in, dp.31in
Later variant: 450 Love Seat, 1960 (19 spindles)

351 Sideboard, 1956-c.1964
Agba carcase, elm top, beech underframe, 3 panelled doors with 2 drawers above, one long, one short, circular handles
ht.33, w.48½in, dp.18in

352 Small Plate Rack, 1956
Shaped sides, open back, single shelf
w.25in

354 Nest of Tables, 1957-94
Oyster-shaped elm tops in 3 graduated sizes
max ht.16in, max w.25 5/8in, max dp.17¾in, med w.19¼in, med dp.13¾in, min w.13½in, min dp.9½in
Original design reissued, 2010, currently in production, 2013 (ht.40cm, w.67cm, dp.51cm)

355 Studio Couch, 1956-c.1985
Bow arms with 11 spindles, elm seatback, foam mattress on rubber webbing, optional back cushions
ht.32in, w.81¼in, dp.29½in
Original design reissued, 2010, currently in production, 2013 (ht.79cm, w.200cm, dp.88cm)

356 Bed, 1956-57
Beech frame, detachable elm head board, foam mattress on rubber webbing
l.77in, w.36in

357 Bed, 1956-59
Beech frame, bow bed end at top with 15 spindles, foam mattress on rubber webbing
l.81in, w.36in

358 Bed, 1956-70
Beech frame, bow bed ends at top and bottom with 15 spindles, foam mattress on rubber webbing
l.84in, w.36in

359 Easy Chair, 1957-70
Curved horizontal seatback with forked struts, 2 uprights, 7 spindles, curved arms on diagonal supports, seat cushion on rubber webbing, back cushion strapped to frame
ht.33½in, w.27¾in, dp.21½in

360 Desk Bureau, 1957
Sits on 379 Side Table or 368 Storage Cabinet: elm carcase, sloping hinged drop-flap door with drawer above, circular handles
ht.14¼in, w.25in, dp.16¾in

361 Trolley Bookcase, 1957-72
4 tapered beech poles supporting 3 elm shelves, mounted on castors
ht.29½in, w.36in, dp.12½in

362 Bookcase, 1957
4 tapered beech poles supporting 5 elm shelves, beech underframe
ht.49¾in, w.36in, dp.12¼in

363 Room Divider, 1957-70
4 tapered beech poles supporting 4 elm shelves above 2-door cupboard, beech underframe
ht.75¾in, w.36in, dp.15¾in

364 Double Bow Easy Chair, 1957-62
Tall double bow seatback, 9 spindles, curved arms on diagonal supports, seat cushion on rubber webbing, back cushion strapped to frame
ht.34in, 28½in, dp.23½in
Later variants with partly upholstered arms: 913 Evergreen High Back Easy Chair, 1988 (ht.39in, w.30½in, dp.34½in); 1913 Evergreen Chair, currently in production, 2013 (ht.108cm, w.77cm, dp.89cm)

365 Quaker Dining Chair and 365A Armchair, 1957-c.1986
Tall arched bow seatback, 5 spindles, oyster-shaped elm seat
ht.37½in, dp.21¾in, w. of chair 16½in, w. of armchair 24in
Two later variants with 6 spindles: 875 and 875A, 1987 (seat w.17¾in); 1875 and 1875A currently in production in ash, 2013 (ht.100cm, dp.60cm, w. of 1875 49cm, w. of 1875A 65cm)

366 Sideboard, 1957
Beech underframe, elm carcase, tall cupboard on right, smaller 2-door cupboard on left with drawer below, circular handles
ht.32in, w.45in, dp.20in

367 Sideboard, 1957
Beech underframe, elm carcase, 2-door cupboards with drawer below, circular handles
ht.32in, w.34in, dp.20in

368 Storage Unit / Sideboard, 1957-58
Beech underframe, elm carcase, 2-door cupboard, circular handles (1957), oval handles (1958)
ht.29in, w.34in, dp.20in

369 Goldsmith's Dining Chair and 369A Armchair, 1957-c.1986
Tall shaped horizontal seatback, 2 uprights, 5 spindles, oyster-shaped elm seat
Seat w.16 5/8in
Later variants: 879 and 879A, 1987 (seat w.17¾in)

370 Windsor Dining Chair and 370A Armchair, 1957-c.1986
Variant of 139 and 139A: bow seatback, 6 spindles, oyster-shaped elm seat
ht.32in, dp.21¾in, w. of chair 16½in, w. of armchair 24in
Later variants: 877 and 877A, 1987 (seat w.17¾in); 1877 and 1877A, currently in production in ash, 2013 (ht.89cm, dp.53cm, w. of 1877 49cm, w. of 1877A 65cm)

372 Windsor Fireside Chair, 1957
Variant of 140: bow seatback, 6 spindles, curved arms on diagonal supports, oyster-shaped elm seat

373 Windsor Rocking Chair, 1957
Variant of 141: bow seatback, 6 spindles, rockers, curved arms on diagonal supports, oyster-shaped elm seat

376 Windsor Dining Chair, 1957-82
Variant of 306: curved horizontal seatback, 4 pairs of crisscrossing spindles, double cross-stick stretcher, oyster-shaped elm seat
ht.31in, w.18in, dp.18½in
Later variant: 811/08113 Chiltern Chair for John Lewis, 2010 (oak or lacquered ash and beech, ht.78cm, w.47cm, dp.45cm)

378 Serving Cabinet, 1957-58
Variant of 330: beech underframe, elm carcase, 2-door cupboard with drop-flap serving cupboard above and drawer below, circular handles
ht.45¾in, w.32½in, dp.20in

379 Side Table, 1957
Rounded rectangular elm top with drawer below
ht.28½in, w.42in, dp.18¾in

381 Panelled Dresser, 1957
Elm, solid panelled back, 2 shelves
ht.19in, w.32in

382 Dining Table, 1957-78
Variant of 263: beech underframe with rafter construction, rounded rectangular elm top
ht.28in, w.60in, dp.30in
Original design reissued, currently in production, 2013 (ht.72cm, w.152cm, dp.76cm); another variant in oak or lacquered beech and ash:

811/08010 Chiltern Table for John Lewis, 2010 (ht.75cm, w.151cm, dp.75cm)

383 Dropleaf Dining Table, 1957-72
Variant of 263: rounded rectangular elm top with 2 dropleaves supported by metal rods
ht.28in, max w.54in, max dp.29½in

384 Dining Table, 1957-c.1994
Variant of 304: oval elm top with 2 dropleaves supported by metal rods
ht.28in, max w.49in, max dp.44 ½in

386 Panelled Dresser, 1957-70
Elm, solid panelled back, 2 shelves
ht.19in, w.42in

388 Nursing Chair, 1957
Also known as 4A/100/388: bow seatback, 5 spindles, fiddle-shaped elm seat with optional drawer below, various finishes, including cream or green enamel

389 Nursing Rocking Chair, 1957
Also known as 4A/100/389: bow seatback, 5 spindles, rockers, fiddle-shaped elm seat with optional drawer below, various finishes, including cream or green enamel

391 All Purpose Windsor Chair, 1957-85
Registered design no. 884,923; also known as Chiltern Chair: curved horizontal seatback, 2 uprights, 3 spindles rising from underframe, shaped elm seat
ht.31, w.15in, dp.17½in
Later variant with 4 spindles: 608 Chair, 1970-c.1983 (ht.30½in)

392 Stacking Chair, 1957-70
Registered design no. 884,892: curved horizontal seatback, 2 diagonal uprights rising from underframe, shaped elm seat, red, green, blue or orange stained finish (1968)
ht.30in, w.15½in, dp.17¼in
Original design reissued, 2002, currently in production, 2013 (ht.77cm, w.45cm, dp.50cm)

393 All Purpose Table, 1957-70
Registered design no. 885,238: rectangular elm top, spindle rack below
ht.28¾in, w.39in, dp.27in

394 Bogey Wheels, c.1957-58
Beech frame on castors for wheeling stacks of 392 Chairs

395 All Purpose Table, 1957-70
Square elm top, spindle rack below
ht.28¾in, w.27in, dp.27in

396 All Purpose Table, 1957-70
Registered design no. 885,969: oval elm top, spindle rack below
ht.28¾in, w.39in, dp.33in

398 Occasional Coffee Table, 1958-61
Rectangular elm top, spindle rack below
ht.14½in, w.41¾in, dp.15in

399 Armless Easy Chair, 1958
Variant of 248 Chair; square seatback, seat and back cushions on rubber webbing
ht.31¼in, w.20¼in, dp.28¼in

400 Chair, 1958-c.1985
Variant of 4A Chair, also known as 4A/400 Chair: bow seatback, 4 spindles, oyster-shaped elm seat, various finishes including enamel and coloured stains
ht.33¾in, w.15½in, dp.14in

401 Preformed Chair, 1958-63
Registered design no. 888,150: beech frame, steam-bent beech spine, elm-veneered moulded plywood seat and seatback Original design reissued as 401 Butterfly Chair, 2002, currently in production, 2013 (ht.75cm, w.48cm, dp.45cm)

403 Easy Chair and Settee, 1958-67
Variant of 245; registered design no. 881,621: upholstered square seatback, curved arms on diagonal supports, seat cushions on rubber webbing
ht.34in, dp.33½in, w. of chair 27in, w. of settee 51in

406 Dressing Table, 1958-59
Beech frame, elm carcase, central drawer flanked by two small vanity drawers with built-in sliding glass shelf, oval handles, rectangular mirror on turned beech uprights
ht.48½in, w.45in, dp.21in

407 Wardrobe, 1958-62
Elm carcase on castors, 2 flat doors, oval handles, beech hanging rails
ht.72in, w.36in, dp.22in

408 Dressing Chest with Mirror, 1958-62
Elm carcase on castors, 3 flat drawers, oval handles, rectangular mirror on turned beech uprights
ht.54½in, w.36in, dp.21¾in

409 Centre Cheval Unit, 1958-62
Low-slung elm carcase on castors, flat drawer, oval handles, tall rectangular mirror on turned beech uprights
ht.59¾in, w.26in, dp.20in

410 Side Cheval Unit, 1958-59
Elm carcase on castors, 3 flat drawers, oval handles, tall rectangular mirror on turned beech uprights
ht.57¾in, w.19in, dp.20½in

411 Side Cheval Unit, 1958-59
Elm carcase on castors, 2 flat doors, oval handles, tall rectangular mirror on turned beech uprights
ht.57¾in, w.19in, dp.20½in

412 Chest of Drawers, 1958-62
Elm carcase on castors, 3 flat drawers, oval handles
ht.26in, w.36in, dp.19½in

414 Dressing Chair, 1958-70
Low bow seatback, 5 spindles, oyster-shaped elm seat

415 Tall Back Easy Chair, 1958-62
Tall double bow seatback with forked struts, curved arms on diagonal supports, seat cushions on rubber webbing, back cushion attached to frame
ht.40½in, w.28¾in, dp.32in

423 Head Board, 1958-67
Accompanies 357 and 358 Beds: ovoid elm board, beech uprights
Full ht.30½in, ht. of board 18¼in, w.39in

424 Head Board, 1958-67
Accompanies 357 and 358 Beds: ovoid elm board, beech uprights
Full ht.30¼in, ht. of board 19in, w.57in

425 Fireside Stool, 1959-61
Beech legs, saddle-shaped elm seat
ht.16in, w.13½in

426 High Bar Stool, 1959
Probably not manufactured commercially; variant without seatback used as draughtsman's stool: beech frame, shaped out elm seat, steam-bent beech spine, solid elm or elm-veneered plywood seatback Recent variant without seatback: 1665 Bar Stool, 2012 (ht.69cm, w.39cm, dp.37cm)

427 Easy Chair, 1959-70
Designed by Lucian Brett Ercolani; registered design nos. 891,887 and 891,888: frame made from turned tapered beech poles, projecting diagonal back legs, seat cushions on rubber webbing
ht.31in, w.20in, dp.30in

428 Quaker Rocking Chair, 1959-c.1986
Variant of 365A: tall arched bow seatback, 5 spindles, rockers, oyster-shaped elm seat
ht.32½in, w.24in, seat w.16½in
Later variant: 889 Rocking Chair, 1987
(seat w.17in)

429 Sideboard, 1958-62
Elm carcase on castors, 2 flat doors with 2 drawers below, oval handles
ht.30in, w.51in, dp.19½in

430 Serving Cabinet, 1958-62
Elm carcase on castors, 2 flat doors with drawer below and drop-flap cupboard above, oval handles
ht.43in, w.32in, dp.19in

431 Wardrobe, 1959-62
Elm carcase on castors, 2 flat doors, oval handles, beech hanging rails, optional interior 4-drawer fitment
ht.72in, w.48in, dp.21¾in

435 Goldsmith's Rocking Chair, 1959-c.1986
Variant of 369A: tall shaped horizontal seatback, 2 uprights, 5 spindles, rockers, oyster-shaped elm seat
ht.33½in, overall w.24in, seat w.16 5/8in
Later variant: 890 Rocking Chair, 1987
(seat w.17¾in)

436 Supper Table, 1959
Variant of 142: circular elm top
ht.17½in, d.34½in

437 Hall / Side / Dressing Table, 1959-62
Triangular section legs, rectangular elm top
ht.29in, w.27in, dp.19in

438 Mirror, 1959-67
Circular mirror on wooden stand
ht.16in, w.12in

439 Drawer Fitment for Writing Table, 1959-67
Sits on 437 and 479 Tables; registered design no. 905,095: elm carcase, 2 side drawers, oval handles
ht.8in, w.27in

440 Small Stacking Chair, 1959-63
Smaller variant of 392: two-tier curved horizontal seatback, 2 diagonal uprights, shaped elm seat

442 Easy Armchair, 1960-67
Variant of 427; designed by Lucian Brett Ercolani; registered design no. 895,821: frame made from

turned tapered beech poles, projecting diagonal back legs, upward-curved elm armrests, seat cushions on rubber webbing
ht.32in, w.27½in, dp.36in

443 Stool, 1960-67
Designed by Lucian Brett Ercolani; accompanies 442 Chair: rectangular beech frame, seat cushion on rubber webbing
ht.15in, w.21¼in, dp.26½in

444 Slide Leg Extending Table, 1960-65
Rounded rectangular elm top extending by telescopic action of under-rails, 2 extra leaves supported by sliding leg stored underneath
max w.88in, max dp.33in

449 Bow Top Chair, 1960-79, and 449A Armchair, 1960-82
Variant of 333 and 333A: curved horizontal seatback, 2 uprights and 5 spindles on chair, 2 uprights and 7 spindles on armchair, oyster-shaped elm seat
(449) ht.31in, w.16½in, dp.19in; (449A) ht.30in, w.21in, dp.19½in

450 Love Seat, 1960
Variant of 349: curved horizontal seatback, 19 spindles, double shaped-out elm seat
ht.31in, w.45in
Original design reissued, currently in production, 2013 (ht.78cm, w.117cm, dp.53cm)

451 Fireside Chair, 1960-79
Variant of 338: curved horizontal seatback with upturned arms, 7 spindles, oyster-shaped elm seat, seat and back cushions
ht.27in, w.21in

452 Rocking Chair, 1960-82
Variant of 339: curved horizontal seatback with upturned arms, 9 spindles, rockers, oyster-shaped elm seat, seat and back cushions
ht.26½in, w.21in

454 Supper Table, 1960-79
Oval elm top, spindle rack below
ht.17½in, w.39in, dp.32½in

455 Sideboard, 1961-94
Registered design no. 905,091; elm carcase on castors, 2 doors flanking 3 drawers, convex profile, oval handles
ht.27in, w.61¼in, dp.19in (1961), dp.18in (June 1962 onwards)
Later variant: 2073, currently in production, 2013 (ht.69cm, w.156cm, dp.46cm)

456 Dropleaf Occasional Table, 1961-70
Long rectangular elm top with 2 dropleaves supported by sliding legs, optional seat cushions stored on spindle rack below
ht.14in, max w.63in, dp.18in

457 Tray Table, 1961-70
Rounded rectangular elm tray top with handle grips, rimmed elm shelf below
ht.17½in, w.28½in, dp.17½in

458 Three Tier Trolley, 1961-c.1994
Beech uprights, 3 lipped elm shelves, mounted on castors
ht.30¼in, w.28in, dp.18in

459 Occasional Coffee Table, 1961-c.1994
Rounded rectangular elm top, spindle rack below
ht.14 ¼ in, w.41¼in, dp.18in
Later variant different legs: 1459, currently in production, 2013 (ht.36cm, w.104cm, dp.50cm)

461 Stacking Chair, 1963-70
Variant of 392: two tier curved horizontal seatback with green colour-coded disc, 2 diagonal uprights, shaped elm seat
ht.30½in, w.15½in, dp.15¼in

462 Stacking Chair, 1963-70
Variant of 392: two tier curved horizontal seatback with blue colour-coded disc, 2 diagonal uprights, shaped elm seat
ht.28½in, w.15½in, dp.15¼in

463 Stacking Chair, 1963-70
Variant of 392: two tier curved horizontal seatback with red colour-coded disc, 2 diagonal uprights, shaped elm seat
ht.25¾in, w.14¾in, dp.13¼in

464 Stacking Chair, 1963-70
Variant of 392: two tier curved horizontal seatback with yellow colour-coded disc, 2 diagonal uprights, shaped elm seat
ht.23¼in, w.13in, dp.12in

465 Stacking Chair, 1963-70
Variant of 392: two tier curved horizontal seatback with white colour-coded disc, 2 diagonal uprights, shaped elm seat
ht.21in, w.12in, dp.10½in

467 Sideboard, 1962-70
Registered design no. 905,092: beech underframe, elm carcase, tall door on right, smaller 2-door cupboard on left with single drawer below, convex profile, oval handles
ht.32in, w.45in, dp.18in

468 Sideboard, 1962-85
Registered design no. 905,098: elm carcase on castors, 3 doors above 2 drawers, convex profile, oval handles
ht.30in, w.51in, dp.18in

469 Serving Cabinet, 1962-94
Registered design no. 905,094: elm carcase on castors, 2 doors in centre, single drawer below, drop-flap cupboard above, convex profile, oval handles
ht.43in, w.32½in, dp.18in

470 Tub Rocking Chair, c.1966-85
Variant of 305: bow seatback, 7 spindles, curved arms on diagonal supports, D-shaped elm seat, seat cushion, optional back cushion
ht.33½in, w.27½in, dp.30¾in

472 Chairmaker's Chair, 1962-c.1987
Registered design no. 905,009: double bow seatback, central splat, 8 spindles, upward-turned armrests extending from central bow supported by 3 spindles, H-shaped stretcher, oyster-shaped elm seat
ht.40½in, w.23¾in
Later variant with hooped underframe: 911 Chairmaker's Chair, 1988, currently in production, 2013 (ht.111cm, w.60cm, dp.63cm)

473 Chairmaker's Rocking Chair, 1962-c.1987
Registered design no. 905,008: double bow seatback, central splat, 8 spindles, upward-turned armrests extending from central bow supported by 3 spindles, H-shaped stretcher, rockers, oyster-shaped elm seat
ht.40½in, w.23¾in
Later variant with hooped underframe: 912 Chairmaker's Rocking Chair, 1988, currently in production, 2013 (ht.107cm, w.60cm, dp.76cm)

477 Double Bow Low Back Easy Chair, 1962-c.1985
Registered design no. 905,006: low double bow seatback, 9 spindles, upward-curved arms on diagonal supports, seat cushion on rubber webbing, curved back cushion strapped to frame
ht.33in, w.28½in, dp.32½in

478 Double Bow Tall Back Easy Chair, 1962-c.1985
Registered design no. 905,007: high double bow seatback, 9 spindles, upward-curved arms on diagonal supports, seat cushion on rubber webbing, curved back cushion strapped to frame
ht.40½in, w.28½in, dp.32½in

479 Hall or Side Table, 1962-67
Registered design no. 905,099: triangular section legs, rectangular elm top with single drawer, oval handles
ht.29in, w.27in, dp.18in

480 Hanging Wardrobe, 1962-67
Elm carcase on castors, 2 doors, convex profile, oval handles
ht.72in, w.36in, dp.22in

481 Wardrobe, 1962-67
Elm carcase on castors, 2 doors, convex profile, oval handles
ht.72in, w.48in, dp.22in

482 Dressing Table, 1962-67
Beech underframe, elm carcase, central drawer flanked by 2 smaller drawers, convex profile, oval handles, rectangular horizontal mirror on beech uprights
ht.48½in, w. 45in, dp.19½in

483 Dressing Chest with Mirror, 1962-67
Elm carcase on castors, 3 drawers, convex profile, oval handles, rectangular mirror on beech uprights
ht.54½in, w.36in, dp.18in

484 Dressing Chest, 1962-67
Elm carcase on castors, 3 drawers, convex profile, oval handles
ht.26in, w.36in, dp.18in

485 Cheval Dressing Table, 1962-67
Elm carcase on castors, single drawer, convex profile, oval handles, tall rectangular mirror on beech uprights
ht.59½in, w.26in, dp.9½in

492 Dropleaf Dining Table, 1964-70
Rounded rectangular dropleaf elm top
ht.28in, max w.49in, max dp.44½in

493 Dining Armchair, 1964-67
Curved seatback with 2 scalloped ladderback slats, upward-curved arms on diagonal supports, oyster-shaped elm seat
ht.29in, w.24in

495 Nest of Tables, 1964-70
5 nesting rectilinear elm tables in graduated sizes, recessed handles
max ht.15¾in, w.20in, dp.12in

499 Windsor Settee, 1964-67
Double bow seatback with 3 pairs of forked struts, 3 splats, 23 spindles, upturned armrests extending from central bow, hooped underframe, kidney-shaped elm seat, seat cushion
ht.34 ½in, w.65½in, dp.32in

501/3 Double Bow Bergere Settee, 1965-70
Double bow seatback, upturned armrests extending from central bow, H-shaped underframe, seat cushion on rubber webbing, back cushions
ht.33½in, w.78in, dp.42in

501E Double Bow Bergere Easy Chair, 1966-70
Double bow seatback, upturned arms extending from central bow, H-shaped underframe, kidney-shaped seat frame, seat cushion on rubber webbing, back cushions
ht.33½in, w.27, dp.36¾in

505 Trolley Table, 1966-72
Beech uprights, dropleaf oval elm top, 2 lipped elm shelves below, mounted on castors
ht.30in, max w.37¾in, max dp.28¾in

507 Sideboard, 1966-70
Elm carcase on castors, 3 doors with 2 drawers above, convex profile, oval handles
ht.32in, w.53¾in, dp.19in

508 Wine Cabinet, 1966-70
Sits on 507 Sideboard: detachable elm cupboard unit with 2 pairs of double doors, convex profile, oval handles

509 Wall Shelves, 1966-72
Shaped sides, 2 shelves
ht.20½ in, w.17in, dp.8½in

510 Slide Leg Expanding Table, 1966-83
Variant of 444: design registration no. 895,789; patent no.891,021: rounded rectangular elm top extending by telescopic action of under-rails, 2 extra leaves supported by sliding leg stored underneath,
ht.28in, max w.88in, max dp.36in

512 Sideboard, 1967-70
Registered design no. 929,521: sculptured beech underframe with legs joined at foot, elm carcase, 3 doors above 2 drawers, convex profile, oval handles
ht.44½in, w.51in, dp.17¼in

513 Dining Table, 1967-70
Sculptured beech underframe with legs joined at foot, rounded rectangular elm top
ht.28¼in, w.78in, dp.31½in

514 Windsor Bow Armchair, 1967-70
Registered design no. 929,522: double bow seatback with upturned armrests, central splat, 10 spindles, oyster-shaped elm seat

515 Segment Shape Occasional Table, 1967-70
Four 515 Tables encircle 516 Table to create Sixsome Supper Table; registered design no. 929,517: sculptured beech underframe with legs joined at foot, curved segment-shaped elm top
ht.19½in, w.36½in, dp.14in

516 Quadrilateral Centre Unit Table, 1967-70
Four 515 Tables encircle 516 Table to create Sixsome Supper Table; registered design no. 929,518: sculptured beech underframe with legs joined at foot, rounded square elm top
ht.19 ½in, w.21in, dp.21in

517 Circular Revolving Tray, 1967-70
Complements Sixsome Supper Table; registered design no. 929,519: circular elm lipped tray
d.21in

518 Bureau, 1967-70
Sculptured beech underframe with legs joined at foot, elm carcase with sloping drop-flap front
ht.40½in, w.32in, dp.17¾in

519 Drawleaf Table, 1967-70
Registered design no. 929,521: sculptured beech underframe with legs joined at foot, rectangular drawleaf elm top
ht.29¼in, max w.84 in, dp.33in

520 Circular Occasional Table, 1967-70
Registered design no. 929,523: sculptured beech underframe with legs joined at foot, circular elm top
ht.19½in, d.33in

530 Small Sideboard, 1968-70
Beech trestle underframe, elm carcase, 2 drawers
ht.31½in, w.44½in, dp.18in

531 Sideboard, 1968-70
Beech trestle underframe, elm carcase, 2 narrow central drawers flanked by 2 wider deeper drawers, convex profile, oval handles
ht.31½in, w.53in, dp.18in

550 Bookcase, 1968-70
Beech trestle underframe, elm carcase, 3 shelves
ht.51in, w.30in, dp.11¾in

554 Easy Chair, 554/2 2-Seater Settee and 554/3 3-Seater Settees, 1968-70
Bow seatback with upturned armrests, central splat and 8 spindles on 554 Chair, 2 splats and 16 spindles on 554/2 Settee, seat cushions on rubber webbing, back cushions supported by frame
dp.30in, w. of chair 25¾in, w. of 2-seater settee 50in, w. of 3-seater settee 66in

555 Circular Dropleaf Table, 1968-70
Beech trestle underframe, circular dropleaf elm top
ht.28in, d.44¾in

556 Refectory Table, 1968-70
Beech trestle underframe, rounded rectangular elm top
ht.28in, w.54in, dp.29½in

557 Tall Ladderback Chair and 557A Armchair, 1968-70
Tall ladderback seatback with 5 slats, oyster-shaped elm seat, available in red, green, orange or blue stained finish

559 Low Ladderback Chair and 559A Armchair, 1968-70
Low ladderback seatback with 4 slats, oyster-shaped elm seat, available in red, green, orange or blue stained finish

560 All Purpose and Catering Table, c.1968-70
Contract table, circular elm top
ht.26in, d.24in

561 All Purpose and Catering Table, 1968-70
Contract table, circular elm top, spindle rack below
ht.26in, d.24in

562 All Purpose and Catering Table, 1968-70
Contract table, square elm top
ht.26in, w.24in, dp.24in

563 All Purpose and Catering Table, 1968-70
Contract table, rectangular elm top
ht.28in, w.42in, dp.24in

564 All Purpose and Catering Table, 1968-70
Contract table, rectangular elm top
ht.28in, w.48in, dp.24in

566 Easy Chair, 1968
Contract chair, square seatback, 5 spindles,
cushions on rubber webbing
ht.32½in, w.24¾in, dp.28in

567 Easy Armchair, 1968-70
Contract armchair, square seatback, 5 spindles,
curved arms, cushions on rubber webbing
ht.32½in, w.24¾in, dp.28in

572 Writing Desk, 1969-70
Elm carcase on castors, 3 drawers on
each side, 2 drawers at top
ht.29in, 46½in, dp.22¼in

579 Gateleg Table, 1969-72
Beech trestle underframe, oval dropleaf elm top
ht.28in, max w.42in, dp.33in

594 Trestle Dining Table, 1969-70
Beech trestle underframe, 3 legs at
either end, rounded rectangular elm top

595 Long Sideboard, 1969-70
Beech trestle underframe, elm carcase, 3
drawers in centre, 2-door cupboards on either
side, convex profile, oval handles
ht.29in, w.86in, dp.18in

608 Kitchen Chair, 1970-83
Variant of 391; also known as Chiltern
High Back Chair (1983): curved horizontal
seatback, 6 spindles rising from
underframe, shaped elm seat
ht.30½in

Below
349 Love Seat, 1956

NOTES

Chapter 1

1 For an autobiographical account,
see Lucian R. Ercolani,
A Furniture Maker: His Life, His Work and His Observations,
Ernest Benn, 1975.

2 A sister, Mary, was born just before the family emigrated. She appears in a family photograph, c.1924, but died some time later.

3 Ercolani, 1975, p.31.

4 Ercolani, 1975, p.35.

5 *The Cabinet Maker*, 12 October 1907, pp.47-49.

6 Because the Salvation Army would not permit Ercolani to keep the cabinet, it remained in their ownership. Many years later Ercolani tracked it down, although it was in poor condition by the time he retrieved it.

7 Ercolani, 1975, p.43.

8 Ercolani, 1975, p.41.

9 Ercolani, 1975, p.68.

10 Paul Ferris, unpublished manuscript about Lucian R. Ercolani, commissioned by Lucian Brett Ercolani and Barry Ercolani, 1968, p.54.

11 Transcript of interview with Lucian R. Ercolani by Paul Ferris, 25 April 1968 (LRE 24, R2).

12 Ercolani, 1975, p.72.

13 Interview with Lucian R. Ercolani, 29 June 1968 (LRE 59, 14).

Chapter 2

1 Ercolani, 1975, p.79.

2 Ferris, 1968, p.54.

3 Quoted in interview with Lucian R. Ercolani, 29 June 1968 (LRE 60, 21).

4 Ercolani, 1975, p.80.

5 This abbreviation was apparently suggested so as not to upset his fellow directors by over-personalising the name. Interview with Lucian R. Ercolani, 30 June 1968 (LRE 62, 39).

6 Ercolani, 1975, p.90.

7 *Furniture for To-Day*, Ercol catalogue, c.1928.

8 Ercolani, 1975, p.93.

9 Interview with Lucian R. Ercolani, 7 May 1968 (LRE 28, 8).

10 Ercolani, 1975, pp.101-102.

11 Ercolani, 1975, p.102.

12 Quoted by Ferris, 1968, p.56.

13 'Built to an ideal', *Furnishing Trades Organiser*, November 1936.

14 'Obituary, Mr.John Wright', *The Cabinet Maker*, 13 February 1954, p.710.

15 Interview with Lucian R. Ercolani, 30 June 1968 (LRE 63, 43).

16 Patent no.24564 is cited in a *Furniture of Today* catalogue, c.1933. Patent no.322174 appears in a catalogue, c.1937.

17 Ercolani, 1975, p.95.

18 Minutes of Board Meeting, 1930.

19 Quoted by Ferris, 1968, p.64.

20 Minutes of Board Meeting, August 1932 (edited).

21 Interview with Lucian R. Ercolani, 23 May 1968 (LRE 47, 19).

22 'Built to an ideal', *Furnishing Trades Organiser*, November 1936 (edited).

23 See Chapter 6.

24 Ercolani, 1975, p.124.

25 *Oak down the Ages*, Walter Skull & Son (1932) Ltd. catalogue, 1932, p.1.

26 Ibid.

27 Ibid., p.4.

28 Ercol's upholstery department continued to be based at the old Skull's factory until 1993 when the building was sold. The staff in this section of the company still to refer to themselves as 'Skull's', even though they have been based at the main works for the last 20 years.

29 Interview with Lucian R. Ercolani, 25 April 1968 (LRE 24, R4).

30 Ferris, 1968, p.97.

Chapter 3

1 'Their dream homes started in the nursery', *Daily Herald*, 8 November 1962.

2 Quoted by Ferris, 1968, p.68.

3 Interview with Lucian R. Ercolani, 25 April 1968 (LRE 24-25, R6-R7).

4 Interview with Lucian R. Ercolani, 16 May 1968 (LRE 40, 65).

5 Interview with Lucian R. Ercolani, 30 June 1968 (LRE 62, 34).

6 Interview with Lucian R. Ercolani, 30 April 1968 (LRE 26, 37).

7 Interview with Lucian R. Ercolani, 29 June 1968 (LRE 61,27).

8 See archive film, *The Chiltern Bodgers* (1935) on Ercol website: www.ercol.com.

9 Interview with Lucian R. Ercolani, 30 June 1968 (LRE 65, 56).

10 Ercolani, 1975, p.169.

11 Interview with Lucian R. Ercolani, 15 May 1968 (LRE 36, 26).

12 Quoted in 'A family of craftsmen', *House Beautiful*, March 1965.

13 'Chapels, children and chairs', *Design for Living*, Ercol catalogue, 1992, p.7.

14 Interview with Lucian R. Ercolani, 15 May 1968 (LRE 36, 25).

15 'The Ercolion unfolds his Windsor tale', Ercol catalogue, 1967.

16 Ercolani, 1975, p.140.

17 Quoted in 'A family of craftsmen', *House Beautiful*, March 1965.

18 Interview with Lucian R. Ercolani, 15 May 1968 (LRE 34, 17).

19 'The Ercolion unfolds his Windsor tale', Ercol catalogue, 1967.

20 'He works with solid wood,' *The Scotsman*, 30 January 1960.

21 'The other elm story', *Forestry and Home Grown Timber*, June-July 1973.

22 Ibid.

23 Quoted by Ferris, 1968, p.120.

24 'He works with solid wood,' *The Scotsman*, 30 January 1960.

25 'Profile of Lucian Ercolani', *The Observer*, 25 January 1959.

26 'The other elm story', *Forestry and Home Grown Timber*, June-July 1973.

27 *Design '46*, Council of Industrial Design, 1946, pp.96, 98.

28 Interview with Lucian R. Ercolani, 24 April 1968 (LRE 23, 38).

29 Quoted by Ferris, 1968, p.121.

30 Interview with Lucian R. Ercolani, 30 April 1968 (LRE 26, 35).

31 Ercolani, 1975, p.154.

32 'He works with solid wood,' *The Scotsman*, 30 January 1960.

Chapter 4

1 *Ercol: The Mark of Good Furniture*, catalogue, June 1951.

2 Ercolani, 1975, p.158.

3 Ercolani, 1975, p.159.

4 'Modern furniture manufacture', *New Homes*, July 1955.

5 'A family of craftsmen', *House Beautiful*, March 1965.

6 Ercol archive material in Wycombe Museum (HIWLH: 1995.79.8.2).

7 'He works with solid wood,' *The Scotsman*, 30 January 1960.

8 'The Ercolion puts safety theories into practice', *Industrial Safety*, October 1961.

9 Ibid

10 Quoted by Ferris, 1968, p.68.

11 Ibid.

12 Ercolani, 1975, p.162.

13 'Their dream homes started in the nursery', *Daily Herald*, 8 November 1962.

14 Interviews with Robin Day, 1999-2000. Lesley Jackson, *Robin and Lucienne Day: Pioneers of Contemporary Design*, Mitchell Beazley, 2001, pp.9-10. It was not until 2001 that Day eventually collaborated with Ercol on an oak chair, produced as part of the Onetree project. See Garry Olson and Peter Toaig, *Onetree*, Merrell, 2001, pp.60-1.

15 Ercolani, 1975, pp.163-4.

16 'New version of the Windsor tradition', *The Cabinet Maker*, 15 August 1958, p.450.

17 Interview with Edward Tadros, 28 March 2012.

18 'Profile of Lucian Ercolani', *The Observer*, 25 January 1959.

19 'Designing comes naturally to Englishman', *Bedding Upholstery and Furniture*, December 1959.

20 'Modern furniture manufacture', *New Homes*, July 1955.

21 Email from Edward Tadros, 1 June 2012.

22 Interview with Mike Pengelly, 4 April 2013.

23 'Modern furniture manufacture', *New Homes*, July 1955.

24 Ercolani, 1975, p.154.

25 Ercolani, 1975, p.160

26 Quoted by Paul Ferris, 1968, p.92.

27 Ercolani, 1975, p.168.

28 Ercolani, 1975, pp.165-6.

29 *Ercol Windsor Contemporary Furniture*, catalogue, May 1957, p.2.

30 Interview with Lucian R. Ercolani, 16 May 1968 (LRE 38, 57).

31 Ercolani, 1975, p.166.

32 *Ercol Windsor Contemporary Furniture*, catalogue, May 1957, p.2.

33 *Art and Industry*, April 1956, p.132.

34 Ercolani, 1975, p.161.

35 Ercolani, 1975, p.167.

36 Ercolani, 1975, p.169.

37 'Profile of Lucian Ercolani', *The Observer*, 25 January 1959.

38 Ercolani, 1975, p.170.

39 Quoted by Ferris, 1968, p.137.

40 *House & Garden*, Summer 1948, p.53.

41 *The Cabinet Maker*, 21 January 1950, p.182 (advertisement).

42 *The Cabinet Maker*, 15 April 1950, p.180 (advertisement).

43 Quoted by Ferris, 1968, p.132.

44 *The Cabinet Maker*, 5 August 1950, p.471.

45 *The Cabinet Maker*, 15 July 1950, p.188.

46 'Invitation from the Ercolion', *The Cabinet Maker*, 10 February 1951, p.493 (advertisement); *The Cabinet Maker*, 10 February 1951, p.604.

47 'The Ercolion makes his Festival Offering', *The Cabinet Maker*, 7 April 1951, p.19 (advertisement).

48 'The Home of 1951', *The Cabinet Maker*, 21 April 1951, p.242.

49 'Festival at High Wycombe', *The Cabinet Maker*, 4 August 1951, pp.418-9.

50 Ercolani, 1975, p.165.

51 Ibid.

52 'Their dream homes started in the nursery', *Daily Herald*, 8 November 1962.

53 'The Ercolion takes the chair', *The Cabinet Maker*, 17 November 1951, p.585 (advertisement).

54 '"Ercol" Furniture Family Brochure', *The Cabinet Maker*, 15 December 1951, p.1009. For a detailed discussion of Old Colonial, see Chapter 6.

55 *Designers in Britain*, no.2, 1949, p.20.

56 'The wooden chair', *Punch*, 19 April 1950.

57 *Introducing the 1957 Range*, publicity leaflet, 1957.

58 'Strength balanced with simplicity', *The Cabinet Maker*, 9 August 1963, p.302.

59 *Windsor Chairs*, catalogue, 1953.

60 'Three chairs for the Ercolion's wedged through seat legs!', *The Cabinet Maker*, 4 July 1953, cover.

61 *Windsor Chairs and Small Easy Chairs and Easy Chairs*, publicity leaflet, 1954.

62 *The Cabinet Maker*, 9 February 1952, p.623.

63 *The Ercolion's Furniture Family Reference Sheet*, June 1953.

64 *Furnishing*, July 1952, p.65.

65 'These three houses could banish depression', *Furnishing*, May 1952, p.371 (139 Chair); 'Leading furnishers equip houses at Olympia', *Furnishing*, April 1953, p.363 (151 Coffee Table).

66 Dorothy Meade, 'Furnishing in the New Towns', *Design*, February 1957, pp.42-7. The house was furnished by a local store called Sheratons.

67 'Taking Contemporary furnishings to London's East End', *Furnishing*, August 1952, pp.94-5.

68 'Bristol sees Contemporary and likes it', *Furnishing*, July 1952, p.64.

69 'Harrods' modern furniture section remodelled for 1952', *Furnishing*, June 1952, p.435.

70 'Contemporary v. Traditional in the Midlands', *The Cabinet Maker*, 3 October 1953, p.54.

71 'Small homes give Jones a sales opportunity', *Furnishing*, March 1954, p.261.

72 Heal & Son publicity leaflets, Archive of Art and Design (AAD 1994/16).

73 'Ercolion has changed position in new display', *The Cabinet Maker*, 26 July 1952, p.342.

74 'This contract department is organised', *Furnishing*, October 1953, p.288.

75 'Warnham Court – Contemporary furniture in a period setting', *The Cabinet Maker*, 26 July 1952, p.317.

76 'Kidbrooke School', *The Cabinet Maker*, 14 August 1954, pp.545-8.

77 Reported in *The Cabinet Maker*, 9 August 1952, p.479.

78 Quoted in *For the Love of Wood*, Ercol publicity film, 1987.

Chapter 5

1 'New version of the Windsor tradition', *The Cabinet Maker*, 15 August 1958, p.450.

2 Ibid.

3 Interview with Lucian R. Ercolani, 29 June 1968 (LRE 58, 9).

4 *The Cabinet Maker*, 20 February 1954, p.913.

5 *The Ercolion Presents his Latest Improvements*, leaflet, 1954.

6 *The Cabinet Maker*, 15 August 1958, op. cit., p.450.

7 *The Ercolion Presents his Latest Improvements*, leaflet, 1954.

8 *The Ercolion Shows his Windsor Chairs and Small Easy Chairs*, leaflet, 1954.

9 *The Ercolion Presents a Pre-View Parade of his 1956 Exhibition Furniture*, press pack, February 1956.

10 'C.o.I.D. at the Brussels Exhibition', *The Cabinet Maker*, 14 February 1958, p.661.

11 'New productions: "Ercol" chairs and tables', *The Cabinet Maker*, 20 September 1957, p.867.

12 'Windsor stacking chairs', Ercol catalogue, 1967, p.32.

13 When the 401 Chair was reissued in 2002, it was renamed the Butterfly Chair, but it was generally known as the Preformed Chair when it was first produced. Although loosely related to Charles and Ray Eames's well-known DCW Moulded Plywood Chair (1946), the shape and curvature of the seat are very different on the Ercol design. The legs and spine are also completely different, both in materials and structurally.

14 Ercol catalogue, 1958.

15 For further information about these designs, see Chapter 6.

16 Interview with Lucian R. Ercolani, 30 April 1968 (LRE 26, 35).

17 Mary Schoeser, *Marianne Straub*, Design Council, 1984, pp.89-90.

18 Email from Sam Reich, 16 January 2013.

19 '"Adventure with colour" exhibition at Coventry store', *The Cabinet Maker*, 27 August 1955, p.680.

20 Alex Gardner-Medwin, 'Furniture survey: Upholstered occasional chairs', *Design*, May 1955, pp.26-7.

21 For seating designs such as the 203 Chair, which remained in production over several decades, webbing configurations provide evidence of the date of manufacture.

22 *And So To Bed*, leaflet, 1957.

23 'ABC of furniture show', *The Cabinet Maker*, January 1962, p.313.

24 'The Ercolion takes wing', Ercol catalogue, 1967, p.24.

25 *The Ercolion Proudly Presents his Ercol Furniture Family*, catalogue, August 1958, p.12.

26 Patent application number 35840/58. Design registration application number 891887/8.

27 'The Ercolion on the anatomy of comfort', *Design*, February 1960, p.76 (advertisement).

28 *The Cabinet Maker*, 20 September 1957, op.cit., p.867.

29 Interview with Lucian R. Ercolani, 30 June 1968 (LRE 62, 38).

30 'A "Play for Safety" exhibition', *The Cabinet Maker*, 21 February 1953, p.841.

31 For the evolution of Ercol's sideboards from 1946-56, see Denise Bonnett, *Contemporary Cabinet Design*, Batsford, 1956, p.184.

32 *The Cabinet Maker*, 19 February 1955, p.895.

33 ''Vantage server', *House & Garden*, 1963 (advertisement).

34 As elm became scarcer during the late 1970s following the arrival of Dutch elm disease in the UK, different timbers were used for the inside layers of the laminates used on cabinets, with thick elm veneers on the outside.

35 *Ercol Windsor Contemporary Furniture*, May 1957, p.2.

36 *The Cabinet Maker*, 26 January 1963, p.309.

37 *The Cabinet Maker*, 28 January 1966, p.250.

38 'The Ercolion unfolds his Windsor tale', Ercol catalogue, 1967, p.1.

39 'Profile of Lucian Ercolani', *The Observer*, 25 January 1959.

40 'Ercolion in the bedroom', *The Cabinet Maker*, 24 January 1958, p.431.

41 'The Ercolion woos the ladies', *House & Garden*, December 1953, p.15 (advertisement).

42 'More sitting room in the sitting room' (advertisement), *House & Garden*, December 1954, p.9.

43 Quoted by Ferris, 1968, pp.19 and 137.

44 'The chair that roared', *Furnishing*, August 1963.

45 *The Cabinet Maker*, 15 August 1958, op.cit., p.450.

46 These statistics were repeatedly cited in press coverage from the mid 1950s onwards, for example in *Art and Industry*, April 1956, p.132; 'He works with solid wood,' *The Scotsman*, 30 January 1960; and 'A family of craftsmen', *House Beautiful*, March 1965.

47 'The chair that roared', *Furnishing*, August 1963.

48 'The Ercolion puts safety theories into practice', *Industrial Safety*, October 1961.

49 'Designing comes naturally to Englishman', *Bedding Upholstery and Furniture*, December 1959.

50 'Modern furniture manufacture', *New Homes*, July 1955.

51 Ercol catalogue, 1966.

52 'Mr L.R. Ercolani, O.B.E.', *The Cabinet Maker*, 19 June 1964, p.729.

53 Quoted by Ferris, 1968, p.145.

54 Ferris, 1968, p.146.

55 *Design*, January 1959, p.32.

56 'A family of craftsmen', *House Beautiful*, March 1965.

57 Interview with Lucian R. Ercolani, 23 May 1968 (LRE 50, 30).

58 'Review of current design', *Design*, July 1959, p.28.

59 Dennis Cheetham, 'Cottage conversion for weekend living', *Design*, March 1961, pp.52-3.

60 'Choosing furniture that will last', *Modern Woman*, April 1962. For an illustration of Ercolani's Windsor chair, see Chapter 3.

61 'Guild Mark Awards', *The Cabinet Maker*, 6 April 1962, p.33.

62 *The Cabinet Maker*, 24 January 1964, p.281.

63 Interview with Lucian R. Ercolani, 23 May 1968 (LRE 50, 29-30).

64 Interview with Lucian R. Ercolani, 24 April 1968 (LRE 23, 38).

65 For further information on this subject and general background to British furniture during the post-war period, see Lesley Jackson, *Modern British Furniture: Design Since 1945*, V&A, 2013.

66 Interview with Lucian R. Ercolani, 30 April 1968 (LRE 25, 32).

67 Interview with Lucian R. Ercolani, 15 May 1968 (LRE 36, 30).

68 'The Queen shows her furniture knowledge', *The Cabinet Maker*, 13 April 1962, p.80.

69 'Profile of Lucian Ercolani', *The Observer*, 25 January 1959.

70 Although these works outings were eventually dropped due to cut backs, Ercol still organises family days for its staff, such as dragon boat racing at Bisham Abbey or It's a Knockout tournaments, where Ercol workers compete against staff from other companies as a fundraising exercise.

Chapter 6

1 *Furniture with a Human Story*, Furniture Industries Limited catalogue, 1937, p.1.

2 Ibid., pp.5-6.

3 Interview with Lucian R. Ercolani, 21 May 1968 (LRE 41, 39).

4 Ibid., p.6.

5 *Furniture with a Human Story*, 1937, op.cit., pp.10-2.

6 Ibid., p.14.

7 Ibid.

8 *The Ercolion presents his Furniture Family*, catalogue, November 1951.

9 Price list for Windsor and Old Colonial Ranges, Furniture Industries Limited, 4 June 1951.

10 *The Cabinet Maker*, 10 February 1951, p.604.

11 'Pre-compressed wood can easily be bent while cold,' *The Cabinet Maker*, 18 June 1965, p.590.

12 *Ercol Old Colonial Furniture*, May 1957, p.2.

13 Ercol catalogue, 1965, p.31.

14 'The chair that roared', *Furnishing*, August 1963.

15 Interview with Lucian R. Ercolani, 16 May 1968 (LRE 38).

16 Quoted in 'A family of craftsmen', *House Beautiful*, March 1965.

Chapter 7

1 'Their dream homes started in the nursery', *Daily Herald*, 8 November 1962.

2 Ibid.

3 'A family tradition', Ercol catalogue, 1986, pp.14-5.

4 Interview with Lucia Ercolani, 29 March 2012.

5 Ibid.

6 Tom Dean joined Ercol in 1949 and was always involved with the timber and manufacturing side of

the company. From 1986-94 he was joint managing director with Michael Evans. Following the latter's retirement, Dean continued as managing director of Ercol Furniture until 1997. After this he was managing director of Ercol Holdings (Ercol Furniture's parent company) until 2002.

7 Interview with Edward Tadros, 28 March 2012.

8 Quoted in 'Case Study - furniture design and the generation game', *Enterprise*, 1 October 2002.

9 Ercol catalogue, 1973.

10 Notes on photographs of ceremonial chairs made for Worshipful Company of Furniture Makers.

11 Ercol catalogue, 1974, p.3.

12 Ercol catalogue, 1988, p.6.

13 'Man's oldest friend', *Design for Living*, Ercol catalogue, 1992, p.30.

14 Quoted in 'Founder's philosophy is key to business success', *Bucks Free Press*, 25 May 1990, p.6.

15 'Chapels, children and chairs', *Design for Living*, Ercol catalogue, 1992, p.12.

16 'A bit of heartache, a bit of sweat', *Design for Living*, Ercol catalogue, 1992 (edited).

17 Ercol catalogue, 1970.

18 When the first prototypes were being developed, they were hidden on the loading bay so the Old Man would not see them. Information from Edward Tadros.

19 Barry made good friends in Japan and would go there quite regularly. David Ross and Christopher Driver, 'Barry Ercolani', *The Guardian*, 18 June 1992 (obituary).

20 'Ercol in Amsterdam Week', *The Cabinet Maker*, 28 May 1965, pp.444-5.

21 'Ercol in N. America: First consignment to three Canadian stores', *The Cabinet Maker*, 5 November 1965, p.311.

22 Ibid. The stores were Eaton's and Simpson's of Toronto and Depuis of Montreal.

23 Ercol catalogue, 1983.

24 Ercol catalogue, 1986, pp.14-5.

25 Ercol catalogue, 1988, p.13.

26 The 913 Evergreen Easy Chair was introduced in 1988. It is now model number 1913.

27 As Pengelly was leaving the room, he heard Ercolani Snr say to his son, 'Look after that boy', so it was no surprise when he was offered a job. Interview with Mike Pengelly, 4 April 2013.

28 With Golden Dawn and Traditional a stain was applied using a pad, worked deeply into the surface of the wood, then pulled back to reveal the grain. As with Natural, they were then wax polished using fine wire wool.

29 Until the mid 1990s air drying was carried out at Ercol's Latimer timber yard near Amersham, bought in 1975 when production was at its peak.

30 Chris Robinson, 'The family firm of Ercol', *Newcastle Life*, May 1975.

31 'Working with the grain', *Design for Living*, Ercol catalogue, 1992, pp.46-7.

Chapter 8

1 Ercol Holdings Ltd. was created in 1983 as the parent company of the various Ercol companies, including Ercol Furniture. The Ercolani family have control over Ercol Holdings through four family trusts. Edward Tadros is the principal trustee and also the chairman of the board of directors of Ercol. Dr Norman Schofield is a non-executive director. Edward's son, William Tadros, joined the board following the death of Lucian Brett Ercolani in 2010 in order to maintain family involvement.

2 Amanda Birch, 'Forestry commission', *Building Design*, 8 November 2002.

3 'Ercol splashes out', *Forestry & British Timber*, 3 December 2002

4 Quoted in *Building Design*, 8 November 2002, op. cit.

5 Interview with Edward Tadros, 28 March 2012.

6 Judy Warschauer, 'Ercol workers may go to four-day week', *This is Buckinghamshire*, 9 May 2003.

7 Interview with Edward Tadros, 28 March 2012, and email from Edward Tadros, 5 August 2013.

8 Nicholas Figiel, Alan Zolik and Chris Huddy

9 Interview with Ruth Wassermann, 1 Feburary 2012.

10 Interview with Edward Tadros, 28 March 2012.

BIBLIOGRAPHY

July Attfield, ed., *Utility Reassessed: The Role of Ethics in the Practice of Design*, Manchester University Press (Manchester, 1999)

Michael Barrington et al., *The Intelligent Layman's Book of British Furniture: 1600-2000*, Intelligent Layman's Publishers (London, 2005)

Stephen Bland, *Take a Seat: The History of Parker Knoll 1834-1994*, Baron Birch (Buckinghamshire, 1995)

Denise Bonnett, ed., *Contemporary Cabinet Design and Construction*, Batsford (London, 1956)

Steven Braggs and Basil Hyman, *The G Plan Revolution: A Celebration of British Popular Furniture of the 1950s and 1960s*, Booth-Clibborn Editions (London, 2007)

Christopher Breward and Ghislaine Wood, eds., *British Design from 1948: Innovation in the Modern Age*, V&A (London, 2012)

Council of Industrial Design, *Design 46*, HMSO (London, 1946)

Council of Industrial Design, *Design in the Festival*, HMSO (London, 1951)

Harriet Dover, *Home Front Furniture: British Utility Design 1941-1951*, Scolar Press (Aldershot, 1991)

Clive D. Edwards, *Twentieth-Century Furniture: Materials, Manufacture and Markets*, Manchester University Press (Manchester, 1994)

Lucian R. Ercolani, *A Furniture-Maker: His Life, His Work and His Observations*, Benn (Tonbridge, 1975)

The Fine Art Society / Rayner & Chamberlain, *Austerity to Affluence: British Art and Design 1945-1962*, Merrell Holberton (London, 1997)

Geffrye Museum, *CC41 Utility Furniture and Fashion, 1941-1951*, Inner London Education Authority (London, 1974)

S.H. Glenister, *Contemporary Design in Woodwork: Volume 1*, John Murray (London, 1955)

S.H. Glenister, *Contemporary Design in Woodwork: Volume 2*, John Murray (London, 1961)

John Gloag, *The Englishman's Chair: Origins, Design and Social History of Seat Furniture in England*, Allen & Unwin (London, 1964)

Michael Harding-Hill, *Windsor Chairs*, Antique Collectors' Club (Woodbridge, 1988)

Lesley Jackson, *The New Look: Design in the Fifties*, Thames & Hudson (London, 1991)

Lesley Jackson, *'Contemporary' Architecture and Interiors of the 1950s*, Phaidon (London 1994)

Lesley Jackson, *The Sixties: Decade of Design Revolution*, Phaidon (London,1998)

Lesley Jackson, *Robin and Lucienne Day: Pioneers of Contemporary Design*, Mitchell Beazley (London, 2001, revised edition, 2011)

Lesley Jackson, *Modern British Furniture: Design Since 1945*, V&A (London, 2013)

David Joel, *The Adventure of British Furniture, 1851-1951*, Ernest Benn (London, 1953)

David Joel, *Furniture Design Set Free: The British Furniture Revolution 1851 to the Present Day*, J.M. Dent & Sons (London, 1969)

Pat Kirkham, R. Mace and Julia Porter, *Furnishing the World: The East End Furniture Trade 1830-1980*, Journeyman (London, 1987)

Gordon Logie, *Furniture from Machines*, Allen and Unwin (London, 1947)

Leonard John Mayes, *The History of Chair-Making in High Wycombe*, Routledge and Kegan Paul, (London, 1960)

Judith Miller, ed., *Mid-Century Modern: Living With Mid-Century Modern Design*, Miller's (London, 2012)

Ella Moody, *Modern Furniture*, Studio Vista (London, 1966)

Garry Olson and Peter Toaig, *Onetree*, Merrell (London, 2001)

The Frederick Parker Foundation, *The Frederick Parker Collection: A Selection of Chairs*, London Metropolitan University (London, 2008)

Penny Sparke, *Furniture: Twentieth-Century Design*, Bell & Hyman (London, 1986)

The Worshipful Company of Furniture Makers, *A Celebration of Excellence 1958-1998*, The Worshipful Company of Furniture Makers (London, 1998)

Dennis and Barbara Young, *Furniture in Britain To-day*, Tiranti (London, 1964)

AUTHOR'S ACKNOWLEDGEMENTS

Having grown up sitting on the 392 Stacking Chairs purchased by my parents in the 1960s, I've had a soft spot for Ercol since my early days. Those chairs deserve a long service award as they're still going strong in my kitchen, supplemented by various siblings from the Windsor Contemporary Furniture Family.

When Richard Dennis invited me to write this book, he had no idea I was already a confirmed Ercoloholic. I am deeply indebted to him for giving me the opportunity to indulge my passion for Ercol and for being such a generous and enlightened patron. Richard has played a pivotal role in this project from start to finish, not just as the publisher, tirelessly beavering away behind the scenes, but as a researcher, drip-feeding me with information, and as an ambassador, offering encouragement and opening doors.

I am indebted to the whole team at Richard Dennis Publications, particularly Michelle Wyatt, who has calmly and efficiently transmitted information and images between all the relevant parties scattered around the country. The book has been greatly enhanced by the photographic skills of Magnus Dennis, whose images form the core of the illustrations. It has been a great pleasure to work with graphic designer Tim Moore, who has risen to the creative challenge of knitting together the text and images in such an ingenious way. His clear and attractive layouts have been carefully honed and he has gone out of his way to satisfy innumerable finicky requests. Thanks also to Sue Evans for proofreading the text, and to Sharon Pearce, Buchan Dennis and Tracie Welch for all their input in putting the book together and sending it out into the world.

Without the support of Ercol, this book would never have got off the ground. Edward Tadros welcomed us at the outset and has remained enthusiastically committed throughout the project. I am extremely grateful to him for making time in his busy schedule and for his attention to detail in checking my text and answering my many queries. Special thanks also to Vicky Tadros for all her help over the last couple of years, particularly for collating images and allowing her collection to be photographed. Visiting the Ercol factory, seeing the furniture being made and meeting the company's employees has been one of the highlights of my research. I would like to thank everyone at Ercol, especially Stella May, Nick Garratt, Ruth Wassermann, Chris Huddy and Larry Parkinson. Special thanks also to Lucia Ercolani and Mike Pengelly for their insights into their careers. I am grateful to Margaret Howell for kindly agreeing to write the foreword.

The book has drawn heavily on photographs from the High Wycombe Furniture Archive. Many thanks to Professor Jake Kaner at Bucks New University for facilitating access to this material. Chris and Liz Clarke at Ercol Collectors have also been extremely helpful in making their unparalleled collection of Ercol furniture available. Thanks are also due to Joseph Harvey at Torre Abbey.

I would like to acknowledge my debt to Paul Ferris for his pioneering research on Lucian R. Ercolani in 1968. Although the book commissioned by Lucian Brett Ercolani and Barry Ercolani to mark their father's 80th birthday was never published in the end, I am grateful to have been allowed access to the manuscript and transcripts of interviews.

Finally, special thanks to Ian Fishwick for sharing my interest in Ercol and helping with my research.

PHOTO CREDITS

The majority of images are from the Ercol company archive and Ercol contemporary furniture catalogues. New photography of the factory and selected furniture is by Magnus Dennis.

The following images have been kindly supplied by those listed below:-
Centre for Buckinghamshire Studies,
Records of E. Gomme Ltd: p11 above, p12 left
Chris Clarke at Ercol Collectors: p49 bottom left and top right, p53 top and centre left, p64 top left and right, p66 centre and bottom, p84 centre, p87, p90 top left, p95 third down and bottom, p97 centre left and bottom left, p101 top right and third down, p102 left, p108 bottom left, p127, p129 above, p134 top left
High Wycombe Furniture Archive at Buckinghamshire New University: p12 above, p18 above right, p33 above, p35 labove left, p38 above left and above right, p39 above and left, p40 centre right, p41 top left, bottom left, top right, p46 bottom left , p58 bottom, p82 bottom centre right, p83 bottom centre, p86 below, p90 top right, p92, p93 above, p95 second down, p97 centre right, p105 left, p106 bottom, p109 top left and bottom right, p113 top left, bottom left, p128 top left and right, p131 bottom right, p133 top left and bottom left, p136 top right and bottom right
Jill Kennington: p4
London Metropolitan University Library: p10 above centre and above right, p43 top left
RHW 12327 copyright of the SWOP Collection managed by High Wycombe Library: p112
Vicky Tadros Collection: p82 top right and bottom far left, p96 bottom left, p101 right second down, p113 centre left
Torre Abbey Historic House and Galleries: p26 right
© As stated by the copyright holder/ Victoria and Albert Museum, London: p152/3